The Andretta Tillman Story

"Making of Beyonce and Destiny's Child"

BRIAN K. MOORE

DOUSIC
PUBLISHING
Spring, Texas
Est. 2013

The Making of a Child of Destiny

ISBN-13: 9780991635580

Library of Congress Control Number: 2014934814

First Printing, May 2014

Printed in the United States of America

Inquiries should be addressed to:
Dousic Entertainment Publishing
Spring, Texas.77379
www.dousic.com

Disclaimer

All the material contained in this book is provided for educational and informational purposes only. No responsibility can be taken for any results or outcomes resulting from the use of this material.

While every attempt has been made to provide information that is both accurate and effective, the author does not assume any responsibility for the accuracy or use/misuse of this information.

In Loving Memory
⚬⚬⚬

I write this book in memory of my friend and partner - the late, great Mrs. Andretta Tillman. You taught me so much about the music industry and how to continuously draw on the internal will to achieve and fulfill our destiny. For that, we say thank you.

To the memory of Dwight and Shawna Tillman, because of Ann's love for you, we were able to accomplish what others said could not be done.

To the memory of others who have touched my life, my Grandmothers Lizzie Banks and Armelda Moore; my sisters Louise and Sharron; all of my uncles, aunts, and cousin of The Moore, Banks, Wooden, Smith and East Lawn Drive families that are resting in the arms of God.

Dedication

I dedicate this book to my wife Cassey for her love and support; to my children Brian and Bryanna; to the children of Andretta and Dwight Tillman, Armon and Christopher; to my father Reverend B.T. Moore, Sr. and his wife, Ada; to my mother, Elizabeth Banks; to my brothers Gregory Moore, Booker T. Moore, Jr., Tony Moore; to my sisters Beverly Caulfield, Armelda Thomas, and Sheila Moore; to my in-laws Sam and Macy Wooden; and to all of my aunts, uncles, cousin, nieces, nephews, and friends. You know who you are.

Acknowledgments

Special thanks to the Brown, Tillman, Knowles, Rowland, Luckett, Davis and Roberson families. Nikki, Nina, Beyoncé, Kelly, Ashley (Tamar), Latavia, Latoya, Lonnie Jackson, Tony Moore, David Brewer, Lynn, Sha Sha Daniels and the guys of Tayste (ToTo, Harlan, Mitch, And A.J.) Thanks you guys for being a part of a wonderful journey to Destiny.

Thanks to Atiya & Ingram, Keisha, and the Dousic Family for your support and understanding. Thank you all from the bottom of my heart.

Foreword

When Brian "Kenny" Moore told me that he was going to write a book about how my mother created the group Destiny Child, I was surprised, relieved, and doubtful. A book on the truth of how Beyonce, Kelly, LaTavia, Ashley, and the rest of the girls became a part of this story was a long time coming. Yet, Andretta Tillman was not here to tell it. So, who better to give the intimate details about the truth of what went on behind the scenes; what better person was there to step up and talk about the journey in such a personal and compelling way, but her friend and partner, Kenny.

The business world knows him as Brian K. Moore. Beyonce, Ashley, and the other girls called him uncle watermelon head. The management team referred to him as Kenny Mo. To me and my younger brother, Chris, he has always been pops as long as I can remember. Although pops was like a father to us, he was my mother's rock of support, confidante, friend and "make it happen" business partner. Who would have known that over 17-years later, we would be looking back and reminiscing the bitter-sweet memories, the dreams, the joys, the heartbreaks, the setbacks, the sacrifices, the lives lost and the victories that so few knew of, let alone willing to tell the truth about.

From the time I was around nine years old, our home was filled with little girls singing and dancing and grown folks telling them how to move. Some faces came and left, but the few who were mainstays and there from the very beginning were almost like part of the family. Kelly even lived at our house for a while. Some may wonder who I am or even who my mother was because the story has changed numerous times over the years, and with those changes there was less and less of her contributions being mentioned. I am Armon Tillman, Andretta's eldest child and just as much as this is the true story about my mother's life and her legacy, it is also about how Destiny's Child start was right in our living room, backyard, and garage. Likewise, this book sets the record straight and brings out the many truths that have been hidden for far too long.

Moore worked with Andretta as her partner up to the time of her death. He worked with Beyonce, Kelly, LaTavia and the others from the time they were nine and ten years of age, and was a staple of the management team during the many name changes that took place from Girl's Tyme to Destiny, to ultimately Destiny's Child. He experienced the many trials and triumphs first-hand as he was co-manager and partner of Tillman Management. Although the name later changed to Music World Management, he remained and continued to work alongside Andretta and Mathew Knowles playing a major role in the strategic development and success of Destiny's Child until he finally walked away from it all.

After leaving the camp, and shortly before bridging his diversified music industry background with technology serving for over 20-years with a fortune 500 tech company, Moore worked as vice president of operations for Eastlon's records management and music portfolio. Like the energy and work ethic that he and Andretta shared which made them effective business partners, today Moore lives, breathes, and eats in the worlds of Music and Technology. He is the president/founder of DOUSIC Entertainment LLC formed in February 2011 and the creator of the DOUSIC concept. DOUSIC aspires to be one of the world's leading social media and entertainment content companies, with unparalleled expertise in the development, production and marketing of digital media, to a global audience across its distribution and media platforms. This Buffalo, New York-born gent who was raised in the Mississippi (Greenwood) Delta, attended Mississippi College.

It was no doubt that it was divinely meant for Andretta Tillman to meet Brian K. Moore. It was also destined that the group become a major force in the music industry under their direction. The reason being is that of the driving forces behind both of their lives, their calling, and their life-experiences. Andretta faced a plethora of complexities and challenges; but her "why" was much greater than the struggles she faced. Her drive to reach the promise was so strong that she refused to let it die, and it just so happens that Beyonce, Kelly, LaTavia, Ashley and even MicHecke Williams, although she became a part of Destiny's Child after Andretta, today are the beneficiaries of that unyielding and relentless force that refused to give in to failure.

Moore does a remarkable job at uncovering the facts with astonishing details of events that are often talked about but shrouded in a dark cloud, whereas the light of truth is hardly recognizable. In the book, he unravels the myths that have been accepted, by providing specifics surrounding various situations and circumstances. One excellent example is that of how Mathew Knowles actually became involved with Destiny's Child in the first place and ultimately a part of the management team and of Music World. He also explains why and how Beyonce became the lead singer for the group, and the circumstances surrounding the group's name changes.

Destiny's Child was one of the best-selling girl groups of all time, and Beyoncé is one of music's greatest icons. Yet, that did not happen in a vacuum and it certainly did not happen at the hands of Mathew Knowles as many may have been led to believe. There had been several questions left unanswered and many hidden truths. However, in The Making of a Child of Destiny: The Andretta Tillman Story, Moore discloses the "unknown" facts which had a tremendous impact on Andretta's life, and the success of Destiny's Child. He presents compelling and in-depth information leaving it to the reader in the end to be the final judge.

This is a relevant story and a liberating one for many who were involved in some way or another. The world through the years have heard whispers of setbacks including the Star Search loss, but no other text out there until now has even come close to lifting the veil and capturing the highs, lows, sacrifices, wins and losses of the journey leading to the beloved group we now call Destiny's Child. As the saying goes, "You shall know the truth, and the truth shall set you free." Regardless of what anyone believes or thinks about the whole subject matter, this book will most definitely captivate you and address the question of what really happened. The truth just is…undisputedly, and it was just a matter of time before it was told.

Moore's passion shines on every page, particularly when he ventures off on side-trips through happier times in young Destiny's Child development. It's filled with romance, drama, comedy, tragedy, ingredients necessary to open your eyes, so that the next time you see Beyoncé or any of the girls from the group; you will appreciate what they went through to be where they are today. Above all, you will learn of a profound love, a love so strong, that could not and would not let the dream die regardless of who did in the process. Many readers will immediately be able to identify and relate to wanting something so bad, to feeling so obligated to keep going no matter what, to loving so hard that regardless of what it costs you, you just keep going.

This is not just a book, it's an experience where Andretta in the spirit, guides the reader through her life and love of something that was and is so much greater than herself. She comes alive within these pages to answer those questions that were left unanswered for the girls, as well as to help each of them and the other people involved move on with their lives and finally live and walk in their true purpose. In doing so, she can finally rest in peace comfortably knowing that the truth was finally told, her destiny reached, and her name placed in the annals of history that the world may recognize the light shining brilliantly behind the "stars" that we see.

From all of us who love Destiny's Child — thank you, Brian Kenneth Moore, for finally speaking up and allowing yourself to be a conduit and a means of access for one of the most incredible love stories ever, to be told, The Making of a Child of Destiny: The Andretta Tillman Story. I shouldn't have doubted that you could do it, not for a minute!

Armon Tillman
Son of Dwight and Andretta Tillman
Houston, Texas

Table of Contents

DESTINY FULFILLED

"We did it! We finally did it! We actually made it happen!"

As I looked upward toward the top of the Toyota Center's dome, water welled up in my eyes, and all I could think about was if only she were here to see that all of the sacrifices and hard work was not in vain. Little girls eight, nine, and ten back then, but today, stars in a beautiful galaxy of people as far as the eye can see. All are here to behold what my friends had been telling me would be the last tour for Destiny's Child; possibly the last time they will ever share the stage together as a group.

With bitter-sweet memories running across my mind, I could not help but to flash back to yesteryear and wonder to myself, do they really know the sweat and the tears it took to get them to this very moment? Do they fully understand the tough times endured by many or the sacrifices made to make this very night possible? Most importantly, do they realize the lives that were lost on this tragic but wonderful journey?

Glimpses of bold colors of red, gold, purple and hints of green, here we are back where it all began – Houston, Texas. The night was August 20, 2005. It was about 90-degrees outside. It was hot and humid, but inside of this home to the Houston Rockets, it was much hotter than outside. In fact things were heating up fast! I finally got up the nerves to go see the girls perform. It had been about eight years since I had seen any of my old team let alone any of the girls in the flesh. Yet, here I was confronted with my own truth. As each song played, I recalled moments in time that pierced my soul like a knife. I cried, I laughed, and I deeply reflected. With each song came a remembrance of those who labored; a realization of the pain and heartache that many faced and an appreciation of it all.

Thinking back to the time I stepped into the picture and the day I walked away, as I looked up to hear and see the energy, the lights, the roaring crowd, I was so proud. Although there were moments where it hurt badly, that day through the tears of joy, I can honestly say it felt so good to finally accept that I was a part of this. It feels so good! And yes! "We" finally did it."

As the stage came up, there stood three young women who were no longer little girls; and two of whom I watched grow up. Little-by-little the hurt, the bitterness, and the pain were transformed into pride, appreciation, acceptance, and more importantly an inner knowing that I played a significant role. The song that kicked everything off was, "Say My Name." Yet, there were many names that one could shout out, and some that certainly went across my mind: Dretta, Lonnie, Mathew, Arne, T-Mo. Each time I heard, "Say My Name," I thought out loud, "Ash, Bey, Nicki, Nina, Kelly, Tavia, Toya, Uncle Watermelon Head, Baldy Locks, and Pops."

While others were jamming to the beat and grooving to the chants of, "Say My Name," I was in many moments at one time while listening with an attentive ear and watching them perform, dancing in unison and working that stage. I shook my head because all of the coaching, the long hours of practice, the changes, the girl talks, the drama, and all the names that could truthfully fill in the blanks to, "Say My Name," there were some really great times.

Back then they were "snotty-nosed heffas" running around during cookouts where we grown-folks gathered around laughing and joking and doing what grown folks do. The children of the families ran and played and did what children did. It was a much needed release for them because although they were young, they worked just as hard as the adults if not harder and were faced with challenges that most children their age were not confronted with. No matter how we as managers, parents, producers, or friends tried to shield them and protect them from the harsh realities of the world, some were inevitably touched by real ugliness and we as a team had to confront it head on and help them move beyond it.

Both good and bad, those times will never be forgotten no matter how many names are omitted from the history. One memory of an unforgettably fun time was after one of the shows, where we all went back to Dretta's, and Tayste was telling me, "Man, K-Mo, Bey is stealing our stuff!" It was too funny! Big A.J., Mitch, Harlon, and To To- they were all characters. A.J. was the church singer. Mitch was the quiet one. Harlon, well, he was the brains, the dancing sex symbol and Ralph Tresvant knock-off. Finally, there was To To, Dretta's brother and cocky lead singer. I don't know who was worse; but one thing for sure, they all were really exceptional singers and each had a great sense of humor.

"Say My Name, Say My Name." As the song was coming to a close, I just laughed to myself thinking back to the crazy times. We called each other every name under the sun, but at the end of the day, we had lots of fun.

There were always ups and downs along the way; and sometimes those downs seemed to overshadow the ups. I was sad to hear that Girl's Tyme, the group that ultimately became known to the world as Destiny's Child, formed and managed by Andretta Tillman from a group of about thirty young girls who showed up one day at a local recreational center hoping to get picked to become a part of a singing group, would be parting ways to pursue their perspective solo careers after this tour. I wasn't sad that they were dismantling. I was saddened because Dretta was not here for the journey.

Although she was the one who without a doubt not only put her money where her mouth was, she also gave many pep talks of the need to stay strong and to keep going. She reminded the team that the show must go on no matter what. It was Dretta who provided a platform and laid a strong foundation for these girls, and she knew a star when she saw one. You had to show up and show out or go home. That's the way it was.

I was sad that she was not sitting in the audience watching them rock that stage like nobody's business and like grown-women who knew exactly how to handle themselves. She would be proud. The crowd was going mad as they were laying it down! Who could have imagined that little Girls Tyme, a cross between TLC and En Vogue would put on their big-girl drawers to ultimately go on to sell more than forty-million records worldwide and a year later receive a star on Hollywood Boulevard's Walk of Fame? Who would have imagined the sacrifices made that started in nineteen eighty-nine would eventually render this level of success and this wide of a following and fan base? Dretta knew. She had an intuitive nature about her. If she said it, you could take it to the bank. No one can argue the point against the fact that she indeed was a launching pad and catalyst to their success; and for her to miss out on this night was disheartening to say the least.

By the time they got to, Lose my Breath, the place was on fire! What a show! What a magnificent performance. I was so proud of them. That was one Heck of a night, and to think, I was a part of it from almost the beginning. It's been a long time, and as the show was wrapping up, I wondered, "Do they really know what happened? Do they really know what's ahead?" Time will tell.

To know where you're going, it's important to know where you've been. While some may say that the past doesn't matter, it is very much relevant. When phenomenal success is achieved, those who labor from the very beginning understand the blood, sweat, tears, and even sacrifices to achieve a dream and claim your destiny! So the past does matter, because it is the very time and season which lays that critical foundation upon which everything else is built.

No matter how high the acclaim we reach, we can never forget those fallen heroes who made it possible for us to be where we are today. In light or the dark and God only knows, one's destiny is always fulfilled. Yet, it is up to us to remember and acknowledge that without those helping hands, compassionate hearts, and hard work, there would not be a platform on which to stand. While many winds do blow, our greatest triumphs lie in the winds that blew to lift us up, to make us stronger, and resilient. Our greatness comes not alone and not merely by believing in ourselves, but rather a combined force where self-belief is matched with others believing in us. Therein are we able to truly reach our destiny.

A child of destiny gives birth to a dream that never died with the dreamer, but lived through a believer who believed that destiny could be fulfilled. So it is, we have indeed come a very long way and through many trials; but we must never forget those who helped us to make it this far. You can never forget those who made contributions no matter how small or great, because regardless, they too played a part in your destiny!

"Say my name, say my name…" Every time you hear that song, there is one name that we shall never forget – Andretta Tillman and this is her story.

MEET THE BROWNS

They say the apple doesn't fall too far from the tree. I guess that depends on what apple you're talking about and which tree. There can be two very different trees in the same back yard and a whole bunch of apples. On the thirty-first day of March nineteen fifty-eight another apple was picked from the Brown Family Tree. Lighting up the room and exposing herself to the world for the very first time was a little, yet strong and courageous baby girl who came to be known as Andretta Brown. She was the eighth child of twelve born to Jimmie and Effie Lue (Buck) Brown. Aside from Ann, the Browns birthed Charles, Jeanette, Glenda (Mop), Arvonette, Jann, Larrell, Mary Joe (May Jo), Lornando (To To), Brenda, Lucretia, and Jimmie Jr. (Bo). From that first day, Andretta's mother knew that it was God's grace and favor shining upon her, and she quickly begin to call little Andretta, Ann for short. I on the otherhand always called her Dretta.

Dretta was born in Whitehouse, Texas population of close to seven thousand people, of which the Brown family made up a good portion of the seven thousand residents. Dretta's family was so large that when all the children and grandchildren came over for dinner or holidays, they would often gather around the picnic tables under the big tree in the front yard.

If anyone from out-of-town happened to drive down Troup Highway, it would not have been out of the ordinary to think that it was a family reunion going on.

The house was surrounded by nothing but woods. There were no neighbors for about two miles, so they could make all the noise they wanted and never had to worry about disturbing the peace, at least not anybody outside that big old slave-looking, ancestral, plantation house. Although it sat on several acres on top of a hill, you could see the ground through the floor. The Browns may have had land, but they were dirt poor.

Dretta's family was not the only large family in Whitehouse though. There were the Pettigrews, the Bowies, and the Stewarts. It was a whole lot of them too, and in many cases it was hard to say who was who because in those families they were all mixed up. That's a tough one to figure out, so we will leave that one right where it is.

Dretta's upbringing was similar to my own. Even though I was born in Buffalo, NewYork, in reality I am just an old country boy from Greenwood, Mississippi. Eastlawn Drive to be exact. Similar to Dretta's hometown of Whitehouse, in my hometown of Greenwood, it was not unusual for couples to have large families. The people were either tilling the land or having babies or a little bit of both. Grocery Stores such as Piggly Wiggly made a small fortune from all the mouths that had to be fed.

People stayed busy. There was no such thing as idle time. No matter the day of the week, there was always something going on. .

Ann was born during a very significant time period, especially for Black America. During the 1950's, the Civil Rights Movement started and the South quickly became a very heated area of the country. Ensuing from an incident in Topeka, Kansas, The U.S. Supreme Court ruled that legal segregation was unconstitutional, and therefore ruled in favor of Brown vs. The Board of Education. Rosa Parks refused to give up her seat in the colored section of a bus in Montgomery, Alabama sparking the historic Montgomery Bus Boycott. As a result, four African

American churches, as well as the homes of Dr. Martin Luther King, Jr. and E.D. Nixon were bombed by four angry whites infuriated over the boycott.

Just up the road from my hometown in Money, Mississippi, Emmett Till, the fourteen-year-old Black boy from Chicago, Illinois was beaten to death for allegedly whistling at a white woman.

While things were feeling the inferno of racial injustice, music was the one thing that could sooth the beast and unite people if only for two minutes and thirty seconds. In the south music was playing a tremendous role in racial integration. One sound that impact both Dretta's and my life was the sound of Berry Gordy, Jr's. Motown. A record company that gave rise to many industry greats such as Marv Johnson, Smokey Robinson and The Miracles, Mary Wells, The Marvelettes, Diana Ross and the Supremes, The Jackson 5, The Four Tops, Marvin Gaye, The Temptations, The Spinners, Gladys Knight and The Pips…the list goes on and on.

Along with the emergence of Motown, racial tension and political upheaval were the news of day. Although Andretta was eleven hundred miles away in this small town near Tyler, Texas, All of these factors created an atmosphere where Dretta would have no choice but to become influential in the world. Her destiny was simply waiting for her to walk in, and our destiny would cross as if ordained by God.

In life, Andretta experienced the highest of highs and the lowest of lows. She met and married the love of her life Dwight Ray Tillman on Saturday, December third, nineteen seventy-seven at New Canaan Missionary Baptist Church in Whitehouse, Texas. She gave birth to two healthy boys Armon, Christopher and on

Tuesday, October sixteenth, they welcomed their little baby girl - Shawna Marie Tillman. Her middle name Marie was named after Dwight's grandmother and she was a beautiful baby.

Dwight taught at Booker T. Washington High School and Ann worked for Houston Lighting & Power Company (HL&P). Ann was a supportive wife that encouged her husband Dwight to not only teach but to chance his dream of working in the music industry.

"What do you plan on doing now that we are here Dwight?"

"What I plan on doing and what I want to do are two different things. I plan to keep teaching."

"I remember you telling me at the church that your dream was to be like Berry Gordy. You said you wanted to manage music acts."

"Yes, that's what I want to do. One day, I will be a famous record executive just like Berry Gordy.

While they kept the dream on the back burner, from time to time Dwight would go and check out acts to quench is thirst until he could do it full time. At this point life couldn't get any better.

On Sunday, October 26, 1986, Dwight and Ann decided to pack up the children and drive to Tyler. When they got to Whitehouse, Dwight ended up staying at her mother, Buck's house with the children, while Ann and her mother went to church. While Dwight was at the house, his friend and Ann's brother-in-law Raymond called to let him know that they were barbequing and since they are already in town, they might as well come on through.

When Ann got back from the church, Dwight told her what the game plan was.

"Hey Ann, Raymond called. Him and Mop are barbequing and asked us to stop by."

"Sooky-sooky now! I'm sooo hungry."

Ann called Mary Jo, then she and Dwight headed over to switch cars and then on over to Mop and Raymond's house. Ann and Dwight laughed and talked on the way to Tyler. She was able to give him some names of singers that were at the church before they pulled up in her sister's and brother in-law's house.

"Hey Shaw Shaw!" Glenda took Shawna out of Ann's arms. "How's my baby?"

"Girl take her"

"Where's your car?" Raymond asked Dwight.

"Man, it started acting up and I didn't want to take the chance on getting stuck on the highway."

"Isn't that May Jo's new car?"

"Yeah, man."

"And they let you drive it?"

"Why not, he knows I'm good."

Dwight, Raymond, Glenda, and Ann sat around laughing and talking. All of the children which included Armon, Christopher, Shawna and their cousin Albert played and ate til their bellies were full. To To was on his way home from the military so they were all excited to see him. .

"I never thought To To would get right…"

Ann started to sing "Straighten up and fly right… I guess the military did him some good."

"Ann, you know To To is still To To." Dwight said laughing.

"He's going over to your mother's, Mop." Raymond said.

"Oh okay…So what ya'll have to drop Albert off, then ya'll running by Buck's then heading back on to Houston?"

"Yeah. We better head on out, it's almost eleven, and that drive can get long when it's late. But I got Ann and the children to keep me company so…I guess it won't be too bad."

Dwight and Ann stood up and hugged Glenda and Raymond, gathered the children and started loading everyone into the car, waved then pulled off, heading back toward Whitehouse.

"Whoo, I had a really good time. I'm glad I came. I'm glad you are with me. Girl I love you, and having you with me makes it worth-the-while."

"Yeah it was good wasn't it? Well, at least you don't have to drive back by yourself. I can't wait to see To To. I don't think he's seen Shawna yet." Ann kissed Shawna on her forehead. This little baby girl was her pride and joy. She sat there stroking Shawna's head while she was sleeping on her mother's lap. The boys were in the back seat playing tap back and forth.

Ann and Dwight were talking and recapping the day when they came to the corner of Loop 323 and West Elm Street about five houses down from Glenda and Raymond's house. When they pulled up to the stop sign Dwight noticed a person driving recklessly looking like he wasn't going to stop.

"Oh My God! He's coming way too fast. I don't think he's going to stop!"

"Move out the way Dwight!"

"He's coming too fast!"

"Ann we're gonna get hit!"

"Oh Jesus!"

Dwight was less concerned about himself, and instead was focused on protecting Ann and the baby. As the on-coming car was speeding toward them, there was little time to do anything but brace for the impact. As he reached over in the attempt to use his body to shield his wife and daughter, the drunk driver struck the vehicle on the driver side, spinning the car completely around and smashing it almost like a sardine can.

Up the street, Glenda was pulling her car into the garage. Before she could get out of the car good and into the house, she heard a big bang. The thoughts running through her mind were, "No, not possible. It can't be." Glenda started out down the street first slowly on foot, then yelled out for her daughter Nicole to follow.

"Nicole!" As Glenda and Nicole started running up to the loop, they saw the blue Ford that Dwight was driving completely mashed in. "No, No, No, No, No!

"Oh my God! Nicole go get your dad, and call 911!"

"Oh Jesus, no Jesus! Oh my God."

Glenda saw Armon and Christopher in the back seat screaming and crying. She immediately ran to them and pulled them out the car. They appeared to only have nicks and cuts. She had them sit down over to the side while she tried to pull Albert out of the backseat who was going in and out of consciousness. Armon and Christopher were crying for their mommy and daddy.

Raymond and Nicole arrived back at the scene. Nicole walked part way down the road to direct on-coming traffic that would not be able to see that there was an accident. Raymond helped get everyone else out of the car.

As Glenda went to the passenger side, she was trying to get Ann to respond. "Ann, wake up! Ann." Ann did not respond but Glenda could see that she was still breathing. Raymond ran to help Glenda pull Ann out of the car. Glenda looked up and saw Shawna laying in the windshield half way in the car and half way out in a pile of shattered glass. The entire car was turned completely around where the side wheels were dangling over a big black hole making it difficult to get to them.

"Oh Raymond, there's the baby!" Glenda reached up to pull little Shawna from the dashboard, while Raymond struggled to get Ann out by himself. Raymond was trying to wake Ann up, but she would not wake up. As Glenda grabbed Shawna, she started crying frantically when she noticed as she could hear only a faint breath coming from Shawna. Her body was listless, barely holding on to life.

Raymond had gotten Ann out of the car and laid her out over in the grass. He then ran over to the driver side where Dwight's head was pressed against the horn causing it to beep loudly. Cars continued to drive by slowly. Raymond tried to get Dwight out of the car, but the door was jammed in too bad. "Dwight, man! Can you hear me?" There was no response.

"Mop, I can't get Dwight out! He's not responding!"

Raymond and Glenda were frantic and Armon and Christopher were horrified not really understanding everything that was going on. They kept crying, "I want my mommy!"

"Why won't my mommy wake up?"

"Oh God, please no! Father God, please have mercy!" Glenda continued to hold Shawna in her arms who was unresponsive. Not even a cry came from her limp body. As she stood there holding Shawna and crying and pleading, she heard the last breath leave Shawna's little fragile body. Little Shawna Marie had just died in her auntie's arms.

"Oh God no! Raymond! Oh Jesus!" Glenda was crying uncontrollably breaking down when the fire department finally arrived, followed almost immediately by the ambulance. The fire department pried the door open to get Dwight out of the car, the paramedics laid everyone else out on the grass to check vitals and to ascertain their condition.

Shortly after, all of the passengers were loaded up into ambulances and transported to the hospital. Shawna Marie Tillman was pronounced dead on the way to the hospital. Glenda was devastated. All she could do was grab her two nephews and hold them tight. She just shook her head and looked up with tears in her eyes. "Poor Ann. Oh God."

Ann was still unconscious, but alive. However there was no news on Dwight.

Glenda called Buck, Jimmie, Brenda, James, Mr. and Mrs. Tillman...

"It's bad. You need to come."

"Well honey what's going on?"

Glenda kept it together long enough to let them know that they needed to get to the hospital.

"The boys are fine"

"We are waiting."

She just couldn't find the words to tell them that Shawna died.

"Where's my mommy?"

"She's going to be okay Armon. We just have to wait honey."

"What about my daddy?"

Glenda couldn't cope with the questions. She left the room to cry while Raymond stood with the boys. As Glenda was coming out of the room, family members were arriving. Brenda and James walked up to Glenda, Glenda whispered to them that Shawna didn't make it, James broke down. James Bowie was a loner but he and Dwight were very close. So when he heard that his daughter didn't make it, he was devastated.

"Oh God!" James broke down and Brenda and Glenda had to take him from ear shot from others standing around.

"Glenda, what about Ann and Dwight."

"Well, Ann was unconscious, when they loaded her into the ambulance. We don't know about Dwight because we really couldn't get to him.

Quickly the hospital emergency room filled with family and friends. Everyone was waiting around just trying to see what was going on. Finally the doctors came out and gave reports.

"Andretta has a severe concussion. There's a lot of bruising, so she won't be able to move much. But she'll be okay. We're going to admit her for a few days. Keep an eye on her."

The family members were anxious but relieved as they continued to hear the doctor's report. "Albert, well he has a pretty bad banged up leg. He'll be okay but he probably won't be playing any more sports…Armon, Christopher…they're fine just a few minor scrapes. We bandaged those up. They can go home."

Mrs. Tillman spoke up. "What about Dwight and Shawna?"

Glenda grabbed Raymond and looked over at Brenda and James.

"Well, we will have someone come out in a moment and give you more information as it becomes available."

After what seemed to be several more hours, the hospital chaplain came over. They pulled the family in a room, and started to speak.

"I'm very sorry. Both Shawna and Dwight suffered major internal injuries. There was nothing that we could do."

"Oh Lord!" yelled Mrs. Tillman, almost passing out.

"Neither survived the accident."

Family members broke down creating a panic. They took the family in the patient room where Dwight and Shawna were placed to allow them to see them. Their lifeless bodies laid there as all machines around them were turned off. "Oh my God! Oh Ann!"

"Oh God, Why?"

Buck spoke up. "Does Ann know yet?"

"No, we haven't broken the news to her.

"Where is she doctor?"

The doctors directed Mrs. Brown, Glenda, and To To to Ann's room. The chaplain, Mr. and Mrs. Tillman, James, and most of the others stayed in the room with Dwight and Shawna, grieving and spending a few moments with them. "So this is it... Lord, my baby...too soon."

Buck, Brenda, Glenda, and To To walked into Ann's room and noticed her groaning in excruciating pain. Buck didn't say a word or show any emotion. She just kept this grave look on her face. Glenda was the nurturer.

"Hey sweetie...You okay?"

Ann groaned in pain. "Oh...uhm...no, it hurts. Where's the children?"

"The boys are out there with May Jo." As Glenda spoke with her sister, you could see that she was extremely saddened and trying to comfort her sister the best she could. They all knew that in a matter of moments, the doctors would come in to give Ann the news about her husband and daughter.

"What? Ya'll looking like somebody d..."

Just as Ann was getting her sentence out, the chaplain, doctors and nurses came in.

"Andretta, how are you feeling right now?"

"Uhm, well how do you think I feel right now?"

Glenda and To To moved closer to Ann, while Glenda stroked her arm.

"Okay."

"Your family took a pretty hard hit."

"Yeah."

"Your boys, they're fine, they just have a few bumps. They can go home."

"Okay."

"You have a really bad concussion, so we're going keep you for a few days...

"Your nephew, he's fine too, okay."

"What about my husband and daughter?"

Tears streamed down Glenda's face as she rubbed Ann's arm more intensely. To To lowered his head. Buck just stared straight ahead, but observing Ann out of the corner of her eyes. It was so hard for them to keep their composure.

"Well, Andretta, that's what we want to talk with you about."

"Okay."

"Your husband and daughter sustained some really bad injuries in the accident. Your husband had two broken arms... both his legs were broken and he had a crushed chest cavity. The injuries were too extensive... We're sorry but...they didn't make it, Andretta."

"Huh?"

Ann starting crying, "Huh?"

Glenda in a low tone said, "Honey they died."

"No! No! Oh God! No not Dwight! Not Shawna!" Ann screamed out painfully loud for her husband and daughter. "Shawna! Dwight! Oh Jesus! No! My baby! Ann was crying uncontrollably. "Please God no!"

Glenda, Buck and To To along with the hospital chaplain just did their best to console Ann as she continued to scream out her husband and daughter's name. "Dwight! Oh God my baby...What am I gonna do....Lord God help me...Jesus...No!"

As Buck stood there firmly looking ahead, barely showing emotion, a closer look exposed that there was a single tear rolling down her cheek.

LOVE LOST

The day of the funeral, the church was filled to capacity as family, friends, colleagues, and students came to bid farewell. Three charter buses were parked outside as the drivers waited to carry those who would leave the service with only a memory of Dwight and Shawna. There was no hollering and screaming, no preaching, no singing, just the reading of the twenty-third Psalms.

"The LORD is my shepherd; I shall not want.
He makes me to lie down in green pastures;
He leads me beside the still waters.
He restores my soul;
He leads me in the paths of righteousness
For His name's sake.

Yea, though I walk through the valley of the shadow of
death,
I will fear no evil; for thou are with me;
Thy rod and Thy staff, they comfort me.
You prepare a table before me in the presence of my
enemies;
You anoint my head with oil; my cup runs over.
Surely goodness and mercy shall follow me
All the days of my life;
And I will dwell in the house of the LORD
Forever."

While all medical indications perhaps might say that she would not physically be able to attend the funeral, Andretta got up and half way through the service to everyone's dismay, walked into the church unexpectedly to see Dwight and Shawna off.

As she walked down the long aisle, flashing through her mind were memories of the last time she took that walk. It was to celebrate a happy occasion. As she mustered up the strength to move through the constant barrage of thoughts of the "I do's," and recollections of those faithful vows she took "until death us do part," she never imagined that in less than ten years she would once again walk down that aisle only to say goodbye forever to her only true love. As she made it to the front, she looked upon their still bodies, placed her hands on her chest, and found the strength to kiss Dwight and Shawna on the foreheads and finally, the ultimate strength to say goodbye.

Things happened so fast. One minute Ann and Dwight were laughing and talking about the day's events. The next minute, life changed dramatically.

As months continued to come and go, Ann was still having a lot of pain and swelling in her joints. The headaches continued and she was often fatigued. Finally, the doctors who previously had chalked everything up to residual feelings from the accident and depression from losing two family members, decided to explore a little further.

"How are you feeling?"

"I am really tired all the time. The headaches seem to increase. My fingers and toes tingle a lot now."

"Uhm. Well Andretta, with the injuries you sustained in the car accident, it is not uncommon to experience aches and pains. You have been through a lot, and it is expected to be somewhat tired. Your body has been under a significant amount of stress physically and emotionally. You had a severe concussion. Uhm. Yes, it is possible that you could have developed migraines. I can imagine you are also experiencing some depression."

"Okay. I just would have thought that some of this would've subsided."

"Well yes, but everyone is different and perhaps your body is responding this way. However, the tingling…uhm. So that with the other symptoms…Well what I would like to do is run a few tests just to be safe and go from there."

"Okay."

"What I want to do is a complete blood work-up and urine analysis. Let me take a look at that then we will go from there. Are you able to go over to the lab today?"

"Yes."

"Good. It will take a few days to get back. If you haven't heard anything within a week, give me a call back. In the meantime, I will prescribe a muscle relaxer to help alleviate any inflammation in the joints, which can also cause some pain."

"Okay."

"So let's see you back here in two weeks."

"Thanks doctor."

"Stop at the receptionist and she will give you the order for your labs."

"Okay, thanks."

Ann headed over to the lab, then to pick up the boys and on home to prepare dinner and face another day in the house that had yet to turn back into a home. Only two days had passed when she received a call from her doctor's office. She wanted Ann to come back into the office. When Ann went back to her doctor's, she learned that her doctor wanted to run more tests.

"Okay, Andretta, we did get your tests back. It looks like you might be anemic. However, one test came back positive and some showed elevations that I think we should explore closer. The ANA test..."

"The what?"

"Antinuclear Antibody...we call ANA for short, came back positive. With the symptoms you are describing and the fact that this test was positive, it makes me want to test further for lupus. Now, understand that many people who have a positive ANA test, do not have lupus, but often people with lupus usually have a positive ANA test."

"Okay so, what is lupus?"

"Lupus is an inflammatory disease where your body's immune system attacks itself...your own tissues and organs."

"So, how do you get it?"

"Well...you don't necessarily have it... that's what we want to test for. But, if there is a diagnosis of lupus, it is most likely that you have had it for a while, and it was just laying dormant and triggered by the accident."

"So what happens if I have it?"

"Well Andretta, like I said, you may not have it but if you do we would treat it and keep the symptoms under control. Currently there is no cure for it so you would basically learn how to live as normal of life as possible with the disease. But again, just because you have a positive ANA test does not mean you have lupus."

"Okay, so now what?"

"Well, I am going to refer you to a rheumatologist. He will do some further testing. But because lupus can mimic so many other things, it may take some time, so you will have to be a little patient."

"I have no choice but to be, do I?"

"I understand. You've been through a lot."

"Doc what could be more devastating than what has already happened?"

Her mind was such that whether she had lupus or not, she would be okay.

"Lupus, forget it! Heck. So what! I have lupus. Well, I don't have my husband nor my daughter; But I have Lupus, I can't trade it all back...Just give me the darn pills or whatever, and let me work to get on with my life!" Ann snapped and really didn't care to hear any more about it.

She didn't want to hear about lupus, she didn't want to hear about who died last week, who was in the hospital, who is depressed, or anything else. That was more of a burden to carry on top of the one she was already carrying. She cared, but she was not interested in hearing anything that made it harder for her to just be okay. She already lost her husband and daughter, and her father was recently diagnosed with lung cancer. So at that junction, Ann was like, "I just don't care."

MOVING ON

After about a year and eight months since the death of Dwight and Shawna, Ann started to suffer from a host of symptoms including chest pains and severe fatigue. She broke out in a horrible rash and was knocked on her back sick and hardly able to move for several days at a time. It was the worst she had ever felt physically. She thought she was going to die. Doctors confirmed that she was having an acute lupus crisis brought on by stress.

While laying in bed recuperating, flashes of Dwight flashed through her mind. All sorts of thoughts flooded her, and she felt the urgency to so something of consequence but what?

A few days later, To To called her telling her about his hot group that she should hear. The conversation instantly brought thoughts of Dwight.

It penetrated her unexpectedly.

"Ann, we're good, I'm tellin' you. Look…right. It's four of us. It's me, Big A.J., Mitch, and Harlon. That ain't their real names but you know…anyway."

"Ya'll have a manager?"

"No see, that's what I'm saying. We can really go places. We need some help though. See Ann, that's where you come in."

"What you talkin' about To To?"

"Naw see, I figure you know a little something because of what Dwight was tryin' to do. But the truth is, we need somebody to back us."

"What you mean invest?"

"Yeah, but it's bigger than that. We want to really do something Ann…But look here, we need your help."

"Aw, man I know you can sing, but what about those other dudes? I don't know nothing about them cats, I wouldn't even know where to start."

"Just think about it Ann."

"Alright To To. Alright. Just shut up."

Ann hung up from To To, but the conversation sparked a lot of thoughts about Dwight and his dream to be like Berry Gordy. To To really got Ann to thinking and she wondered, "Why now? What is this really about?"

Then a few days later her friend Denise called. She opened the conversation as usual, and it appeared to be no big deal.

"Hey Ann."

"Hey girl. How are you?"

"I'm good, just been working on trying to pull this group together."

"What group?"

"This girls group. We have some girls, they're pretty good, but it's tough though."

"Why?"

"Well you know, the music industry ain't easy to break into, and right now you got all these boy groups out there, but there aren't any girls out there. You have a few but, not many."

"Yeah, I noticed that."

"So Deena and I have been working on putting this group of girls together. Our thing is like, it's the girl's time now, so we had some initial auditions to try to put a group of girls together."

"Oh okay. So how's it going?"

"It's going…but the thing is…we really need some help because we got a few people on board and we got some girls, but in truth, we don't have the money it's going to take to really do things…you know, to go any further."

"Wow, Denise, that's something because my brother just called not even a week ago saying the asking the same thing."

"What did he say?"

"To To told me he had this group of guys that were really good, but they needed some help. Based on what he said, ya'll saying the same thing. Is it that hard?

"Well…see…"

"When Dwight was doing it, I mainly stayed at home with the kids. I didn't really know what the deal was, I just supported him. I listened to some of the artists, but I was not really into it like that. When we drove back to Tyler that night, it was one of the few times I even went with him."

"Wow, Ann that's deep."

"I don't know a darn thing about the music industry, and you and To To bringing this to me like I'm some record producer. I don't know anything about that stuff."

"Girl, the truth is, we need some money to take these girls to the next level. I can't say we know a whole lot, but we've gotten this far. I figure with the financial backing we could take them places."

"Okay, so what you saying?"

"I'm asking would you be willing to invest or help."

"My brother asked me the same thing. Uhm…let me think about it."

Over the next couple of days, Ann thought about an up and coming gospel singer she had just heard, Kathy Taylor, To To and Denise. She asked herself if this could possibly be a sign.

Certainly it must be and Denise just put the icing on the cake and confirmed that possibly, it was for Ann to pick up where Dwight left off. She knew nothing about the music industry, so she understood that if she was going to help, then she must know and understand what she is helping with and how the game was played.

Ann thought, "I have the resources, I have the time, and I have my husband's dream...alright...let me get into this and see."

Ann purchased a book entitled, Music Industry 101. It was helpful in bringing about a better understanding of how to break into the music industry and provided simplistic explanations on everything a person needed to know. It was a comprehensive guide which ultimately became Ann's bible for the music industry.

It took her no time to read the book. Every night when she would usually be overwhelmed with thoughts of Dwight and Shawna, Ann read through the book and in doing so learned about points, distribution, promotions, distribution deals, and a whole list of other things that helped her to understand that this could not only be a great investment, but it could also be an avenue to bring their dream back to life. The book brought new meaning into Ann's life. This helped her to feel closer to Dwight and after reading the book, she knew that this was the right thing to do.

Ann reached a turning point in her life. So when she called Denise back, she shared the good news with her.

"Yes."

"Alright! So, when did you want to come and see them?"

"How soon will you be ready?"

"We can do this Saturday because we're already getting together. We'll make sure everybody's there."

"Alright."

On Saturday, Ann met up with Denise and her partner Deena. There she also met Alonzo Jackson, but they called him Lonnie. He was from the stable of Oakland Bay Area producers. She also met Anthony Moore who they called T-Mo, a songwriter. Denise and Lonnie were also songwriters. Ann met the group of girls that Denise had been talking about. What Ann learned was that there were two groups they were trying to blend: The Ultimate Masterpiece and Girls Tyme.

The Ultimate Masterpiece consisted of sisters Nicki and Nina Taylor, ages twelve and ten, who were both background vocalists, dancers and rappers. Then there was Latavia Robertson and Chris Lewis, both nine years old, and also background vocalists, dancers and rappers. Finally, the Ultimate Masterpiece consisted of Millicent Laday, who was eight. She was a D.J., Hypemaster, background vocalist, and rapper. Girls Tyme included Beyonce "BK" Knowles, who was nine; Stacie Latoison, eleven; and Jennifer Young, twelve. All three performed lead and background vocals.

So the idea that D & D Management had was to sculpt these two groups into a harmonious blend to present in one "unique" show that provided hype and entertainment consisting of singing and dancing. The goal was to "provide listening pleasure through radio, video, and live performance."

As Ann sat there watching the girls and observing the dynamics between Lonnie, T-Mo, Denise, and Deena and their approach with the girls, she saw a lot of gaps based on her understanding of Music Industry 101. She realized that she could actually do this, but if she was going to put her money behind something like this, she and Denise had to come to some sort of joint management agreement. Ann learned that no contracts were signed with Girls Tyme, the team wasn't getting paid, and there were no real plans for the girls past what she already saw. It was clear that Denise didn't have the resources to take things to the next level.

Ann gave Denise feedback and she didn't bite her tongue in doing so. Ann's position was, "if I am putting the money on the table, then some things need to be adjusted." So after the rehearsals, Ann and Denise sat down and had a heart-to-heart discussion.

"Okay Denise. I'm willing to help, but I believe there need to be some adjustments that will make things better and help this thing take off."

"Alright, tell me what you are thinking."

"Well first we need to agree on some type of co-management arrangement."

"Oh, no that's cool."

"Okay, then there need to be some contracts in place if you want to do this thing the right way."

"Okay."

"This is the other thing…it's too busy. Ya'll got too many moving pieces. It looks like ya'll trying to create some Parliament Funkadelic act with these little girls."

"Ann you are crazy."

"No for real. I see what you are trying to do and I support you on it. But I just think it's too busy and you need some stronger vocals. So what I would suggest is to hold some more auditions and let's pull some things tighter together. What do you think?"

"No problem. Look we need help. We need the money and if you are willing, hey, let's do it. You come in as a manager. I'm not able to do it by myself."

"Okay so if you are cool with that, I will get the paper work together and let's do this thing the right way. I want you to understand that it's gonna happen, and once it does take off, you will always be there. You will always have a place. I don't want you to think because I'm bringing the money to the table that I am just gonna push you aside. That sure ain't gonna happen. You get me? So our understanding is our understanding. You get me?"

"Girl yeah. The truth is, we need the help, and I'm glad it's you."

"Alright, let's do it."

Denise embraced Ann. "Thank you so much Ann. I really appreciate this."

"Hey, the biggest thanks would be to make this successful."

Denise nodded her head in agreement, and they left.

When Ann made it home later that night, she delved even deeper into Music Industry 101. This time it was with much more intention and purpose. She was even more determined to make their dream live. She read Music Industry 101 from front to back and from that moment on, she never put it down. Ann thanked God for the signs and the wonders. She finally heard her husband's voice. He was still present in her heart and so was his dream. With water welled up in her eyes, she looked up to the heavens and said to her husband Dwight, "We are gonna do this."

DO DREAMS COME TRUE

For Ann, "doing this" meant much more than just managing a group. It was something much bigger for her. As she studied Music Industry 101 in great detail, it became the standard operating procedure of how she conducted her business affairs. Her belief was that it was crucial to her success. As she stepped into the role of not only investor, but manager of the process and the group, she went to work to ensure that everyone at the table knew and understood the principles contained between its pages. She wanted her team to know it like the back of their hands. She made it a requirement for anyone that came on board or worked on the team to read it.

Although D & D Management with Denise at the helm started out with eight girls, Ann was fully aware from a business standpoint, that there were some major changes that would need to take place in order to take the girls to the next level. There needed to be stronger lead vocals and more continuity. Some things needed to be tighter and streamlined to help them reach the level of success that she envisioned.

Internally, Ann knew star potential when she saw it, and to be able to maximize on that star potential she did not hesitate to make those necessary changes. So, the first thing Ann did was establish a strong team. From a production standpoint, she felt that Lonnie was her guy. It wasn't necessary for her to look past him and go find someone else. She knew Lonnie was the one. However, she also knew that it would be hard dealing with him because he was arrogant and pompous and wanted everything his way.

"Lonnie, you are getting on my last nerves. You might be a good producer, but you better piss or get off the pot. It's my money and if you wanna get paid, you gonna do things my way, kapish? You feel me?"

Ann struggled early on dealing with him and there were constant squabbles between the two. There were many times Ann had to tell Lonnie off and show him who was running things. He thought when Ann first stepped into the picture that because she was a woman she would back down. She quickly set him straight and went toe-to-toe with him each time he tried to push the envelope.

T-Mo came on as a writer. He was Lonnie's yes man and whatever Lonnie said to write he wrote. So by checking Lonnie, Ann in essence checked T-Mo too. Once Lonnie realized that Ann was forking over the money, his loyalty shifted. Yet, Ann knew that Lonnie was for Lonnie, so she did not bite her tongue with him.

"Lonnie stop being a jerk, man. Sit down and listen to me! I'am running this show."

"I got you Ann."

Lonnie was a good producer. He had a West Coast flavor with an old school meets real funk sound. But she didn't care about how good he thought he was when she trying to get something done.

"You gonna get in line. I don't care about how good your skills are. In fact if you are so good then get to work and give me the music we need."

Ann was no joke and not someone to take lightly. She had a very clear picture of what she wanted. As she stepped up her game, Denise faded into the background. She was always there in the wings but her role became more silent. She was good about the process and moved aside so that Ann could work her magic. However, Ann's focus was to play off of Dwight's vision of having a Motown type of stable. So every move she made was stable-wise and not act-wise.

When Ann stepped in, she had more of a vision with all the acts and not just the girls. She secured Tayste, which featured her brother To To. Then she started working with Girls Tyme. The two acts were the core foundation and grassroots of the stable of Tillman Management. The stable later became known as Tillman Management/Girl's Tyme Entertainment, and then from those two acts, Ann built everything else.

Ann paid Lonnie and T-Mo up front for songs they wrote and produced and had an agreement to get points on the back end. She had the skills and an uncanny ability to move people and make them comfortable so that she could get what she wanted.

Tayste was showing real promise. With A.J. and To To doing lead vocals they were just as good if not better than groups out at the time like Jodeci and Boyz II Men. They worked hard to improve their stage presence so they would be a complete package.

Tayste went into the studio and Lonnie and T-Mo started laying down tracks. Tayste was showing outstanding potential for being a top mainstream act. They were tight, had a dynamic sound, and amazing presence. Her vision for them was to be the next hot male group. They had a New Jack feel and after trial and error they came out with the hits songs, "Groove Me One More Time" and a hot ballad performed melodramatically by To To entitled, "I Wanna Be Loved Just by You."

Around the same time, Ann was molding the girls and getting them ready for the studio. The team worked with both the guys and girls hand-in-hand all the way. With the success that

Tayste was having, other groups started looking toward Tillman Management for opportunities. Someone approached Ann about one group in particular called H-Town. Tayste had already produced hits and was going strong. When she took a look at H-Town, Ann felt that Tayste was equally good if not better than H-Town so she was very comfortable in not pursuing them. Although she later regretted the decision because H-Town became a huge success in the music industry releasing great hits such as "Knockin' Da Boots."

While Tayste was already recording, there was still some work that needed to be done with the girls group before they were anywhere near ready to go into the studio.

Ann's vision for the girls was to produce a group that was a cross between SWV and EnVogue with an Emotions type harmony. Tillman Management was to become a hit machine just like Motown.

She moved forward with that mindset, and further auditions and house cleaning dwindled down the original eight girls to the best six. Ann was looking for the "best of the best" and to get to that point, she made the necessary adjustments. Mediocrity was not an option.

So from the auditions, two girls were selected, Kelendria Rowland and Ashley Davis. Chris, Millicent, Stacy, and Jennifer were not part of the plan for the girls group being formed at the time. However, the team maintained the idea of possibly circling back after launching other acts. Ann took care to deliver the news to the girls and their parents. Even though the decision to release the young girls was difficult for Ann, the ultimate goal to fulfill the dream weighed more heavily on her mind.

"This may be a difficult situation for some of you, but we are in the business to create the greatest group in the music industry. You will either be a part of it or you can get gone."

As Ann spoke with the girls and their families, she was kind and caring, but very direct as to not mislead anyone.

"The music industry can be a very tough nut to crack. My intentions are to crack it wide open. So this is not personal. It is about business, and no matter how fond I am of any of you, it must be about business because it is only sound business decisions that will help us to achieve what we are after."

Everyone listened as Ann continued to speak frankly.

"Does this mean that I am saying those not moving forward will not make it, no. What I am saying is that at this time, Tillman Management will not be moving forward with you. However, when we launch additional acts in the future, we will definitely consider you."

Ann was about the business of creating a successful group that would sell in the industry. She was sensitive to their feelings, but at the end of the day, it was about business and as a new person coming in to help, she had no loyalty to anyone who was already involved. She took the best of what was there. Denise was in agreement and supported her willingly. So the group Girls Tyme was formed and consisted of Beyonce, LaTavia, Nicki and Nina, Kelendria who was called Kelly, and Ashley.

Once Girls Tyme was formed, there was a meeting so that everyone had the opportunity to meet everyone else. This included the management team, the artists, and the parents. Once the formalities were handled, Ann put the girls through a boot camp where she and Lonnie worked to help sharpen them as a group. Lonnie worked on the vocals to make sure they were straight and the harmony tight. Ann also brought in David Brewer as a vocal coach to help them strengthen any areas of weakness.

"Okay, David. What I am looking for is the kind of harmony that the Emotions have. I know they're sisters, but I want these girls to sound like conjoined twins. Every note sang with precision."

"You got it babe!"

The girls rehearsed, rehearsed, then rehearsed some more. They worked on choreography along with Keith from Tayste. Lonnie was Ann's taskmaster keeping them on point with the dancing and the singing. They worked hard.

At a certain point in their development, after rehearsals, the team put the girls in front of people to see what the response would be. They performed at places like Greenspoint Mall and Sharpstown Mall. Ann rented venues such as the Shape Community Center and the Jewish Country Club off Braeswood. Ann also would get the club houses of apartment complexes where the girls lived if the parents had access. Ann's goal was to create a buzz. As the girls continued to develop, they created a following by going around town and performing.

However, Ann had to find something solid for the girls and get them into the studio. The flow of the group at this junction placed Ashley as lead vocalist. Beyonce performed back-up vocals and co-lead. LaTavia was a rapper and hype master. Nicki and Nina were dancers, and Kelly performed background vocals.

"Look girls, I know it's rough and I know it's hard, but I believe in you. We believe in you."

Ann instilled in the girls a deep passion to keep working and by working hard now, they would ultimately become successful.

"You are going to be great one day. I promise you that. Just stick with it, be disciplined and things will happen."

Ann became sort of a surrogate mother to the girls. They fell in love with her and started wanting to stay the night at her house. They practiced every day so the parents were able to get to know her. No matter how hard the girls worked, they never wanted to go home. The girls' parents trusted Ann's guidance. Anyone who knew Ann understood that she loved those girls dearly. They were like one big happy family and Ann's house was their second home.

Ann had a special connection with the girls, even more so than the guys. She gave them extra attention and a little extra of whatever else there was to give. It appeared that the girls began to fill the void of something that was missing in Ann's life. As time went on, and as I came to know Dretta personally, it was very apparent that Girl's Tyme filled the void of her baby girl Shawna.

These little girls filled her house and her heart. Everyday she was with them and the more time she spent with them, the more she loved them. Her life soon began to revolve around this new found love affair with not just one little girl, but several. While no one could ever take the place of Shawna, Beyonce, Ashley, LaTavia, Nicki, Nina, and Kelly all became Ann's little girls in another way. For Ann, this was the first time since their death that she was feeling Shawna's spirit in the house.

"Baby, no one can take your place. Mommy misses you. Tell God I thank him for placing these six beautiful little girls in my life."

Ann observed the girls' musical ability, but she also watched them like a proud mother. Sometimes if you looked at her closely as the girls were singing and dancing, you could see water in her eyes. There were a couple of times that Ann would call Shawna instead of the girl's name and have to quickly correct it.

"Shawna...Lord Jesus..., I mean Kelly come here."

The girls were used to Ann calling them each other's name, so it really did not register to them. But for Ann, when she hugged them and encouraged them, she was doing so as if it was Shawna, and that is the love that both the parents and the girls could feel. There was nothing fake about Ann's love for them, and at any moment she would have taken any of them into her home as her own. For in spirit, they all represented an aspect of her baby girl and she pushed them as if it was Shawna she was pushing to become better and to hang in there.

Everyone was working really hard. As Ann looked at what was in front of her, she had Lonnie producing, T-Mo writing, and David handling the vocals. Everything was together except someone who knew how to go out and get investors. So a man named Lynn came to the table to complete the inner circle of managers. He seemed to be well connected with corporate people who had money and convinced Ann that he could take the work produced by Tayste and get investors.

When everyone heard the tracks from Tayste, they got really excited. Lynn convinced a group of white businessmen to invest. Unbeknownst to Ann, Lynn formed Encore Records and took the tracks from Tayste and got investments for Encore Records. He continued to go out and hustle for other investments for his company using Ann's artists. He played two ends against the middle. He somehow convinced a group of investors to lease the twenty-fifth floor of the building on Highway Ten to erect a sign saying, "Encore Records" on the outside of the top of the building for all the world to see. It gave the appearance that Encore Records was this big conglomerate.

Aside from not knowing of Lynn unscrupulous antics, Tayste was happy. The girls were happy. Everyone was seeing progress. Most practices took place at Ann's big house on Strawgrass Drive. With all the movement going on breathing life back into her and Dwight's dream, the house was also coming back to life. As Tayste rehearsed, all the other girls would be running around and playing. Beyonce would sit quietly in a corner studying the boys carefully while they performed. She loved To To and the vocal runs that he could do.

"Hey To To, why this little girl keep staring at us?"

"Man, A.J. She ain't studden you. She just likes what we do."

"No man, look at her, she stealing our stuff."

"Man you crazy."

"I'm tellin' you To To, man she takin' our stuff. Watch, I'm tellin' you man."

"Come on A.J. pay attention, Bey ain't thinkin' about us."

"Alright, don't say I didn't tell you."

It was evident from early on that Beyonce wanted to hone her skills by studying Tayste and other performers, but A.J. saw it as Beyonce' stealing their style.

ALL IN THE FAMILY

It was a whole lot going on in Ann's life, yet a very happy time for her. She was really starting to move and shake and get things going, but she felt she needed someone else to help focus on the management aspect of the business. In the end, that person would be me.

In March of nineteen and eighty seven I finished my U.S. Airforce career in Osan Korea. Before leaving I made contact with my one of my best friends Cassey, who was always a willing and trusting ear and shoulder if I needed it.

"Kenny Mo, why don't you come to Houston to see how you like things here?"

"You know Cat that might not be a bad idea."

"I cannot imagine you going back to Indianapolis or Greenwood. Honestly, Kenny Mo, what's there for you back in Mississippi? If you don't really know what to do, come here."

Cassey and I were childhood friends. We'd known each other since we were about eight-years-old. Cassey was Miss Greenwood High School and a very beautiful young woman. If people today saw a picture of her from back then, and could observe her carriage, they would probably say she reminded them of Jackee' Harry from the hit show 227. As she gets more mature, she might remind you of the actress Jennifer Lewis. Either way it goes, she is a superstar and will always be in my book.

Anyway to go back a little, after high school, I went on to play college football at Mississippi College for three years before enlisting into the service. Cassey became a flight attendant and moved from Greenwood, Mississippi to Houston, Texas by way of Orange County California.

Cassey was a constant friend all the way from childhood to adulthood. We stayed in contact with each other throughout. It didn't matter whether I was in college or in the service, we never lost contact. Little did she know but she helped me to get through some really tough times. When Cassey invited me to Houston, given our history, I had to seriously consider the option.

"Alright Cat, it might not be such a bad idea. I'm really not sure of what direction to take. I keep asking myself, 'Do I want music or do I want football?' You know though either way, Houston may be a good move. I have a friend who plays for the Houston Oilers. I've been getting in shape anyway so…"

"Kenny there are a lot more opportunities here. You can stay with me until you find a place. You know it's not a problem Kenny Mo, I gotcha, you know that."

"Alright, Cat, then it's settled."

I was determined to have some type of a career in the music industry. After all this was one of my true passions. A rich man once told me, "If you do what you love, you will always be rich, and the money will come."

So as I was leaving Osan Korea, my mind was made up to take over the music industry. I was full of confidence, so full that the last thing I told my friends as I left Korea.

"You are gonna look up one day and see my groups names up and lights."

As I was flying from Korea, I kept asking myself can you back up all that talk, because to be honest I did not know a soul in the music industry. So my plan for the moment was to get a job, and have a talk with some of my old football friends. As I prepared to board my next plane from San Fransico to Houston, some of the Flight Attendant stopped me at the door and asked me, "Are you Kenny Moore?" Shocked I replied yes, while thinking to myself what have I done? One of the Flight Attendents replied "Cassey sent us to pick you up, and bring you home." She then sat me in a first class seat, and provided all the star treatment that goes with it. As the flight took off I begin to think wow is this a sign that this type of life style is waitng down the road?

After arriving in Houston my quest had begun as Cassey and I start to build our lives together. I searched for jobs all around Houston, anything so I could moonlight as an entertainment manager. I finally landed a stable job as a probation officer for Harris County Probation Department. So it was time to for me to chase this music thing, but I still had one little problem "*I didn't know anyone in the music industry.*"

Then one day an opportunity appeared. Cassey told me of a friend of hers named Troy who was a musician. While talking with him Cassey told him I was an entertainment manager, and that we should talk. So after several phone calls he decided I knew enough about the music industry to help him and his band mates when they come to Houston.

I was not one for being nobody's flunky, but I had to start somewhere. So as the time came for me to finally meet Troy, and his band I was asking him for the bands name and he would laugh and say "you will see". He said my assignment was to go down to the club and make sure it was up to standards. My question was "up to standards for whom?" As I arrived at the club called Main Event, it was the best looking club I had ever seen coming from Greenwood. I was excited that it was a first class venue. Then I saw some posters of the show for tomorrow night. The poster said *"The Gap Band & Yarbrough & Peoples."* I was like "hold up, wait a minute, I'mma hook up with the Gap Band & Yarbough & Peoples? "Oh My goodness!" I started running in place and screaming, *"Yes, Yes, Yes"* I'm now in the music industry!"

Troy played for the Gap Band and his sister Alisa, who we called Lois, was one half of the group Yarbrough and Peoples. They produced such hits as "Don't Stop the Music." Troy mentioned that Yarbrough and Peoples, along with Charlie Wilson and the Gap Band would be coming back to The Main Event.

As we made plans, Cassey's older sister decided to drive down to attend the show as well. Just like her sister never traveling alone, she showed up with some guy by the name of Foley. They showed up mainly to see the concert.

Everybody was in for the show, so I barbequed that day and packed some up to take to Troy who had already had my famous barbeque over the summer and loved it. So of course, I couldn't get in the door of The Main Event without his share. It was just understood that whenever we saw Troy, we had to have some of my barbeque with us.

They killed it that night! We all got to laughing at me bringing barbeque with me, but someone ended up giving Charlie Wilson a taste of it, and that was all it took. Charlie was like, "this is some good food. Where is the barbeque?"

"Well you know there is more where that came from."

"Well where is it man? Bring it on."

I invited all of them over for barbeque, and they accepted. So Cat and I went on home to get everything set up and Troy led the crew over after they broke everything down. About an hour later this big tour bus rolled up I-45 to Imperial Valley Drive to the Hollywood Apartment complex. Cat's sister and Foley were outside talking and when the bus doors opened, out popped Troy, Lois, Cavin Yarbrough, members of the Gap Band, and Charlie Wilson. Foley looked at her and was like, "Dang, what is happening here?"

He was shocked to see the Charlie Wilson's tour bus stop almost in front of the complex. When I saw it pulling up, I came outside, shook Charlie's hand and said, "Come on man, let's go gets some grub." Charlie and I walked inside together talking and laughing. Everyone was having a great time gathered around the complex pool and enjoying the food. The whole time Foley was watching and digging the scene. It was as if he was saying, "Dang, he must be well-connected."

I noticed that Foley was checking out my every move that evening. As soon as an opportunity arose, he came over to where I was and started telling me about his cousin who is in this group, being managed by some woman named Ann.

"You seem like a good person to know."

"Oh yeah? Why is that?"

"My cousin Keith is in this group. You know, they're just getting started. Maybe you can help them."

"You don't say."

"Well, right now, he's being managed by some woman. I want to introduce you to my cousin. I think maybe you can help them. Seeing you know some people and all... you know what I'm saying?"

I did not take Foley that serious. I thought maybe he was talking out the side of his mouth, but I did agree to meet his cousin.

"Set it up. I'll see what I can do."

"Alright, done deal. I'll call my cousin and we'll get a time together."

After the Charlie Wilson's tour bus left and the apartment was cleared, Cat's sister and Foley stayed a little longer before heading back to Dallas. Foley called his cousin Keith later that evening. I spoke with him briefly and learned that he sang in a group called Tayste, they had been in the studio recording, produced a couple of songs, but were interested in setting up a meeting between me and a woman by the name of Andretta Tillman. Keith talked to me about the group in a little more detail and told me to call him Harlon. He also mentioned somebody named To To and then put him on the telephone. When I spoke with To To, he told me that Andretta Tillman was his sister and managed his group and another girl's act, but he was interested in working with me.

"If you are connected like that, I'm interested in seeing how you can help. Ann's my sister, man. Let me call her and set up a meeting between the two of you and see what's up."

"Alright To To. No problem man. You got my details. Give me a call and let me know what's up."

Cat's sister and Foley got on the road and headed back to Dallas. Within an hour of them leaving, To To called me back and said he had a meeting set up between me and his sister and gave me the details of where to meet. I hung up the telephone and turned to Cassey and said, "It's on baby!"

And....that was that!

HERE WE COME

The next Saturday I met with Harlon and To To early afternoon around eleven. When I walked into the place, there were two young men about five-feet, nine inches tall. One was a brown-skinned dude with what many would refer to as "good hair." The other was dark-skinned and wore a pony-tail. During the introductions I learned that To To was the dark-skinned one, and Harlon was the one with the "pretty boy" persona.

The three of us sat and talked for awhile. To To and Harlon discussed what they were looking for while I listened.

"We're happy with Ann, man. I don't want you to get us wrong. Foley told me you had it going on and so I thought it would be a good idea to meet in person and see what was what."

"Well Harlon, here I am, whatcha working with?"

"Kenny, that's your name, right?"

"Yeah."

"Okay, Kenny, Ann's my sister right? And she's a good manager. We're happy with her you know, but we were maybe looking for somebody like yourself to come in and maybe co-manage us… something like that…you know what I'm saying?"

"Alright."

"We've already been in the studio, and recorded some stuff, but we want to go real big. We're looking to get things moving a little faster and stronger. We want a major record deal and we… well…we think maybe you can help us with that."

"Well, To To, you got the meeting set-up with your sister?"

"Yeah, man. Right after we leave here, we're gonna go over to Ann's house, right. She knows that we're coming by, so…let's do it."

"Alright then, let's go."

We all shook hands and headed over to Ann's. We pulled up into the driveway of this big beautiful house in a really affluent neighborhood. This is the first time I had the opportunity to meet Andretta Tillman. When we arrived, she answered the door and motioned us to come into the living room and sit down.

"Hey, sis, this is Kenny Moore. Kenny, this is my sister Ann. Like I was telling you she manages us. Ann, Kenny here is the one we were telling you about who worked with Charlie Wilson, the Gap Band, and Yarbrough and Peoples."

Ann nodded her head. She showed no emotion. She smiled cordially and I could tell she was receptive. Although, while To To and Harlon was doing most of the talking, she didn't say much; she mainly listened carefully. As they were speaking, she would occasionally look over at me and she looked me straight in my eyes as if to see right through me. I looked her straight in her eyes too. I was always told by my football coaches to look a man straight in their eyes, no matter who they were or what color they are. Of course Ann was no man, but she was a strong Black woman who you could tell was not on any B.S. She was serious about what she was doing and it was easy to tell that she was sizing me up, but also keeping an open mind to sincerely see how I could assist.

To To and Harlon pretty much echoed what Foley had told them about my contacts and that they thought I could help them do things on a much larger scale and expand what they were trying to do. The four of us continued to talk for a few minutes and when they saw that Ann and I were comfortable with each other, they left the room so that we could talk it out and see which way to go from this meeting forward.

"Well, Kenny, the way we have to do the deal as managers is to get things on the back end because there's no upfront money to be had right now. Can you work with that?"

"I'm cool with that."

"You know Kenny, you got writers points, producer points, and record label points...you know we can squeeze our way into getting some points if we could do our own productions or split it."

Ann was very clear in terms of what she was doing and what she wanted to happen. I continued to listen as she was laying out a detailed plan for me to understand how she was working. "If we could get access to a recording studio that would allow us to get all the recording done that we needed, and if they would be willing to get their money on the back end, then we could produce final product and take those to the record labels."

"I see what you're saying."

"Yeah. See, Kenny, I'm not looking to just get an individual record deal. I'm more concerned about getting distribution deals and getting my artists signed to major labels. So, how do you think you can help us achieve that objective?"

"Well, I do know some contacts, some football players and people like that. So we may have some means to capital and some people willing to invest."

"Okay. Well, I do have a team in place. What I would like you to do is come over and meet with the team, if that's alright with you. Let's see how you bond and everything. See if you can work with the team in place and see if they feel you and if you all can work together."

During the conversation, Ann reeled me in as we jumped around from subject-to-subject. We talked about a lot of different things. Then out of the blue, she started laughing hysterically. I looked at her and was thinking, "What is wrong with this crazy woman?"

When she finally got her composure, I was still sitting there looking at her not quite sure what to think. She was finally able to get herself together to talk start talking to me again. "Kenny?"

I looked at her sort of sitting back a little gauging what's going on and answered cautiously. "Yes Ann?"

"You really don't know about music points do you?"

"What?"

"You really don't know anything about points and how producers and writers get paid do you?"

"I know they get royalties and everything like that. Whatcha trying to say Ann?"

Ann got up and left the room and left me sitting there. I didn't know what to think. I was sitting there in the room alone for about five minutes before she returned with a book in her hand.

"Here, I'm done reading this. Why don't you take it home and start polishing yourself up on how everything works...on how the points system works, so when it's time for us to get paid, we know how we're gonna get paid."

I took the book about the music industry out of her hand, and we just laughed it off. I was cool with it. It wasn't that I didn't know what I was doing, I just needed to learn a little bit more about the music industry for where we were heading. Ann was cool. I wasn't sure what to expect from the meeting, but we did click. While it was a good one, I didn't think it was anything major, but I guess Ann thought I could actually help them.

"Well, Kenny, I think you are the guy to help get us on down the road. What do you think?"

"Uhm. That's cool with me Ann."

"So, can you come back here on Tuesday? We have a weekly management meeting, where the rest of the team will be here and you can get a chance to meet them and see how you blend."

"Sure, see you then."

To To and Harlon came back in the room. They walked me to the door and I headed on home. Cassey and I chilled the rest of the evening laughing and talking about the activities of the day. The weekend flew by and Monday quickly rolled around. Before I knew it, it was about seven-thirty and time for me to head over to Ann's to meet the rest of the management team. I walked up the walkway and rang the doorbell. When I walked in, I could see that they were in a heated discussion already. They were discussing Girls Tyme, getting them into the studio and whether the songs they had were good enough.

"Ann, we ready to go. We really need to take the girls out to California, the Bay Area. Let's take them to The Plant. I got the connections..."

Lonnie was still talking when Ann interrupted him to introduce me to the group. "Hey ya'll, I want to introduce the newest member of our team. This is Kenny."

Ann could barely get my name out before Lonnie chimed in. "...Who in the heck is he? What do he do? Why we need him? Who is he..."

Lonnie started a barrage of negative reception which was followed by Lynn, then T-Mo.

"What does he do, I'm getting' the investors and everything, Lonnie's producing, T-Mo's writing..."

"Yeah, I'm writing…so what is he a writer…you not happy with my writing?"

"We don't need nobody else…This food cut up enough ways already."

Ann kept her cool, although you could see a look on her face like she wanted to say, "If these niggas don't shut the heck up…embarrassing the heck out of me. Ain't got no home training."

However, she was very professional and once they all aired their feelings, she explained to them what my role would be. "Well, Kenny is going to help me with the management."

They all looked at each other, then Lonnie spoke up. "Help you with the management?"

Lonnie turned to me. "Who have you managed?"

"Well…I haven't persay managed anybody. I've worked with Yarbrough and Peoples, Charlie Wilson, the Gap Band…"

"I know Charlie, I ain't never heard of you. I know Charlie. I know the Gap Band. I ain't ever heard of you."

I sat there listening to them act a fool and talk to me like I was nothing. I turned to Ann and said, "Look Ann, I didn't agree to come here to get abused."

"Ya'll chill out. Chill out. Kenny's part of the team and that's it."

I could see that Ann had her hands full with Lonnie. He was hot-headed and ignorant. The thing is he seemed to always lead the pack on being disrespectful.

"Just stay out of my way. Let me do what I do."

Lynn piggy-backed off of what Lonnie said. "I don't think you can do what I do, you know…whatever… I'm the mover and shaker…so…"

I just looked at them and sort of blew them off. "Well okay…cool. I'll get in where I fit in. I'll just sit back here and listen to ya'll."

So we finally went on with meeting, discussing the next steps, the girls getting into the studio and the progress of Tayste songs. There was a lot of back and forth and then Ann spoke up.

"Lynn, how are we coming on the investors?"

"Oh…uh…uh…yeah. They just put up…uh…the Encore Records building sign. My thinking is we can sign the girls and the boys to Encore."

"You ain't no record label, Lynn. What do you think you can do for us?"

"Well, I'm just saying, if we can sign to them, then we can go and do a distribution deal."

It was a lot going on in the meeting. Lynn was pissing Ann off with his antics. Lonnie was cursing and going back and forth. "Naw, ain't no need for it to be like that."

Then Ann finally reeled everybody back in. "Look, we are gonna do it like this…We're gonna go…we really need to go get the money. I can't keep forking over all this money. We really need to go get access to a studio where we can get the girls and Tayste in there on a regular basis and keep rolling."

Everyone was sitting and listening to Ann as she was handling her business. They dared not interrupt her at this point because she had just slapped the trump card on the table – her dishing out the money. "We need to convince the studio that we'll pay them a little bit up front, but they can recoup their production costs and everything on the back end after we sign the deal."

Ann was working to set up sort of a bartering system. You could tell that the team was not too pleased. The meeting ended with everyone rolling their eyes at me. Lonnie, turned to T-Mo.

"This sucker don't know jack!" I tell you now he don't know nothing."

He then turned to Ann and started questioning her judgment. "I don't know what you doing Ann, I don't know whatcha doing."

"Lonnie, this is my show, not yours. So shut the up please!" You getting on my last nerves crying like some pissy wet baby."

That meeting was tough but Ann was a safe haven and backed me all the way. She did not allow them to bull-doze or bully me just because they were already a part of the team. They were intimidated and thought that I was coming in to steal their thunder. So, by Ann telling them I would be helping her to manage, they moved out of the way. From that meeting I started attending the meetings every week as a co-manager to Ann.

Now, the Saturday following the first meeting I attended with the management team, Ann had everyone over to her house for a rehearsal intertwined with a barbeque and a welcome to the team reception. It gave me the chance to meet all the families and everyone else associated with both Girls Tyme and Tayste. It also gave the groups the opportunity to practice for the show they had scheduled the next day at one of the community centers and the management team to let everyone know what they would be doing before Sunday.

When my family arrived at the picnic, it was a beautiful sight to see. All the families were gathered around and children were running and playing. It was really nice. I was looking forward to becoming a part of the whole process. I didn't doubt for a moment that my family would become a part of Ann's family and the entire music family of Tayste and Girls Tyme.

Ann took me around and introduced me to everyone. It was the first opportunity I had to meet everybody involved with Tillman Management and Girls Tyme Entertainment. The adults were in various groups talking when I came in with my family, while the children were playing. Ann took me around to introduce me to the parents first who were all in little cliques.

Kelly and her mom Doris were standing off to the side. "Hey Doris, this is Kenny. He will be joining the team to help manage the girls. So Kelly, you will be seeing a lot of Mr. Kenny because he will be working with you as well. Kenny, this is Doris, Kelly's mom. Kelly sings back-up."

"How ya'll doing? It's nice to meet you. This is my wife Cassey and our son Brian."

"Hi, nice to meet you. Welcome."

"Thanks."

After meeting Kelly and her mother, we walked off to continue the rounds of introductions. As we walked on, Ann was telling me about the type of girl Kelly was. "Now Kelly is quiet, but she's a sweet girl."

"Now Ann, you know sweet ain't gonna get her down the road, right?"

"I know, Kenny. You're right. We got somebody working on that."

Ann led me over to the next group of parents. Tina Knowles was standing with her little girl Solange talking with Carolyn and Nolan Davis. "Hey Tina, Carolyn, Nolan this is Kenny. He's my partner and will be managing with me. Kenny, this is Tina Knowles, Beyonce's mom, and this is her little sister, Solange. Beyonce is sort of like a co-lead."

Before Ann even had the chance to introduce the other two parents standing there, Carolyn interrupted extending her hand forward assertively to shake my hand. "Hi Kenny, I'm Carolyn Davis, Ashley's mother. This is my husband Nolan. Ashley is the lead singer in the girl's group."

I was taken aback by her abruptness and "everyone needs to know me" attitude. "Okay…uh…well, this is my wife Cassey and son Brian."

Tina spoke up. She was a really sweet person. She and Cassey hit it off immediately. "Welcome aboard Kenny, welcome Cassey. It is really good to meet you. Thanks for helping the girls out and Tayste of course too."

Cassey smiled as she responded to Tina's polite and tactful demeanor. "Thank you Tina, it is very nice to meet you…you as well Carolyn and Nolan."

As we're walking away, Ann rolled her eyes up in her head. I said, "Ooh wee…"

Ann shook her head and said, "Yep, that's Carolyn." We all chuckled as Ann kept talking.

"Now Tina…she's cool. She ain't on that…Her attitude is that she is just here to support her daughter. She's very helpful…always asking if there is anything I need. She ain't on that my kid need to be in front mess. Now that Carolyn, that's another story."

I learned as Ann took us around meeting everyone, she was very outspoken and straight forward with me. This was a great quality I found encouraging, since we would be working so closely together. Next Ann took us over to meet sisters Charlotte, Cheryl, and Yvonne. Charlotte was Nicki and Nina's mom. Cheryl was LaTavia's mother; and Yvonne was Lonnie's special friend. She knew Houston very well so whenever Lonnie was in town, Yvonne took him around. Also standing over with them was LaTavia's step father, a Houston police officer.

"Hey. How ya'll doing today? This is Kenny. He's going to be working with me managing everybody."

Almost in unison, they greeted us.

"Hi."

"How are you doing? This is my wife Cassey and our son Brian."

LaTavia's step father shook my hand. "Good to meet you, man. Talk to you later."

"Cool."

As Ann was taking me to meet the girls, she yelled for her son. "Armon! He came running over to his mom. "Huh?"

"Take Brian to go play."

"Okay...you wanna come with me?"

Brian went willingly to Armon, while Cassey made her way over to where Tina and Carolyn were talking. Ann took me over to meet the members of Tayste first. As we headed in their direction, Ann was pointing the boys out to me. "You've met To To and Harlon already. That over there is A.J. And Mitch. Mitch is Harlon's younger brother. Now you know To To's my brother. His little black behind thinks he's the bomb, but he can sang his tail off. Harlon, well...he thinks he's part of New Edition or something. I think he thinks he's Ralph Tresvant or somebody."

I laughed as Ann was describing the boys' personalities. She kept a straight face and that made it even funnier.

"A.J. All he wants to do is eat and sang." Now he can sang, but I gotta hide my food else he will eat me out of house and home. Watch him Kenny. You think I'm kidding. Every time you seeing him, he is gonna be eating on something or talking about he is hungry. You watch and see."

Ann had me laughing as she kept going on about the boys. "Kenny you think it's funny, don't you. You gonna see what I'm talking about. It ain't gonna take long either…and then…that Mitch …he gonna go wherever Harlon says go and do whatever he says do. The good thing is though, you ain't gonna have a problem with him. Just reel Harlon in, then you got Mitch. You got me?"

"Hey ya'll, this is Kenny."

They all shook my hand. "Hey, man it's good to see you again."

"Alright To To, Harlon. Good to see you again too. Am I gonna get to see your moves today?"

To To spun around with some dance moves. "And you know it!"

They all laughed as the other boys acknowledged me.

After meeting the rest of Tayste, Ann took me over to meet the rest of the girls. I had already met Kelly when she was standing over by her mom. "Hey girls, this is Mr. Kenny. You gonna be seeing a lot of him. He's my partner and going to be managing you all as well."

Ann started pointing out the girls one-by-one. "Kenny this is Ashley, Beyonce, LaTavia, Nicki and Nina. You've already met Kelly."

"They ain't twins neither Mr. Kenny. I just thought I say that before you asked." LaTavia said in a self-assured manner.

"She older than me." Nina said pointing at her sister with her one hand on her hip and rolling her head. I looked at Ann to keep from laughing. I was thinking to myself, "These little fast tail girls. I bet they can sang their butts off though."

It was easy to observe that Latavia was the most outspoken of the bunch. As we stood there talking with them before they started to practice she was cracking jokes. She was not shy at all. Kelly looked like a little scared mouse. Beyonce laughed, but kept whispering to LaTavia. Ashley was a little "miss diva." She had no problem carrying the jokes on.

As Ann and I were walking off. She started to share with me her take of the girls. "Alright Kenny, those are the girls. They are good girls for the most part, but they each have their own personality as you can see. I'mma let you work that one out on your own...it ain't gonna take you long. You gonna see a lot more when they start performing."

"What do you mean Ann?"

"Well look...Ashley, she's the lead singer. You already met her diva mama. Like mother like daughter. You better watch out for her mama. She's a Hollywood momanager. She is one of them that think Ashley should have her own dressing room. But, I don't need to tell you that, you saw that already."

We just laughed. Ann continued to give me the blow-by-blow about the girls. "Now Ashley can sing, but she's stiff on stage. Beyonce...she's background, but we let her do leads some... but Bey...she's a sweetheart. She is always willing to work hard and Tina is just as nice as they come. Her dad Mathew comes from time to time mainly for the shows though."

"Okay."

The groups started dancing and rehearsing. When I glanced over where the girls were, Beyonce stuck out like a sore thumb. "Ann, why that little girl bucking so hard?"

Ann fell out laughing when I said that. "Kenny, that's just Bey. I told you she works hard."

"Naw Ann, she just bucking and popping every thang. She just wild with it."

She just continued to laugh at me going on about how this little girl was dancing. "Well, that can become a problem, Ann."

"Why?"

"Well if you got all the other girls standing there and then she's bucking so hard, she kind of upstaging the other girls and the unison don't look right."

"Okay, okay, good eye, Kenny. Yeah, we working on that."

We laughed over Beyonce for a moment, then Ann continued to tell me about the girls. "Now Kelly, like I told you earlier. She's a sweet girl."

"Okay...well...like I said...sweet ain't gonna get you down the road. She needs to have some talent."

"She got it. I just gotta get it out of her."

"Okay."

"I've been working with her. I'mma get it out of her. I got David working especially with her to get her to come out of her shell."

"Okay."

"Now LaTavia..."

"Well, Ann...that one don't need no introduction. She introduced her self. She's strong. Her personality is big. That little girl tickles me. I can see she works hard."

"Well you know, LaTavia she is the face and spokesperson for 'Just For Me' hair products. It ain't nothin' to go in the house and see her on the commercial during Soul Train."

"Okay. So she's doing some things then?"

"Now Nicki and Nina, everybody think they are twins. They work hard at the dancing and stuff. They're real. For them it's all about the program. LaTavia is their first cousin. Their mama's are the sisters."

"Okay."

"All the families are on board. Everybody get along pretty well. There are no real issues on that front. Of course..."

"Ann you don't even have to say it...As long as everybody stay out of Ashley mama's way..."

"Ashley's too. She just like her darn mama."

I shook my head. "Huhm."

I took everything in that Ann shared and observed the girls. They practiced hard and were ready for the show. The next day Cassey and I went to the show. This was the first time that I saw the acts actually perform on stage and in front of an audience. I saw them practice, but at the show, they rocked it! Tayste was on fire! They sang their butts off. Ann had some great acts, they just needed to be polished around the edges. From what I saw, they had talent and they were bound to go places. It was their destiny.

After the show, the management team met the following Tuesday as usual. They discussed that Girls Tyme needed to go ahead and get into the studio. It was apparent that it was time, and I was surprised that they had not recorded anything yet. The team agreed that Girls Tyme just needed a couple of songs to get them started. Tayste had already produced some tracks and they just needed to get into the right hands.

During the meeting, Ann also raised the issue about investors again. Lynn as usual was he-hawing around, not really giving a concrete response. He always got squeamish whenever Ann brought it up. You could tell she was pissed, but she kept her cool. The more Ann saw how Lynn was operating, the more leery she grew of him. After the meeting, she called me at home.

"Kenny, hey look, I want to start pursuing other investors. I don't want to keep leaving this up to Lynn. I don't trust him."

"Okay…"

"I'm tired of his games. We need to get some investors and stop playing all these games. Lynn is full of it and we need some other investors outside of what he's working on. Do you think you can you reach out to some of your contacts?"

"Yeah, my friend William plays for the Oilers. Some of them are already investing in singing groups. I'll get on it."

"Thanks, Kenny. I ain't playing around with Lynn, he's too darn shady for my liking. He's on some other mess. But you wait. He gonna screw up, and I'mma screw him up."

"I hear you, Ann."

I remained neutral because I could tell that she was really upset. After I hung up from her, I reached out to my boy William. He mentioned that Earnest and some of the other teammates had made some investments in the music industry, and while he was not in the position to invest, some of the others might be willing to explore options of investments or partnerships. William invited me to bring the boys over the next weekend for the gathering they were having.

So that next weekend I took the boys to the party. Everybody was having a good time. Tayste had their tracks with them. Although they didn't perform live for the team, William made sure their tracks were heard. Many of the team members were like, "Man this is hot!"

"Yeah, this is tight."

Haywood, Earnest, and William were really digging the tunes. "Hey man, ya'll got some more songs?"

"We working on some." To To responded.

"Tell you what, I'm really interested. I mean, this is tight."

"Okay."

"What we want to see is for ya'll to put a little more leg work in, come up with some more songs, then come back and let us see what you come up with."

"Cool."

Tayste was excited. You could tell that Earnest, William and their teammates were serious. "Kenny, man you really got something there."

"I know man, and this is not the half of it."

"Alright… alright. Let's see what ya'll come up with."

The response regarding Tayste was very favorable. So we left the party on a high and ready to kick it up a notch. The guys went to work on the suggestions that the Oilers made to them. Meanwhile, Lonnie and T-Mo was working on some things for the girls. Things were coming together.

Eventually, Lonnie and T-Mo came up with this little bubble gum track about world peace and a few other songs. The girls practiced their new songs until they were seamless, and then went into the Digital Services Recording Studio in Houston to lay down the tracks. With everything going on and a major buzz being created, Ann began to raise the bar in terms of their performances and where they performed. It was about star power and she was out to claim it. She knew she had some hot acts and her goal was to let the world know.

One of the first major performances for Girls Tyme was at the George R. Brown Convention Center during the Houston Black Expo. They rocked three shows that day opening for Jennifer Holliday and Chris Walker. After the girls performed, Ann debriefed them.

"So, how do you all think you did?"

"Well Miss Ann, I could have been a little tighter on my note."

"Okay Bey, what else?"

"Well, I think we need to get sharper with our dance moves. We weren't all on the same beat."

"What about you LaTavia?"

"I think, Ashley needs to loosen up a little bit more. She sounds good but she needs to not be so stiff."

"Okay...anyone else?"

"We just need to work harder."

"Well, Bey...I think you all did great. So, if you feel you need to work on those areas then you know what you need to do. I advise you all to study Jennifer and Chris. See how they work the stage and connect with the audience. Look at how they hold the mic. I want ya'll to study them closely. See how they act on stage. It could be you girls. As a matter of fact, it will be you girls if you keep at it and keep working hard."

Bey immediately went and sat in the audience to watch Chris Walker perform and then Jennifer Holliday. She did exactly what Ann said. Ashley and LaTavia got side-tracked and ended up walking around signing autographs. It was a good show all-in-all.

After that day, the girls worked harder so that they could be more on point for the next show. Nicki and Nina worked with Beyonce and LaTavia to get the steps down and crisp. They had to work with Beyonce so that she could blend her dancing more as to not upstage the other girls. They had a time with Ashley. That child did not have much rhythm at all when it came to dancing. The girls could hardly stop laughing when trying to help Ashley get the moves down. Poor Kelly, everybody yelled at her. That might have had a little to do with her confidence and self-esteem.

The girls took the criticisms from the last show and fine-tuned their program to be ready for the Juneteenth Special at the Brown Convention. This time they opened for rap artist Das Effex. They nailed it and went back to practice fired up and geared up for their appearance at KTRK Channel 13 ABC Affiliate on Good Morning Houston and then Cross Roads, another local show. Both Girls Tyme and Tayste were on fire. Tayste had their tunes, but the song that T-Mo wrote, entitled, "Sunshine" was a crowd favorite for the girls.

"The song we're about to sing…"

Ashley stepped up to the microphone and then all six girls would light up the audience with the words and melody of the song.

"…that all the homeless people across the world. Also the young children at heart…"

"Sunshine, you light up my way
The children of the world reach out to you.
Your light, it's a sunny day
When all the boys and girls can laugh and play

Only chase the clouds away;
Shining through the hearts of people.
Those who think will never heal;
Thinking bout the better ways to read.

Let your wings of golden love shine;
Gather those who live without a home.
Let them know;

They're never truly alone.

"Sunshine, you light up my way
The children of the world reach out to you.
Your light, it's a sunny day;
When all the boys and girl can laugh and play... "

The song hit home in the heart of the people, and to hear it coming from young people made it even more impactful. It was like Girls Tyme's version of "We are the World."

So "Sunshine" consequently, ended up becoming Girls Tyme anthem song. Each time they performed, they sang it. Ashley took the lead and Beyonce had this small piece with the harmony.

It was a busy summer for Tillman Management and Girls Tyme Entertainment. Things were progressing quickly. With the hype and the response from the people, Ann was having more and more conversations with a woman by the name of Teresa who lived in California. Teresa told Ann that she needed to think about getting the girls in some of the showcases in California where people in the industry could see and hear them.

In addition, Lonnie was continuing to pester Ann about going to one of the big time studios. Ann did not totally dismiss Lonnie, but she knew that what came with the big time studios was also big time money and she believed that before they went that route, there were some other avenues that could be explored.

Ann valued what Teresa had to say. She felt that perhaps Teresa could possibly bring another perspective, another face, and other options to consider. So from her conversations with Teresa, Ann started working on getting the acts in front of some of the big wigs in the industry. The only way that would happen is if she explored taking the groups to California and getting in on some of the action where the real action was happening at that time.

Tayste and Girls Tyme were growing in leaps and bounds and gaining a following. They were working hard for the big time and Ann believed it was time for big things to happen. So, instead of giving in to Lonnie's pressure, Ann used her own contacts to access the necessary information to place her performers on a much larger stage.

A LOOK INTO THE FUTURE

Ann became ever so focused and aware of the importance of placing the acts on a stage where they could be seen by the right people in the industry. Her contact Teresa became a wealth of information and support in this regard. Teresa worked with Sony Music and also did some work for Columbia Records and Epic.

"Andretta, many of the talent scouts and A & R people come to the various showcases to discover new and upcoming talent."

"Okay."

"What I'm saying dear is that to really get your girls out there, I recommend you bringing them to California and see how they fair in this environment."

"Okay. I hear what you are saying Teresa, how do we make that happen?"

"Let me gather some information, and get back with you. The bottom line is, you really won't know what you have until you first put them among acts in their league, and second, hear what the music execs have to say about it. At the end of the day, we need them to bite."

"I hear you Teresa. I don't want any wasted trips. I want to play smart. The girls are talented. I know I have something here and I want to give them every shot I can to help them gain the success I know they can achieve."

"Well Andretta, the only way to do that is to bring them to compete with the big boys – generally speaking. It can be a tough game. You can have a talent, but until you place that talent side-by-side with other top talent, you are not able to have a realistic perspective. The showcases allow up and coming talent to showcase themselves and have people in the industry seriously take a look at them…"

"Okay…"

"…so, if I were you, I would do whatever I could to get them out here. Let me do some checking to see what is happening, and I will get back with you."

"Thanks Teresa, I appreciate all the help."

"Okay, dear. Let's talk soon."

Ann became very vigilant about creating solid opportunities for the girls and being smarter about doing things. She was not interested in being pressured into making moves that were irresponsible or just to appease someone's ego. So Ann took a hard position against Lonnie and his bullying tactics. Ann played by the book, the Music Industry 101 book that is, and empowered herself with information so that she could effectively help her acts break into the business. After all, it was business and she was determined to fulfill her and Dwight's dream. Every move she made, she made with him in mind and she replayed the countless conversations the two of them often had.

"…See baby, there's this man named Gavin right? I think his name is Bill Gavin. He's this old dude…teacher who turned to radio. He plays a lot of music by Black artists and provides opportunities for Blacks to break into the music industry."

"Uhm…okay Dwight…"

"It's like this Ann. This guy produces this report right? It's called the Gavin Report or something like that. All the people in the industry…I mean all of them Ann, even these big time record labels…read the report. They swear by it. They listen to what this dude has to say. He's considered the most powerful person in the business. He says who is good to listen to and who is not."

"Huhm, Dwight, that's interesting."

"I know Ann. If Gavin says you are good to listen to, then labels are more apt to pay attention to you."

"Uhm."

Ann was snapped out of her reflective daydream by the ringing of the telephone.

"Hello."

"Andretta?"

"Yes?"

"Hello dear. This is Teresa. I've got some good news for you."

"Great, I could use some."

"Well...there's this showcase coming up here in July. The Gavin Showcase is one of the top showcases here. How soon can your girls be ready?"

"Teresa, we've been ready."

"I know it doesn't give you much time, but I was able to get you a spot in the showcase. I'll send the details. In the meantime, make sure everything on your end is where it needs to be. Here's your chance."

"Thanks!"

"Hey, no problem. Let's do this. If you have what you say you have, then you are where you need to be. Make sure the girls are as polished as they can be. This means their stage presence and personality, costumes, vocals, how they perform as a group...make sure everything is on, because this is the real deal dear. There will be many people watching and listening. When I say many people, I mean the ones who really matter."

"Okay...I hear you, Teresa."

"Talk to you soon, sweetie."

Ann hung up the telephone and yelled out loudly. "Yes! Heck Yes!"

Armon and Christopher ran downstairs like something was wrong. "You okay ma?"

"Yeah, Armon. I was just excited."

"About the group?"

"Yep."

"I'm glad mommy. I like to see you happy."

"Oh Chris…me too."

Ann patted Christopher on the head and shooed them both back upstairs to play. She was extremely excited, and could not wait to share the good news with the girls and the team. As everyone arrived that evening for practice at her house, they noticed something in her countenance, but could not quite put their finger on it. When I arrived, Ann pulled me aside to let me know the news before she shared it with everyone else.

"Before ya'll start practicing tonight, I have some things I want to speak to everyone about."

"Okay Miss Ann, what did we do now?"

"LaTavia, why you think there's a problem? I got some great news guys!"

"Okay then, what is it already. Spill the beans."

"Hold your horses Bey…I spoke with one of my people in California today, and guess what?"

"Come on Miss Ann…stop playin' with us…"

"Okay…Okay." Ann was excited and laughing at the same time. She was really proud of both the boys and the girls, but she was having a little fun with them.

"Okay, great news…Girl Tyme will be performing in the Gavin Showcase in California."

"What's that?"

"Well Bey, the Gavin Showcase is only one of the biggest and most important showcases there is for artists."

The girls started jumping up and down and hugging each other. Everyone was excited. Lonnie was looking like, "How in the heck did she make that happen?"

Tayste was happy for the girls, but they were looking at each other as if to say, "What about us?"

Ann, paying attention to everyone's body language and response to the news, spoke up.

"Now Tayste, there is no need to worry or feel left out. We're working on some things with you too. For this showcase, I was able to get the girls in, but again we are working on setting some things up with you all."

Lonnie spoke up. Ann could feel a little sting in his tone of voice. "When is it Ann?"

"It's in July. So we have a lot to do to make sure the girls are ready. They will have the chance to perform two songs. They need to nail both of them, because there will be some big wigs watching. So Lonnie, T-Mo, David, I am going to need you to step it up."

Lonnie looked at T-Mo, and mumbled under his breath. "Whatcha mean we have to step it up. I got my stuff together."

"I heard that Lonnie."

He scratched his head but did not respond because the children were present.

"We gonna be stars!" Ashley said rocking back and forth rhythmically like she was about to jump double dutch or something.

"Being a star will take a lot of hard work girls. And like I said before, the hard work will pay off. Just keep your head on straight, stay humble and hone your craft. So ya'll go on and get to it. Kenny, Lonnie, T-Mo, Lynn, David, I need you to do what you do. Work with the girls, and let's do this."

Both Girls Tyme and Tayste left the room to go start practicing. Ann continued speaking with the team for a few more minutes before they went to watch the practice.

"Okay ya'll. We need to work with Ashley. She is a little stiff and we need to get her looking better on stage. She has a great voice, but I need her to loosen up a bit. Bey needs to tone down shaking and popping. Kelly...she probably needs the most help. David, I really need you to work with her. She has to come out of her shell. No weak links. We need to tighten it all the way up, you got me? I'm gonna work on getting some outfits for them. I'm thinking of something a little mannish, but girly-girly at the same time."

Ann took the driver seat and started delegating and assigning things for the team to do. She was not shy about it and the closer she got to the goal, the harder she worked, and the more she reflected on Dwight. "Okay, we have barely a month before this showcase. Me and Kenny will work to get the travel details sorted out, and speak with the parents. I need you all to focus on what you do best and let's make it happen!"

The girls had less than a month to get ready for the Gavin Showcase. Ann and I spoke with the parents about the showcase and everyone started preparing for the trip to San Francisco. The closer it got to the date to head out, the more intense things became on the management team. However, the girls were excited mainly about flying and performing in California. I'm not sure what it was, but for them, going to California was a symbol of success. Although the Jackson Five started out in Gary, Indiana as part of the Motown stable, for the young people, California and the Jacksons appeared to be synonymous.

Ann remembered seeing photos of the Jacksons performing in some powdered blue duck-tail suits with sparkles on them. She envisioned the girls wearing something similar but maybe with some leggings to add the feminine touch. Ann went on the hunt to bring her vision alive and rounded up some really neat white tuxedo jackets, blouses with bowties, along with stretch pants. She found them at some pageant place and had them altered with sequins. Ann took the girls to get their nails done, their hair done, facials, on little shopping excursions around Houston, and everything else she could think of to set the tone for them of what to expect in the near future, and also to help build them up.

Word got out that Girls Tyme was performing in San Francisco at the Gavin Convention. That created an even bigger buzz, because anyone in radio or the music industry understood that the Gavin Convention was a really big deal and a great opportunity for any artist that was fortunate enough to be able to perform at such an auspicious event. I often wondered then if the girls or their parents even really knew how big of a deal it was. I wondered that then, and I wonder that today. Even now I ask myself if they realize the wonderful opportunity that Dretta gave them and the mighty door she opened for them back in nineteen ninety-two.

The stage any of those girls stand on today is a foundation that Ann built. She invested in their future as if she was investing in her own daughter's future, and as she did in Armon and Christopher's future. Those boys may have lost a dad and a sister, but over time they gained Uncle Kenny and several other "little sisters" who invaded their house almost every day after school and everyday in the summers, helping to turn their house back into a home again and to give them the platform to follow and capture their dreams. It was truly destiny in the making!

The harder the girls worked, the more Ann pampered them. She wanted them to feel the reward of hard work. She dressed the girls from head to toe, buying them little trinkets and pretty little things as if she were playing dress-up with her Barbie dolls, very similar to how she did with Shawna. Ann's daughter was the most, well-dressed two-year-old there was, and there was no doubt about it, Girls Tyme would be too if Ann had anything to do with it. The next few weeks were all about preparation for the performance at the Gavin Showcase.

The night before everyone was to fly out; Ann had the girls do a dress rehearsal at her house so that the team and the parents could look at everything together. They looked hot, like little stars. "Okay girls, just like you did tonight, do that and then some in San Francisco. Own the stage you got it? Good job Kelly, you lookin' good baby girl, you hear? Don't be afraid to shine. Thanks LaTavia and Bey for helping to get things on point. I'm proud of you. I'm proud of all of you."

Everyone was happy with the entire presentation. Now it was up to the girls to give a solid performance. The families headed home for the night to get ready to fly out in the morning. They all said their, "see ya tomorrows," and "see ya laters."

"I wish you were going Mr. Kenny."

"I know Bey, but next time, alright?"

I turned to Ann. "Well, this is it. You got it?"

"Yep, I got it. But we're gonna have to learn more about each other so even when you're not present, I can know what you're thinking and visa versa. You are the only one in this bunch I can really trust."

"You'll be alright, Ann. I'm a phone call away."

"I just know Lonnie gonna be on some bull. I have to keep him on a leash this trip. I'm supposed to see Teresa when we get there...touch basis with her. I haven't met her face-to-face so I don't want him acting out."

"Let me know Dretta...see you when ya'll get back."

The next day, Ann called me from the airport. All the parents were bright and chipper. The girls were excited to be performing in California, but Ann wanted to make sure they were not tired from the flight and everything. San Francisco is in a different time zone than Houston. So, their little bodies will be two hours ahead for an already long day.

Ann called me periodically during the day to fill me in on what was going on. The day moved quickly and Ann made sure to help me feel as if I was there. It was finally time for the girls to perform at the Gavin Showcase.

"Kenny?"

"Yeah."

"Hey, this is Ann. They're about to perform."

"Okay, you're recording it right?"

"Yeah."

"Good. They need to be able to look back at it to improve. No matter how good they are, they can always get better."

"Alright, I'm going, I will talk to you later."

"Okay, bye."

"Bye."

Several acts performed, and then it was time for Girls Tyme to grace the stage. The girls came out wearing their sequined white tuxedo jackets, nice shirts, bow ties and some leggings. Ann found exactly what she was looking for. They all had big hair. They looked like little ladies dressed all in white. They had a Jackson Five persona just with six girls instead of five boys. As Ann took one look at the girls as they were coming out, she knew that they were going to be stars. Just as she was imbibing in the moment, the girls broke the silence in the room.

"The song we're about to sing...*Sunshine, you light up my way. The children of the world reach out to you...*"

Ann was more nervous than she had ever been watching them perform. The parents were amazed at how polished the girls looked. The harmonies were on point. *"Only chase the clouds away...Shining through the hearts of people...Those who think will never heal..."*

Lonnie and T-Mo were fixed on the girls to see if they hit every note on point. Ann was looking around to see if she could gauge the expressions on various people's faces. *"Let your wings of golden love shine...Gather those who live without a home...Let them know...They're never truly alone."*

"Sunshine" was their mantra. The audience was mesmerized at the amazing talent of such young girls. They hung onto every note in amazement. It was almost the same expression that Berry Gordy had when he finally listened to the Jackson Five demo performance sent to him. When the girls sang that one part of the song where Beyonce came in, she belted the note out and owned it! Girls Tyme turned the place out! They left their signature in California that day. The energy that consumed the room when they sang was captivating. It was too much for their parents to take in all at once. They had seen their children perform before in front of people, but never like this and never on this level. You could tell by the expressions on their faces that the realization of what was happening to their little girls was only beginning to sink in.

Once Girls Tyme finished singing, Beyonce took control of the mic. "We would like to thank our managers Andretta Tillman and Kenny Moore for making this possible. We also want to thank our producer Lonnie Jackson."

The audience cheered. The girls had such a presence and maturity about them; it was as if they were already stars. After they left the stage, the parents went over to their children and hugged them and told them how proud they were of them. Ann talked to the girls. "That's what I'm talking about girls. You killed it!"

When the showcase was over, Teresa and Ann connected. The two of them spoke briefly after the initial "how are you…finally nice to put a face with a voice" tune. Ann introduced Teresa to the girls. "Great performance girls. You should be really proud of yourselves."

The girls shook their heads and smiled. Teresa expressed the thumbs up to Ann. "Okay dear, great job with the girls. I'll put out some feelers and give you a call."

"Thanks Teresa."

No sooner than Teresa walked away, as Lonnie and Ann were standing near the girls and their parents, someone else approached them. "Hello, I'm Arne Frager with the Plant Recording Studio. You got one heck of a show there."

"Thanks. I'm Andretta Tillman, their manager, and this is Lonnie, producer…And this is…"

"I know who they are; I won't forget these talented young ladies."

The girls just blushed. Arne handed Ann his business card and invited her to bring the girls to the Plant to do some recording. "Well Andretta, get in touch with me."

It turned out that Arne was the director of the world famous Plant Recording Studios in Sausalito, California. As the parents were watching the attention the girls were getting from different people in the business, some of them had immediately begun to try to jockey their way to the forefront. Carolyn and Cheryl started asking Ann what they could do to help. Mathew started offering unsolicited advice. Carolyn made it her business to point out that it was her daughter's group. Ann could see already what was coming down the pipes with this crew.

Lonnie was no better. He immediately started pressuring Ann about the Plant. "See, I have a contact who works with him. You know Dwayne Wiggins of Tony! Toni! Toné!" I can use him to set it up."

"Thanks Lonnie, the man just gave me his card not even five minutes ago."

She shook her head at how some of them were acting. After the crowd began to die down some, Ann rounded up the girls and motioned for everyone so they could leave the venue and get back to the hotel and get ready to leave out the next morning. Once they got to the hotel, Ann called me.

"Hey Kenny."

"Well?"

"They killed it man! They torn the house down for some little girls from Texas."

"Did anyone approach you after the show?"

"Yeah, actually they did. I finally met up with Teresa in person. She mentioned that she would put out some feelers to see what some of the executives thought about the performance."

"Okay."

"I also met this man named Arne Frager. He is with the Plant Studios in Sausalito. He invited us to come and do some recording. No sooner than the man gave me his card, Lonnie's got to going."

"What did he say?"

"He mentioned Dwayne Wiggins and how he can set up the Plant through him. Lonnie why the heck I need him to set it up when the director just gave me his card. Ignorant butt-hole...anyway..."

I just laughed because when Ann got to going, she went there. "...And all of a darn sudden every body want to be Mr. and Mrs. What can I do for you? Heck, go find some darn investors that's what they can do."

"What time does your flight leave in the morning?"

"I have to check the exact time, but we'll talk when I get back."

"Alright take care. Don't let them get to you too much."

"Alright, Kenny thanks. I'll talk with you when I get back."

Ann and the rest of the crew flew out that next morning. It was only a matter of a few days when Ann received a call from Teresa.

"Andretta?"

"Yes?"

"This is Teresa. How are you dear?"

"I'm good thanks."

"Well, I have gotten some feedback from various people in the industry. The response is favorable. Do your girls have demos?"

"They have done some recording...but not a full demo."

"Well we need to push forward some great demos that can be sent to various executives and have them take a listen. My recommendation is to get on that right away and not to let grass grow under our feet. I think we have something here and I want to help in any way that I can, if you'll let me."

"Of course. Arne Frager gave me his card, and invited us to come to his studio to do some recording."

"Yeah? Okay Arne is with the Plant right?"

"Yes."

"Well my suggestion to you is to get on that right away. Once you get some great recordings, it will be easier to communicate with the big boys."

"I'm on it."

Ann followed Teresa's advice. She pulled out Arne's card and arranged for both Tayste and Girls Tyme to go to the Plant. Arne agreed to work with her on the recording by Ann paying up front for the studio costs, but getting points on the production aspect on the backend. So, no sooner than they returned from one trip, Ann and her team was heading back to California. She shared the news with the team at the next meeting.

"Okay, I got some news and feedback from the Gavin Convention!"

"Ann before you get on to your news, I've got a question."

"Okay Lonnie, go ahead."

"Look, I spoke with Dwayne Wiggins. He said he can make some things happen so we can go to the Plant and do some recording. You ought to let me go ahead and set that up. If we really serious about this thing, then we need to move like we serious."

"What are you sayin' Lonnie?"

"What I'm saying is if we gonna do this thing here, we need to do it right. I was talking to Carolyn and some of the others and...?"

"So whatcha saying? I don't know what the heck I'm doing?"

"Look here Ann, all I'm saying is we need to move a certain kind of way, Ann, and I think if you let me set the Plant up...uh er...handle this you can see some..."

"What T-Mo? I see you over there nodding your head in agreement. What do you have to say?"

"Oh yeah...uh, I agree with Lonnie. We need to move now after Gavin and all. Did you see the response?"

"Okay. Does anyone else have anything to say right now? Lynn? Kenny?"

"Naw Ann, come on let's move forward."

"Thanks Kenny...Okay, Lonnie I hear you about the Plant, but pressuring me is not going to get things done any sooner..."

"But all I'm sayin' Ann is..."

"I don't understand why I have to keep telling you this is My Company...and I know how to run My Company." "You just make sure you handle your stuff. Produce and let me manage."

"See I told myself tonight I was gonna be cool, but you keep messing' with my job and I got my job handled. Just make sure you handle yours."

I just shook my head at the whole situation. Lonnie had been pressuring Ann to no end to set up the Plant. Ann already filled me in on the arrangement she made with Arne to go to the Plant. I was simply waiting for Lonnie and the rest to shut up so she could share it with the rest of the team and clue them in on where things were. "Go ahead Ann...continue."

"Okay, Lonnie...I don't need you to set the Plant up with Wiggins, I've got that covered. We have a date for Tayste and Girls Tyme to record at the Plant. I've just been tryin' to tell that all darn night. If you can shut the up for two darn minutes."

Lonnie and everyone else started looking around at each other surprised. Ann had already scheduled the trip to the Plant and the team had less than two weeks to get things organized. Ann needed to share the pertinent information, so that they could in turn tell the groups and their parents the following day at practice. She wanted to ensure the entire management team was on board. So after the management team was informed of the news, the groups and their parents were let in on the excitement.

"We have some great news for you. Both Tayste and Girls Tyme will be going into the studio to record a full length demo. The major tracks will be laid at the Plant, the others we will do here in Houston, and then mix the two."

"Wow!"

"Yay..."

Everyone in the room was excited about the news. "Girls Tyme turned some heads at the Gavin Showcase. You all did a fantastic job and things are really moving. So you are heading to the big time and this is real and it's getting serious. I hope you're ready."

"Okay Ann so what will Ashley's group be recording?"

"Well Carolyn, Girls Tyme will of course be recording "Sunshine." The rest of the songs, we will get with Lonnie and T-Mo on that...put together a hit list maybe even do a work up on some other songs. That will be determined moving forward."

"Okay so, when does everyone fly out?"

"That's a good question Mathew. Everyone will not be flying out. Only the lead and co-leads of both Tayste and Girls

Tyme will be going to California this trip, and then of course the management team."

"Okay."

"So, as much as we would like the parents to be there, it's going to be a hectic schedule. We need to get in and get out as soon as possible and minimize the costs. We don't want any distractions. We want everyone's attention to be on producing a great album all the way around."

Everyone seemed to be cool with what Ann was saying. "Well let me know if there is anything I can do."

"Thanks Mathew, the main thing is to support the groups and of course we still are looking to bring additional investors on board. That is always a factor."

"I'll keep that in mind."

"Yes, please do."

The groups practiced for the evening. Armon had already grabbed Brian out of my hands before the night even got started. It was a good parent meeting and rehearsal. Everyone was cooperative, or at least as cooperative as expected. For the most part we all had a great time that evening. All the parents were in attendance as well as Cassey. I was feeling really good about everything and looking forward to continued work with Ann and the acts.

From the time I came on board as part of the management team, things were moving rather quickly. I hadn't been on the team a good three months and already we were seeing some amazing results and more importantly some great relationships being formed. Aside from some of the parents' evident vying for closeness to Ann and to create their own opportunities to be "in the mix," things were going well. Tayste, Girls Tyme, Ann,

Armon, and Christopher were becoming a very big part of mine and Cassey's life.

During a break in the rehearsal, Ann ensured everyone had a cup of something to drink in their hands. "So let's celebrate everyone! Tayste and Girls Tyme…Destination - Sausalito, California. Here we come!"

"Cheers!"

"Hear, hear!"

The next week or so was hectic for everyone involved. However, that did not minimize the excitement of recording at the Plant. When the time came, To To and A.J. flew out with Lonnie and T-Mo. David was unable to go. The guys left a few days earlier so that Lonnie and T-Mo could do some pre-recording production and tighten up on some of Tayste's recordings. That way when Ann and I arrived with the girls, all their stuff would have been wrapped up and out the way.

The rest of the crew met at the airport. Ann and I arrived first at the airport. Shortly after Mathew, Tina, Carolyn, Nolan, Ashley, and Beyonce arrived, ready to go. Carolyn was making a fuss all over Ashley, fixing her clothes, sweeping her hair over from her eye. Mathew and Tina were excited for Beyonce. Tina's disposition was more a support for Beyonce because this is something she wanted to do. "Have fun baby. And…behave don't give Miss Ann or Mr. Kenny a hard time. You hear?"

As we were organizing the tickets and luggage, Cassey and I went over to upgrade the tickets to first class. Ann arranged for a limo to pick us up on the other end when we arrived. She wanted the girls to know what it felt like to be stars. She worked hard so they could experience the whole "kit and caboodle." She wanted to teach them how to handle themselves when they did in fact become famous.

Once the tickets were sorted and the luggage checked, we all headed on to the boarding gate where our flight was scheduled to take off. Beyonce was wide-eyed and bushy-tailed looking around Houston Intercontinental Airport. There were loads of people flying that day and she was captivated by the whole scene. As the airline staff got on the the speaker to begin calling for boarding, the hugs and kisses goodbye took place. The parents waved and blew kisses at their little pre-teens as they were heading up to the agent to hand them the boarding passes. Back then, there were no security check points to have to go through. So the parents were able to walk clear up to the gates to watch their children board.

"You remember what I told you Bey?"

"Yes, ma'am. Love you daddy."

"Alright now. You know what to do."

Beyonce nodded her head in response to Mathew. Ashley hugged her mom and dad and as we were preparing to board the plane, the questions started coming. "Mr. Kenny, why aren't the other people getting on the plane now?"

"Well Bey, the lady only called first class people to board now."

"What does that mean?"

Ashley jumped in and responded to Beyonce's question. "Those are the most important people Bey."

Beyonce scratched her head. "Oh...Well...Mr. Kenny?"

"Yes Bey?"

"Aren't they important too?"

Ann looked at me and smiled, then proceeded to answer Beyonce's question. "See this is what happens when you become famous Bey. Everything is first class and you don't have to wait in long lines and things like that."

Beyonce seemed more concerned about the other people than feeling like a star. Ashley on the other hand was a different story all together. "We gonna be stars Miss Ann?"

"Yep."

"And people are gonna have to wait for us to go first…that's cool. I think I can get used to this!"

"Yes Ashley. And because you are going to be a star, you are gonna have to know how to act."

We headed down the jet way and onto the plane. Beyonce was still taking everything in around her. Ashley sat next to Ann on the plane, while Beyonce ended up sitting next to me. "You wanna sit by the window, Bey?"

"Can I?" She said smiling.

"Of course you can."

"Okay!"

Beyonce hopped over by the window and I moved to the aisle seat. Ann and Ashley were sitting across from us. Ann sat on the aisle seat as well. Beyonce was looking out the window watching everything going on outside the plane. I was getting everything settled so when the plane took off, I could close my eyes and get some much needed shut eye. Beyonce watched the plane take off. She was preoccupied with all the activity from the handlers outside the plane working to the take off.

"Wow! It looks like a map. You see that Mr. Kenny?"

I looked out the window and smiled at Beyonce. I was glad she was excited but I was looking forward to some chill time. Once the announcement came that we no longer had to keep our seats in the upright position, I exhaled and leaned back in my chair, closed my eyes, and relaxed. I was comfortable and feeling really good. It was a wonderfully quiet moment. With all the hustle and bustle to get to the airport, getting the luggage checked, getting through security and all the other tasks that had to be handled, I was well ready to sit back and sleep during the flight. Just as I sighed from relief and turned my mind off, this scratchy little ten-year-old voice resounded. "Mr. Kenny?"

I opened one eye and looked at her at the corner of my eye, then turned to her. "Yes Bey?"

"How long will it take to get there?"

"About four hours."

"Oh. Okay."

Beyonce went back to looking out the window. I leaned my head back and closed my eyes again.

"Mr. Kenny?"

I opened my eyes back again. "Yes, Bey?"

"What's the studio like?"

"I'm not sure since I haven't been there before. But I'm sure it's nice Bey."

"Is it big?"

"I'm sure it is. They do a lot of recording there."

"What's the hotel like?"

"It's nice."

"Is it big?"

"I'm sure it is."

"Oh...Okay."

She then turned and started looking back out the window. I closed my eyes again. After about ten minutes when she did not ask me anymore questions. I settled back down to relax. Finally, I was able to get some rest. I took another deep breath in and on the exhale, that little voice sounded again. "Mr. Kenny..."

"Will this darn girl shut the heck up." I was thinking to myself, but then responded politely.

"Yes, Bey?"

She asked me question after question. I thought to myself, "Don't this girl ever shut up?"

That went on for about an hour. Then finally at some point she either drifted off to sleep or was hypnotized from looking out the window. Either way she finally stopped asking all those questions and I was finally able to get some shut eye before landing in California. I knew that in about three more hours, things would start to change drastically for these little girls, and I wanted to be well rested.

Ann looked over at me. "I see Bey finally settled down."

"Thank God. I didn't know when she was gonna stop."

We both laughed quietly as to not disturb the girls. "You know Kenny, we will be looking back on this five years from now laughing, don't you?"

"You're probably right, Ann. But for now...Heck...I wanna get me some darn rest. I'll see Sausalito when I wake up."

The Plant...here we come!

TAKING THE LEAD

Ann and I landed in San Francisco with the girls. We retrieved our luggage and as we looked in the direction of where passengers were waiting to be picked up, we saw a man fully suited up holding a sign that read, "Tillman Management & Girls Tyme Entertainment." As he assisted with the luggage, we followed him to the doors. When we walked out the door, there parked right in front was a long white stretch limo. The girls yelled almost in unison, "Limo!"

"That's for us, girls."

"For real Miss Ann?"

"Yes Bey, it's for us."

"That's cool."

When Ashley realized that it was for us, she snapped her fingers and tossed her head back. "Now that is what I'm talking 'bout."

Beyonce was excited about the limo ride, but she was more fascinated with the surroundings. She was into what the people were doing and how they were. Ashley on the other hand was more into things and the hype of it all. We were headed to the Claremont Hotel.

When we arrived, we walked into the lap of luxury of five-star quality. The girls were wowing all the way up to the door. The hotel was huge; sitting on several acres of land and every square foot of it was beautifully landscaped. It had tennis courts, swimming pools, a hair salon and spa, a full service workout room, and a host of other amenities that if time permitted, we could definitely enjoy.

We finally got checked-in. Our luggage reached the room before we did, but it was nice watching the girls taking it all in. The hotel had plush carpet and was furnished exquisitely. We stayed in a three-bedroom suite. It was very spacious with a full size living room, a dining area with a full size dining table, a kitchenette and separate bedrooms and bathrooms. The room had an amazing balcony that overlooked the San Francisco Bay area. It was just the place to stay and relax for the girls' first real studio experience in the big leagues.

When we opened the doors to the room, Ashley ran throughout the entire suite. "This is fabulous! We even have our own bedroom and beds!" She said mimicking the playful voice of a rich lady. Beyonce looked around then plopped down on the couch and started talking about the flight.

"Mr. Kenny, you know that picture you took of me on the airplane sitting by the window?"

"Yes, Bey."

"Well, I wanna have it."

"What do you mean you wanna have it."

"I wanna have it, so I can put it in my scrap book."

"You have a scrap book, Bey?"

"Yeah, don't you? I wanna have the picture to remind me of the airplane ride and of you and how you let me sit by the window. That was nice. When I grow up, I can look back at it…and say, 'Mr. Kenny took this picture and he let me sit by the window.'"

When Beyonce said that to me, it really touched me because here was this little ten-year-old child who was not even the least bit concerned about all the great things happening to her, but rather very sensitive to the people around her. Even at that age, it was easy to see that she was humble and not at all letting the idea of stardom go to her head.

"Wow, Bey. I'm flattered."

"Ah you just a softy Mr. Kenny."

Beyonce and Ashley continued to sit on the couch. We weren't scheduled to go into the studio until the next day, so it was about getting prepared and resting up for a full day of studio work the following day. Ann's idea was for the girls to relax and enjoy this lesson in first-class living.

"Girls, you know this is just the start of it, right? You're gonna have to work hard."

Both Ashley and Beyonce nodded in agreement acknowledging they understood what Ann was saying to them.

"When I become a star, I am gonna live like this every day." Ashley said matter of factly.

"Miss Ann, how do you think the studio will be?"

"Well Bey, it will be a lot of work but you can do it. I believe in you."

"Has anybody famous ever been in there?"

"Yes."

"Who?"

"Well Bey, let's see…Stevie Wonder,…uh… Let's see who else…Prince, …a lot of famous people have recorded at the Plant. You just have to wait and see."

"Wow!"

"What you mean wow, Bey…Girls Tyme…duh…we are stars too."

"Ashley…"

"Don't Ashley me Beyonce Knowles…we are gonna be stars."

Ann and I just looked at each other observing the girls interaction with one another. I just shook my head. That little Ashley, I was thinking to myself, "That little girl is already in diva mode. Woo wee, that one is something else, and a little self-centered too."

Having a son was a whole different experience than dealing with little girls. However, Ann was enjoying every moment of their exchange. She found it to be funny. I looked at Ann and mumbled. "You think this is funny, don't you?"

Ann shook her head and smiled.

"Hey girls, you know this is big time right? You already gettin' your shot."

Ashley didn't respond; however Beyonce spoke up. "Yes, Mr. Kenny. Thank you Miss Ann for helping us and making it possible for us to do all of this."

"Honey, the only thing I do is what good managers do. It is up to you to work hard, hone your skills and refine your craft, and prove that you deserve to be where you are. You have a great voice and a beautiful heart. You can do anything you put your mind to. All you have to do is work hard, don't ever forget that."

Beyonce took every one of Ann's words to heart. You could tell that she was listening and thinking about what was said. Ashley was sitting there twirling her hair and seemingly somewhat disinterested in what Ann was saying or distracted by all the material things around her. Either way, she was not fully present in the moment. Finally, Ann spoke up. "Let's go get us something to eat."

After about an hour or so, we went to have an early dinner at one of the fancy restaurants. After dinner we came back to the hotel to relax. As the night was winding down, we were all sitting around watching television. Ann was going through some paperwork and getting things ready for the following day. Beyonce was snuggled up on one of the chairs with a pillow while Ashley was stretched out on the couch with her glass. I decided to steal some quiet time to myself, think about my wife and son, chill for the rest of the evening, and get ready for the next day. "Well Ann, I think I'm gonna have me a glass of scotch and go sit out on the porch."

"No problem, Kenny."

"If you need me, you know where I'll be."

I got my glass of scotch and went and sat outside. I realized that I needed some ice, so I headed back inside to get some ice. As I headed toward the kitchen, Ashley raised up. "Hey you, get me some more ice water!"

"What?"

"You need to get me some ice water."

Now growing up in Mississippi, all I could think about was little kids stayed in little kids place. Don't talk crazy to grown folks or the old folks. Ann looked up at me from her paperwork. I guess she recognized with both of us being from the country, and all, that this was going to set me off. I had been cool, ain't said nothing to nobody. Ann jumped up as I fixed my mouth to respond to Ashley.

"Little girl what you say?"

"I said get me some water."

"Let me tell you something..."

"Kenny, Kenny, come on...step back outside..."

"Naw...Heck naw..."

Ann pushed me outside. She was laughing at me. I snapped. "What the heck wrong with that little girl. Didn't her mama teach her to respect her elders?" I was on a roll. "Ann, she was already getting' on my last darn nerve. Now this little diva think she gonna talk to me like I'm her staff or busboy!"

"I know Kenny…"

"Does she know who I am?"

Ann started laughing harder as I was going off.

"You gonna let that little brat talk to me that darn way? Who the heck she think she is?"

Ann was still laughing. "I know Kenny…"

"That little pint-size brat. Think she runnin' something all got-darned ready. Who the heck she think she is?"

Ann was holding her stomach by then.

"I'm Kenny Mo. I didn't come out here to be ordered around like some lackey, by a twelve-year-old girl!"

Ann was on the floor laughing. I was still going off. She was dying laughing. "Okay, Kenny…Okay!"

"Ah naw! Who that little thang think she is. I ain't no yes man, and I ain't no busboy!"

Ann was laughing uncontrollably.

"…Never was, never will. In fact if I wanted to be a star, I can be a star. But she think she is the bomb."

"I know, Kenny, I know…okay, okay, okay. Calm down, just calm down. She's just a little girl."

"I understand, but she act like a grown woman. She's talkin' to Kenny Mo! Kenny Mo. Don't nobody talk that way to Kenny Mo!"

"Kenny, why are you talking in third person?"

"What are you talkin' about Ann?"

"Why you talkin' in third person?"

"What do you mean in third person? How am I talking in third person?"

"...You said... what you talkin' about... don't nobody talk that way to Kenny Mo..."

We both fell out laughing. "Ooh I'am! Whoo..."

"Calm your country tail down!"

So Ann and I sat there for awhile. Ashley and Beyonce saw all the commotion. Ann went back inside to get some ice water. She got me my scotch. We just sat on the balcony drinking and talking. We went back inside after about an hour of laughing and talking. Ashley spoke up.

"Was anybody gonna get me some water?"

"Heck naw, get yourself little up and get your own darn water." Ann said half way laughing.

That little incident put an end to Ashley's thinking that she was going to be a prima donna. The whole time while this is going on, Beyonce's eyes was bucked wide open like, "What the heck...I know not to do that..." After Ashley got her water, and we all sat down together. We all realized just how funny it was and started laughing at the situation. Beyonce really thought it was funny.

"You see Mr. Kenny? His water head was just moving and everything."

They all were laughing. "What ya'll laughing at?"

"You was out there... Your neck was just rollin' and your head looked like it had water in it."

"Shut up Bey."

"We gonna start calling you Uncle Watermelon Head."

"As long as ya'll do what ya'll supposed to do, and as long as you handle your business...you can call me Uncle Watermelon Head."

We all agreed to that. It was getting late so we all turned in for the night. The next morning, the limo came to pick us up and we headed on to the Plant to start the session. The ride through the hills of South Sausalito was absolutely beautiful. When we arrived at the facility, it was like the "Holy Grail of Music." When we walked in we saw the host of entertainers who have journeyed through. The Stones had been there, Mariah had been there. Stevie Wonder recorded the "Songs in the Keys of Life;" Prince recorded "For You;" Luther Vandross recorded "Songs," Mariah Carey recorded "Music Box;" Aretha Franklin recorded "Who's Zooming Who;" and Kenny G recorded just about all of his stuff at the Plant. Everybody had been there.

This was the first time that I met Arne Frager. Arne was your typical Californian hippie type dude. He was a white gentleman with gray hair, yet a pretty nice guy.

"Hey girls…good to see you again. I've heard a lot of good things about you. I'm excited to have you here."

Arne explained to the girls what they would be doing. As Arne was talking, Lonnie walked in.

"Alright girls. Let's get in there."

They went through a barrage of songs. Ashley sang her heart out. They ran Beyonce back and forth in for background vocals as we went along. This happened for about two to three days non-stop. Everything worked out well and they were satisfied at what we had gotten. So we packed up and flew back to Houston.

At the conclusion of the studio visit we left there with two of Tayste's songs being mastered - "Groove Me One More Time" and "Love Just by You." We also ended up getting a couple of tracks done for Girls Tyme as well as leaving with some show ready material and tracks for the girls to use for live performances. That was helpful because it allowed us to better prepare for the live showcases.

The team and parents were excited. The acts were excited as well. Once we arrived back into Houston we arranged a listening party at Ann's house to listen to the tracks. We had a great time. Lynn was glad because it gave him additional material to pursue investments.

"This is great. It will help get more investors."

"That's good Lynn, but I wanna say this to everyone on the team. Bringing some solid investors on board is important. So this is something that I want all of us thinking about."

Lynn was uncomfortable with it, but Ann gave him a look like as if to say, "Shut up because if you was on the job, you would have done it by now."

The night went on and everyone was feeling pretty good about where things were.

About a week and a half later, Arne called Lonnie and gave him some preliminary feedback from the initial recordings at the Plant.

"I just wanted to follow-up on the package that was sent out. I sent it to several record labels. I hadn't heard back from any of the folks I sent it to with the exception of Darryl Simmons. He's over at Atlantic."

"What did he say?"

"He loved it. He passed it on to Sylvia Rhone and Merlin Bob in the New York office. I plan on following up with some of the other folks to get an answer."

"So, what now?"

"Well, Lonnie, I did have a long conversation with Ruth Carson. She is one of the three managing partners at De'Passe Entertainment. She was also at the show to see the girls. She was not particularly impressed with Ashley or Kelly's stage persona, and she was not excited at all about Ashley on tape. She feels the real stars are Beyonce and LaTavia. We will discuss that later."

"Yeah, yeah, I see what you're saying."

"I think you need to get the girls back out here. Utilize the background more in the lead and that will help strengthen the sound on tape so the group can break out and obtain a major record deal."

"Okay Arne, let me see what I can do. I'll talk with Ann and see what she says."

Lonnie called Ann and told her what Arne said about the feedback he was getting. He also told Ann that Arne suggested that the the girls go back out to the Plant and tighten a few things up, mainly pulling in some of the background vocals to do more lead as well. "Arne said that there is a lot of interest from industry executives but there were a few things to tighten up on."

"Why didn't Arne call me, Lonnie?"

"I called to see what the deal was and what the feedback was, so he told me. I'm sure he was going to give you a call or something. All I know is he thinks we can get the girls a major record deal but it was suggested by some of the others in the industry who heard the tracks to bring the background vocal to the lead a little more."

Ann received a letter in the mail not too long after that telephone conversation with Lonnie. The letter was addressed to Alonzo Jackson in care of Ann Tillman. When Ann read the letter she was wondering what was going on because based on some of the things in the letter, it was easy to see that Lonnie and Arne had been communicating and there was some other things going on that she was not aware of with respect to Lonnie. After reading the letter, although she was questioning some things, Ann decided to go ahead and take the girls back out to the Plant to re-record some of the songs.

Ann called me to inform me we needed to go back out to the Plant to re-record some things and what some of the music executives were saying. So we packed our bags and in a matter of a few days we were headed back to Sausalito, California. Mathew and Tina, Carolyn and Nolan, Beyonce, Ashley, Ann and I met at the airport again. Mathew left and came back with flowers in hand for both Beyonce and Ashley.

Tina was standing off to the side talking to Beyonce with tears streaming down her face.

"Sweetheart, you know you don't have to do this if you don't want to."

"I'm fine mama."

"Are you sure. You know you don't have to go if you don't want to. I can work harder here."

"I promise, I'm okay."

Cassey comforted Tina to let her know it was going to be okay. "It's alright girl, Bey's gonna be just fine."

"They are just so young to be doing all this traveling and being away like this. I'm not there with her. Her father's not there with her."

"Tina, I promise you, as long as I have anything to say or do with it and as long as I'm alive, I promise I will never let anything happen to Beyonce. Do you hear me?"

"Thanks, Kenny."

"Honey, it's gonna be alright. When my husband says he promise, he means it you hear?"

"Thanks Cassey."

Tina stood there crying. She was having difficulty keeping her composure this time. It was like she was not going to see Beyonce ever again. We talked to her to calm her down to let her know that it would be okay. Then we went ahead and boarded the plane. We finally touched down in San Francisco and got checked into a hotel. Ann went the route of saving resources and we checked into a hotel that was more reasonable with respect to cost. Our main focus was on getting the re-recordings done and get out without spending an arm and a leg.

The next morning we arrived at the studio with the girls. When we walked in Lonnie and T-Mo were already there. Ann and I looked at each other because we could feel something in the air but at that time it was not quite clear. As we continued on with the day, we learned that Arne and Lonnie had gotten together and formed A & A Music. They went out to have Girls Tyme sign a production contract with A & A Music. That way, when the girls blew up, Arne and Lonnie would be a part of their production team. The letter that Ann had received at her home addressed to Lonnie was from A & A Music, but Ann had not realized at the time that it was a company formed by Arne and Lonnie.

It was not until the studio that Ann realized what the real situation was and the contracts that were sent to Houston from A & A were from both Arne and Lonnie. The day at the studio, they pulled Ann aside to speak with her about it. Ann conferred with me, and together we went ahead and agreed that it should be okay. However, Ann was full of questions in terms of how Lonnie was operating. He was not upfront about what was really going on.

When A & A contracts were sent to Houston for signatures, Ann also went ahead and laid out the contracts for Girls Tyme to sign the Tillman Management/Girls Tyme Entertainment contract as well. Ann was making sure to cover all bases. As things were becoming more serious and we were planning major record deals for the girls, Ann had to take into consideration that the girls were minors. Although the parents had been on board, it was necessary to go to the Superior Court of Los Angeles and get authority from the court in the way of a "Right to Work" contract for the girls to be able to work.

We had to get Mathew, Tina, Carolyn, Nolan, Cheryl, and the rest of the parents to sign on the dotted line, and then go back to the Superior Court to get the authority to even sign the girls to a contract. All of this paperwork was handled and sent by the attorneys involved in the process prior to us flying back out to Sausalito to go into the studio again.

After all was said and done, the girls ended up signing a production contract with A & A Music and a management contract with Tillman Management/Girls Tyme Entertainment. The Superior Court of Los Angeles approved the contracts and at that point the girls were legally and officially signed with the two entities.

This time at the Plant, we went all out. Although we anticipated on recording a full load of songs the first time around, we ended up only recording a few. However, this time at the Plant, things were much more serious and we actually ended up recording a ten song collection. The interesting thing is, Ann and I learned that T-Mo, who had written all of the songs that the girls recorded, also signed a contract with A & A Music as well. The writer's deal he signed, confused Ann and me because from where we were sitting, they gave the impression that they were all one team. Yet, this trip manifested something very different.

"Ann, why did T-Mo sign a separate contract with them for writers?"

"I thought that was weird too, Kenny."

"It is. It would seem to me that if they have a production deal, Lonnie is the producer, T-Mo is the writer...I would figure that they were collectively a part of A & A."

Ann decided to do some more investigation and pulled T-Mo aside and started asking him some questions. She was feeling something real shady going on. "Boy, let me see what you signed."

T-Mo got the contract for Ann to look at. She started reading through it, and then she turned to me. "Huhm...Kenny, look at this contract."

Ann then handed the contract to me and I looked over it. I read through it and didn't say a word. Ann handed it back to T-Mo and told him thanks. When Ann and I got back to the hotel, I spoke up. "Ann, I think T-Mo sold all his royalties for a dollar. Did you see that?"

"Yeah, that's what I read too, that's why I wanted you to read it."

So after Ann and I talked, we went back to T-Mo. Ann approached him. "Tony, do you realize that you signed all your royalties away for a dollar?"

"Naw, naw, Lonnie and 'em said we gonna work all that out it was just a standard contract we were signing."

That whole thing raised a red flag for Ann and me. "Darn, Ann that is some screwed up stuff!"

"Look, Kenny anything, I mean anything, any contracts or whatever the heck it is, we both get copies to review it and make sure we are on one accord. We review everything that way we can make sure we are protected. And that way if I miss something or you miss something, we can pull each other's coat tail."

"That is really screwed up! That kind of stuff pisses me off."

"Why are you so upset about it Kenny? Heck T-Mo walked into that stuff on his own. He's always going along with Lonnie. I can see why you would be like...well, I guess I just don't understand why you are as upset as you are."

"You know Ann, years ago back in Greenwood, Mississippi, there was this man named Willie Cobbs who owned this barbeque joint on Walthall Street called CC Bar B Q. Anyway, he used to tell everybody that came in who would listen that he wrote this song called "CC Rider". He would always say 'that white man stole my song.' He kept saying it over and over again, 'I wrote CC Rider...I'm famous ya'll just don't know it because that white man Perkins stole my darn song.'"

"Wow!"

"Heck yeah. When I think of stuff like how David Ruffin died broke...come to think of it a lot of famous people die broke. I'm not with takin' advantage of people. It's just wrong."

"I hear you."

"So, this bull stuff with Lonnie and Arne...it ain't cool to me. This is one of the reasons I wanted to be in management so that I could keep people from getting screwed over."

Ann and I continued to talk for hours telling each other stories about how and why we got into the music industry. "Music was in my blood. My whole darn family sang. Not to mention, my husband's dream was to become the next Berry Gordy! He worked hard at it after he lost his teaching job."

"Heck, music was a part of my upbringing too. I'm a preacher's kid..."

"No way..."

"Yeah I am. Heck I come from a family of preachers. B.T. Moore Jr. and Sr. were both Baptist preachers. Music was a big thing in my family."

"Huhm. I guess this was just meant to happen then. Kenny, I tell you...if Dwight was alive...Shoot, I can't imagine what he would be saying right now."

"How did he die?"

"It was a car accident. We were on our way back to Houston from seeing some singers at the church...well he didn't go to the church that day, but I did. We went over to my sister's house for a barbeque..."

"What is this about incidents around barbeque?"

"I know right? Well we had just left my sister's house when it happened."

"Wow! I'm sorry to hear that..."

"Yeah, it was rough for a long time. I had a daughter too, she was two."

"Wow Ann, that's gotta be hard."

Listening to Ann talk about Dwight and Shawna got me a little teary-eyed. We talked about so many things and we both learned that we had a lot in common. It also gave me insight into why she was so passionate when it came to the girls and the difference that she showed with them and Tayste. Ann motioned her fingers like she was holding a cigarette, she leaned back, and said something totally off beat, yet deep to break the seriousness of the moment.

"Music is my muse."

We both laughed and immediately came out of that conversation. It had gotten really intense for a moment.

"See, you know what I'm gonna start calling you from here on out?"

"No what?"

"I'mma start calling you Dretta. Cause you remind me of my older sister. You got drive and you're a dreamer like me...so yep...your gonna be Dretta."

"Uhm...Alright."

We both sat there quietly for a moment, and then Ann spoke up.

"Darn, Kenny...I mean this stuff is happening right before our eyes. That contract...man that is some real screwed up stuff. I can't get over that."

"Yep! We better polish up our game."

"You ain't never lied. This is for real and these guys are out to get it. So let's keep our eyes open."

"Definitely."

"Alright then Kenny, what's your opinion of Lonnie?"

"Lonnie to me is all about Lonnie."

"What about Tony?"

"Ann, shoot...T-Mo is too dumb to even know what he's dealing with. But I do believe he is a good-hearted person. He's just a dumb ass."

"...and Arne?"

"Arne's tryin' to make the hit. He's had all these acts come through the studio, but he's never been a part of the hit."

This is where our friendship really began to flourish and we got to know one another. She asked me about Lynn. I told her I believed that Lynn was a crook. "We really need to keep our eyes on Lynn. Feed him with a long-handled spoon."

Ann and I decided to run it and work together. "Kenny, let's do this thing right. We don't have to do bad business to be successful and to help the girls or any of the acts for that matter get to where they're going."

That day, Ann and I made a commitment to one another to do our best to do things the right way and have each other's back.

The next day Ann and I headed back to the studio. We had been spending on average about ten hours at the studio each day. We had run through "Take 'Em to Another Level", "Teacher Fried My Brain", "6524287", and about seven other songs. Finally on the third day, Ann and I were watching the recording session. Ashley was in the booth. They were recording this one song when Lonnie kept stopping Ashley and making her start over. "Stop, do it again!"

"They said Jala…"

"Do it again.."

"They said Jala was…"

"Stop! Again!"

"They said Jala was the first girl you…"

Ashley kept starting over and over and over again. Lonnie kept stopping her. Finally after about ten times, everyone got pretty fed up with the process. Lonnie was being hard on Ashley. Beyonce was sitting in the back with me. She was fidgeting and rocking with impatience. As if to say, "Hurry up and get it so we can move on…dang!"

Ann was sitting in the middle. Arne, Lonnie, and T-Mo were up on the board. Because it was so expensive to record, we established a rule that if any of us had any comments, we would make those comment during the breaks or after the sessions. Now the more Ashley kept messing up, the more Beyonce kept fidgeting. "Bey, what's wrong with you girl."

Beyonce gave me this look as if she wanted to say, "What the heck you think is wrong with me?"

"Bey, can you do that?"

"Yes sir."

"Now Bey, you know the rules. If you say you can do it and I stop this session...they gonna cuss me out. Now do you hear me little girl? I'mma ask you one more time...can you sang that song?"

"Yes sir."

"Alright then."

I leaned forward to get Ann's attention and we started whispering back and forth.

"Ann..."

"Shut up ..."

"Ann..."

"Kenny shut up now...we got this session going on."

"Ann, listen to met. The girl screwin up in there, let Bey do it."

"Uh uh."

"Look, Ashley screwin' up in there; let Bey do it."

"What?"

"Let Beyonce sing it."

Ann turned around and looked at me then looked at Beyonce. "Bey, can you sing that."

"Yes ma'am Miss Ann."

"Okay, now don't you mess it up."

"I won't Mrs. Ann."

Ann interrupted the session. "Hey Lonnie..."

"Got darnit didn't I say don't nobody talk during my session...Shut up!"

"Lonnie..."

"Didn't I say don't be talking during my session?"

"Look I'm paying you! Listen to what I gotta say!"

"What!"

"Let Beyonce do it."

"Beyonce?"

I then spoke up to back what Ann was saying. "Yeah, Lonnie let..."

"You shut up!"

Lonnie was not trying to hear what I had to say. He was upset because his session was interrupted. "Man, let Bey do it!"

Lonnie looked over at Beyonce. "Bey, can you do this song?"

"Yes."

Lonnie yelled for Ashley to come out of the recording booth. Ashley came out and came and sat on my right. Beyonce was sitting on my left. So they started talking and giving Beyonce the pitch. Then Lonnie motioned for Beyonce to go into the booth. Beyonce went into the booth and on the first take, she nailed it. "They said Jala was the first girl you kissed and ooh I wish it was I..."

The pitch that Beyonce did that song in reminded us of the ten to eleven-year-old Michael Jackson. She sounded almost identical to how he sounded back then. Beyonce sang with control and with passion. After Beyonce nailed that song, Lonnie got started. "Hold on...let's go back on this other song."

After that, we went back over and over the songs. On every song where there were parts that he didn't like, he pulled Ashley's voice off and replaced it with Beyonce's voice. We all were excited, but at the same time, the more they pulled Ashley's voice off and put Beyonce's on, I watched Ashley's facial expressions and body language. It was ripping Ashley's heart out bit-by-bit.

"Dretta, that's enough."

"What?"

"That's enough."

I was looking at Ann and then looking and nodding at Ashley to signal Ann to look at Ashley.

"Dretta, they takin' the girl's voice off of every song…that's enough!"

We called a recess and the team went into the break room without the girls.

"I'm putting her on every screwin' song."

"Yeah Lonnie, I agree she does sound great."

"I understand Lonnie, I understand Arne…but Dretta…look, you can't take the girl's voice off of every song and have her just do background. Leave her on a couple of tracks and then we can go from there."

The conversation was heated and everyone was putting their thoughts on the table. Arne asserted himself and was all about the business of the matter. "Look here, the people I am hearing from… they like Beyonce."

Lonnie was backing Arne up. "Yeah, there's big people in the industry and they ain't interested in Ashley. They want Beyonce and LaTavia. See I tell you… what we need to be doing, we need to get LaTavia's ass out here… get her on tape doing the rap parts."

"Ann, Kenny, this is business and while it may be a hard decision to make, the truth is I've been in this industry for a long time and I have been talking to several executives and you have something, but the something you have has been doing backup. And what they are saying is the back up is really your lead singer and well…"

Ann listened to everyone go back and forth. After hearing what everyone had to say, she finally decided to just stop the session for the day. We went back to the hotel room. Things were pretty quiet. Ashley and Beyonce didn't really say much. It was easy to see that Ashley was totally heartbroken. Beyonce was sensitive to what had happened. I felt sorry for both of them.

Ann started talking to Ashley telling her everything was going to be okay as they pretented to watch TV, while Beyonce and I sat on the patio and watched the sunset. "Bey, you know…you didn't do nothin' wrong. You did what you had to do. It's all good, okay."

"Okay."

"We'll straighten it out."

Beyonce didn't really say anything. She just looked and you could tell that she was feeling sorry for her friend. The truth is, this situation showed the girls the two sides of success. One minute Ashley was leading songs, and Beyonce was singing back-up. The next minute Beyonce was leading and Ashley was doing back-up. It was truly a hard lesson on how the girls handled both situations. "Bey, the truth is baby girl…someone has to do the lead and someone has to do back-up. That's the way it is sometimes and in this case…well that is what happened. But it'll be okay."

What happened was bound to happen at some point, especially the way Lonnie and Arne had been pushing the fact that industry executives wanted to hear more of Beyonce. I thought Lonnie was too tough with Ashley. I don't believe he was sensitive to the situation at all, and for him it appeared to be more about getting the hit and the deal. Ann and I were concerned about the deal, but we were concerned about not breaking anyone's spirit as well.

Ann gathered both Ashley and Beyonce together in the hotel room. "Look girls, you both are still my lead singers. There are going to be some songs you lead on Ashley and there will be some songs you will lead on Bey. We have to do what's best for the team...but you both are the lead singers. One's not more important than the other. You got me?"

Ann worked to get Ashley's spirit back up. Initially when we went to the Plant, it was about getting her album recorded, so we needed to begin prep work for when we got back to deal with the parents. Yet, in us working hard to keep things in perspective, Lonnie was pressuring Ann about LaTavia. He and Arne stressed to Ann the need to get LaTavia out to get her on the tracks. After a heart-to-heart, Ann and I both agreed that from a business perspective it needed to be done.

Ann called Sheryl and arranged for LaTavia to fly out to Sausalito. Toward the end of the week, Latavia arrived and came into the studio to do some rapping on some of the songs. After that, we all packed up and flew back to Houston that Friday. As we were preparing to leave, Ann and I worked on damage control for when we got back. What happened was not expected and we knew that while some parents would be excited, others would be upset. Carolyn was not an easy person to deal with at times, and we knew that she was going to have a real problem with it. In as much as it was tough to deal with her personality, it was going to be equally difficult to keep Mathew in check.

As we were leaving the Plant, the tracks started going out to various labels. Before we even got back to Houston, things were already popping off. The word that kept coming back was "Beyonce... Beyonce... Beyonce..." Ruth Carson agreed to "present" the girls to five major labels that De'Passe had connections with and would assist in securing a record deal with a guaranteed two to three hundred thousand dollars per album, three videos per album with budgets of one hundred thousand dollars per video, and guaranteed outside promotion budget.

To package the act the way several of the music executives were suggesting required Girls Tyme to emphasize Beyonce and LaTavia at the forefront and this would give Ann the greatest chance of getting Girls Tyme signed with a major label. It was a delicate situation.

"I know what Ruth is suggesting of course; that's easier for her to say. We don't want to slight anyone or cause any hard feelings. But if we want to have a successful group then we have to approach this from a business point of view and do whatever is necessary for the best of the group."

"I know Arne."

"Good. It's up to you Ann and Lonnie to smooth this over politically so that no one gets upset. After all what we are seeking is in everyone's best interest since it is a six girl group. In essence, the label would be committing to spend over a million dollars to break Girls Tyme into radio and on MTV."

Ann and I discussed the matter in detail on the plane back home. "Okay, Kenny, what are we going to say to the Davis'?

"Shoot I don't know…Heck…"

Ann and I just shook our head. "Alright Ann, look… let's pretty much tell them what you told the girls. They both are the leads…"

"You know Carolyn is going to be pissed because Ashley isn't on the lead. Also with Beyonce going to the lead, how are we gonna deal with Tina and Mathew?"

"Dretta…listen. It is what it is. You know Carolyn is going to be Carolyn and start tripping and might threaten to take Ashley out the group. With respect to Mathew...well, I'm not really sure, he seems okay."

"Yeah…"

"My suggestion is we should give them as-needed information. In other words, give them information on a need to know basis and be really careful what we say. You don't want to give too much information because you are not sure how they will handle it. On the other hand, you need to tell them something. Just be careful on what you say and how you say it."

"Okay Kenny, but what are we going to tell them?"

"Well I think we should tell the Knowles that there is a lot of excitement about Beyonce and we are going to have her do more lead than before. We should tell Sheryl that we really are gonna need LaTavia to step up to the forefront and that we are going to put more spotlight on her. I think we should tell Carolyn and Nolan that Ashley is still one of our lead singers, but we are going to change things up a bit."

When we got back, we set up the listening party. Ann tried to do some preliminary damage control prior to, but there was just no way around the issue. As we were sitting there at the gathering, everyone was there listening - Ann, Lonnie, T-Mo, David, Lynn, the parents, Tayste, and the girls. All persons were on deck. There was a lot of excitement in the room. However, after about the fourth song, you could see Carolyn's expression start to change. There were just so many songs that Beyonce was singing the lead on. Ann saw it coming and was prepared for it.

Carolyn didn't make a scene but it was obvious that she was not happy. Ann and Carolyn went off to the side. They discussed the situation. It did get a little heated though.

"Carolyn, I promise you Ashley will get back out front."

"You all should have told me. If I had known this would happen..."

"We'll get everything worked out, alright?"

Ann was able to talk with Carolyn and Nolan. Next she went to speak with Mathew and Tina. "The industry feels your daughter will be the next big star."

There was a lot happening at one time. The rumors then started to fly. Either Lonnie or T-Mo put out that the executives didn't want Ashley or Kelly in the group. (Of course Lonnie was cool with the new line-up because of Yvonne). Also Nicki, Nina, and LaTavia were cousins and Yvonne is Sheryl's sister and Lonnie's special friend, so they all were cool with at least one of them making it to the forefront.

However, between the rumors, the attitudes, and the flexing, it was very challenging to handle. Ann was excited about the deal and put everything on the table. She initially did not anticipate that Mathew and Tina would be an issue; but she miscalculated that one. "Ann, I think it was a mistake to tell Mathew and Tina everything. Mathew is gonna be a problem. You watch and see."

We moved the group forward working through the challenges. During several rehearsals and it happened quite often, Lonnie would get upset and talk to Ashley and Kelly very harshly. "Nobody wants yo darn ass in the group no way. So get your stuff together."

Ann saw how Lonnie talked to Ashley and Kelly. Ann often had to step in and cover Kelly and help to build her self-esteem.

"The sooner we can get you all on board, the sooner they can become stars…Heck most of you are just along for the ride…so ride. But ride right."

"Lonnie! You are along for the ride. Stop talking to them girls like that."

During that time Ann protected Kelly, so much so it was like Kelly became her daughter. She became extra nurturing to both Ashley and Kelly. All of the girls continued to work hard and we eventually began to push through the controversy. As things moved on, the dynamics of everything started to change as well. We worked to get the girls industry polished.

The subject of another California showcase came up. We wanted to avoid it because of the expense, but it was likely in order to close the deal we would have to do another one. To get the girls up to par, we put them before a live audience at least twice per month and they had daily rehearsals. They also performed at the Sammy Awards. This was Beyonce triumphant return and she was very excited about this particular performance because it was the Sammy Awards where her music career first started. Girls Tyme also did a back-to-school concert. They were getting sharper and looking more polished on stage.

Around this time, Kelly's mother decided to move back to Atlanta. This almost put a wrench in things because we were in the middle of negotiations.

"Doris, let Kelly stay with me. I'll take care of your daughter. I will look after her like she is my flesh and blood. Things are getting really serious and we are about to close a record deal. Now is not the time to move away."

"I am moving Ann, I don't want Kelly to miss out or ruin her chances, but I'm leaving."

"Leave her with me. Please let her stay. She can live with me. She's gonna make it. I know she will. Your daughter is gonna be a star. Trust me on this. I know one when I see it."

Ann and Doris continued to discuss the possibility of Kelly staying with Ann. They ultimately worked through the situation. Doris agreed to let Kelly move in with Ann. It was a hard decision but Kelly was willing to stay while her mother moved. Regardless of her mousiness, Kelly wanted it just as bad as any of the other girls, and she too was willing to make sacrifices.

At this point everybody wanted it, and was not holding back about it. Every night we were laying the ground work with the music executives. One evening after getting off the line with some of the people from the industry, I was over to Ann's when she got a call from Mathew wanting to set up a meeting.

"Kenny, that was Mathew. He wants to set up a meeting. What do you think that's about?"

"Well, knowing Mathew, you can about guess."

"Uhm."

Ann ended up meeting with Mathew the next day. "You know Ann, Beyonce has now become the focus of the group, I think you should let me help manage."

Ann looked at him as if to say, "Screw you and get the heck out of my house."

But she knew she couldn't say that to him no matter how much she wanted to say it.

"Well Mathew... uh...No. We have everything we need. I appreciate everything and you offering, but we don't need a manager."

"Well...uh...Ann..."

"What do you bring to the table?" We have everything set up, everything is ready to go. It would only get things off focus and disrupt everything we are already doing."

"Oh, Uhm...okay. I appreciate you meeting with me."

"No problem."

The conversations with Mathew wanting to become a part of the management team kept surfacing over several weeks. Ann was exerting a lot of energy keeping him at bay. Unbeknownst to Ann, the heavy schedule, the stress, and lack of rest had taken a toll on her physically. As a result she fell into a Lupus crisis and ended up being taken to the hospital where she was admitted. When I found out that Ann was in the hospital, I immediately went up to see her.

"You look like crap! What! You forgot to comb that nappy ass hair. Don't be breaking down on me now."

"Screw you Kenny!"

We both laughed. "Don't be in here got-dammit feeling sorry for your self either... Heck. Get your butt up and out of here. You think you on some darn vacation or something."

Ann continued to laugh. "Kenny, stop."

"I'm serious girl. You left me with the animals at the zoo. You ain't paying me to deal with that stuff. You better get yourself up."

Ann and I laughed and talked over the week while she was in the hospital. We became much closer during that time. Cassey also came to visit her. Ann knew that she had real friends in Cassey and me.

No sooner than Ann was discharged from the hospital, Mathew came calling Ann to meet with her again. This time he threatened Ann to take Beyonce out of the group if she did not make him part of the management team. "Either you let me co-manage, or I will take Beyonce out of the group. It's simple as that."

Ann called me to let me know what was happening.

"Kenny, I done paid every bill for all this stuff. The showcase, the studio, the hotels rooms, the flights...paying to fly Lonnie and T-Mo back and forth from Houston to California. I paid everything and this dude is gonna try and muscle me like that.

Lynn has his tail between his legs for being found out as the shady screw up he is! I cannot even get out the darned hospital for five minutes before this mofo come calling me with this stuff!"

"I told you Dretta, you would have some issues with Mathew. It was a bad move to tell them everything like that."

"You're right Kenny. And Lynn's behind done stole my checks and writing hot checks! Gotta deal with that stuff too!"

"We either have to have some investors or stay on course with this. And we don't have any investors and we can't lose Beyonce."

"Kenny...Mathew wants fifty-fifty management."

"Well, what do you want me to do? I can leave and ya'll just handle it."

"No...No, I need you Kenny. You're the only person I can trust.

"Okay..."

"Would you agree to split my half of management with me like we have with the overall management?"

"Dretta, no that's not fair to you. We did all this darn leg work and got all this stuff ready, and he wanna come in just because he's the child's parent? That doesn't mean he should come in and take half...I tell you what, if you give him half, you just give me ten percent of what you get on Girls Tyme and we will go fifty-fifty like we agreed on Tayste and everybody else."

"...And you are okay with that? Will you have a problem working with him?"

"I won't have a problem working with him. He seems like a nice guy. He might be on some bull...but he seems like a nice enough guy...you know I mean...whatever it takes, Dretta. I'm with you. I do understand it is his daughter."

After our conversation, Ann met with Mathew and agreed to let him become a co-manager with her and me as part of the management team with respect to Girls Tyme. So to secure Mathew's point, contracts were drawn up to reflect that Mathew and Andretta were the managers of the group Girls Tyme.

After the other parents saw that Mathew had gotten his way on the management team, they started to attempt to flex their muscles as well. Carolyn and Nolan thought that if they could bring some investors to the table or make some sort of connections that it would help Ashley get more lead time. They had no idea of what the industry executives were saying about Ashley.

"Hey Kenny man, Alexander O'Neal is gonna be having a show here. That's a friend of mine. We grew up together. You know I can make that connection. He got some connections in the industry as well and maybe we can use that avenue to get a deal."

"You know Alexander, Nolan, man?"

"Yeah, we're real tight. He's a friend of mine. Like I said, we been friends since we were young."

Mathew had no problem asserting himself as part of the management team. It was a good mix because he was able to bring that corporate dynamic to the table.

"That sounds good Nolan."

"Yeah, yeah. I can set that up for us. I got my connections too, you see. Alexander and I go way back."

"Well then...word... let's do it."

Lonnie, Mathew, Nolan, and I went to the show. We got to the door and had to pay to get in. Lonnie said, "Nolan man, we got it goin' on. Why we gotta pay to see this nigga?"

"Just come on in man, I got it."

We went in, sat down and had some drinks. We sat there laughing and talking. We were having a great time when Lonnie started to kick things off.

"Man, that negro's coked out…look at him. He's coked out. He ain't what he used to be."

Lonnie was steady shooting him down. Mathew was playing the diplomat.

"Hey, ya'll he probably still have the avenues."

I spoke up as things were getting louder. "Well, let's keep it calm. We can't judge a book by its cover. Let's just see what it's gonna be."

As we were sitting there, Nolan seemed very nervous. He was trying to get it right. This was his opportunity to show his usefulness. We sat through the whole show. Alexander did okay, nothing really to brag about. After the show, we were waiting on him to come off the stage. Nolan said, "Let me go talk to him."

We were standing right behind Nolan as he approached Alexander O'Neal.

"Alexander…Alexander!"

Alexander looked at Nolan all dazed. "Hey man, what's up."

"Its Nolan man…it's Nolan!"

"What's up homie…good to see ya."

Then Alexander just walked off. We all laughed at the situation. Nolan was humiliated. Lonnie really got to going then. "Oh, man, we came down here for this stuff! Heck, he can't do nothin'!"

We walked on and Nolan was like, "Man, ain't this some bull!"

"Man, we done wasted a whole night…let's go!"

"Man, I can't believe that idiot acted like he didn't know me!"

I laughed and chimed in. "Nolan, that cokehead didn't act like he didn't know you...he didn't know you."

We all fell out laughing and teased him about it. Lonnie wouldn't let up. "Man that dude right there so coked out! That sap sucker didn't know you from Adam."

"Nolan, didn't you say that was your childhood friend?"

"Mathew man, yeah, he is."

"Well, that dude right there ain't no childhood friend."

We laughed the rest of the night and on the way home about that night, making the best out of the situation. However, it shot Nolan's credibility all the way down. Although nothing came of it, Ann and I had another plan in place to take the girls to go see William and work with Rob, Troy and Yarbrough and Peoples.

In the meantime, nothing was going to stop Ann from closing the deal. Arne had arranged another showcase, so we worked to get the girls ready.

GOT TO GIVE HIM MORE

Arne insisted that Ann needed to have the girls perform in yet another showcase so that the industry folks could take a look at them again, especially since several adjustments had been made according to the feedback received.

"Andretta, Ruth seems to feel that she can obtain the kind of commitment we're looking for at these labels, but in order to close the deal, she believes the girls should put on a live show in Los Angeles. These folks are concerned with the look and performance and the video isn't strong enough to do it or turn the necessary heads."

"What are you proposing Arne?"

"Well, obviously I would like to obtain the deal we want without going through another expensive showcase and that's still a possibility. But I do believe it's important for us to pursue all available options and help that we can get to reach our goal."

"Arne, I've been the sole upfront investor and I'm spending a lot of darn money. I have foot many of the bills and my thoughts are if we can do it without the showcase that would be ideal."

"I understand Andretta. David and I are exploring the possibility that we can get one of the interested labels to foot the bill to bringing the girls out to L.A."

"Okay."

"In any case, let's talk soon."

Once all was said and done, Arne worked with Ann to schedule the girls to perform as a featured attraction at the BMI Showcase in California. This was a showcase that allowed unsigned talent an opportunity to perform in front of industry heavyweights. It is one of the most powerful music licensing organizations affiliated with the largest groups of songwriters, composers, and publishers that exist. It just so happened that Girls Tyme was the spotlighted act and some of the major players were aware of them as there was already a buzz.

After having opened up for Jennifer Holiday, Chris Walker, Yo Yo and others and performing at events such as the Sammy Davis Jr. Awards, Astroworld, the Black Expo, Juneteenth celebrations, and a beauty pageant, BMI was a natural progression and the preparation for it was similar to other showcases.

As rehearsals continued with a particular emphasis on BMI, Beyonce and LaTavia became more visible, while Ashley, although she continued to sing lead on some songs, was down-played. All of this was to make the deal happen and do what was in the best interest of the group. The girls prepared hard to put their best foot forward to get the major record deal. While there was much talk surrounding their talent in the industry, no major deal had been signed yet.

By that time, everyone was getting used to Mathew being a part of the management team. Although he raised a lot of hell in order to get his way onto team, he initially came in as a quiet observer, taking note of how things were managed. Mathew appeared to bring a positive mix to the table because with him came the corporate experience and he was able to assist with additional structuring.

As everyone was preparing and working hard for the BMI Showcase, Lonnie was flying in and out of town, while Mathew and David were placed in charge of the rehearsals. Ann and I continued to work on the business side of things. With

Beyonce taking a more prominent role in the group and Mathew and David running the rehearsals, Mathew wanted to move rehearsals to his house. He and David convinced Ann that since most of the other girls lived closer to him on the South Side near the Houston Medical Center, and David was living with him as well, it just made sense to move rehearsals to his house. Although LaTavia also lived on the North side, it was no problem for Sheryl to get her daughter there, but Ann had difficulty getting Kelly there because she did not get off work until around five o'clock.

"Come on Ann, you live on the North Side, you and Kenny are the only ones that live in that direction. Make it easier for everyone."

"I hope ya'll know you getting on my last nerves. Mathew, all of your darn questions, and needing this or that and wanting this or that, ya'll making me sick. I'mma move the rehearsals to your house since I put you in charge of the rehearsals, but I'm gonna be on your butts like white on rice and I don't want no stuff. This is an important showcase and we need to close the deal."

"Ann, I need to know everybody you talkin' to and communicating with. Who are the main ones you dealing with?"

"Mathew, you mind the rehearsals and right now just leave the business side to me and Kenny. Get the girls ready to perform. That's your focus right there."

After Ann consented to the rehearsals being moved to Mathew's house, practice beefed up and everyone was buckling down to be in top performance mode. However, that still wasn't enough for Mathew. Next, he and David begin pushing for Kelly to move. They argued that transportation was impacting the rehearsals.

"Look Ann, we need all the girls in one place. With them in one place, we can focus more on the rehearsals, have as much time with them as we need, and vocal training and transportation won't be a factor because all the girls would be there."

"Darn it, I told Doris that I would see after her and that I would treat her like my own daughter. I can't say that I would allow my own daughter to go live with you, Mathew. Is you crazy? What are you trying to do?"

David chimed in to support what Mathew was saying.

"I don't see what the problem is. Mathew and Tina have two other daughters."

"Look Ann, Bey, Solange, and Tina are there. I am surrounded by a bunch of darn women. What could happen to her? Come on now, be reasonable. I think the real concern with Kelly should be here with Armon and Chris."

"What the heck is that supposed to mean?"

"Well Ann, it's no secret that there is some physical attraction between Kelly and Armon."

"What are you trying to imply Mathew? They are kids."

"Yes and kids are kids and when you have males and females in too close corners, it can be an ingredient for disaster."

"Heck, if you take that logic, Mathew, there are just as many men who be messing with little girls, so don't give me that mess."

"What are you tryin' to imply, Ann?"

"Just what I said. Don't be trying to justify Kelly coming to live with you and Tina because of my boys, when there is two grown ass men over at your house who ain't related to her either. So don't come with that bull. I'm not saying you will, but as a mother, I weigh everything. Let me think about it, and I'll let you know."

"Alright."

Ann was getting stressed out over everything going on. Initially she only had to deal with Lonnie's pressure, however now Mathew was also pressuring her. Between Lonnie, Mathew, Lynn and now David, it was wearing her energy down because she felt she always had to look over her shoulder with them. It appeared that since Mathew came on the management team, she was having more Lupus flares.

Ann and I discussed Mathew's questions frequently. "Kenny, why does this man keep asking me all these questions all the time?"

"Who?"

"Mathew! He wants to know who I'm talking with in the industry. He keeps asking me their names, contact information and what they're saying to me. It is beyond him being Bey's father. He keeps hounding me for information that really is not for him to concern himself with... Then he had the nerve to say it would be best if Kelly come and live with him and Tina, and insinuated something about Kelly and Armon."

"For real?"

"Yeah. On top of that he keeps using Bey as a trump card because he knows that they are interested more in Bey and LaTavia. I told you that he called Teresa and Arne didn't I?"

"No you didn't tell me that Ann. What did he call them for? See, I had a feeling you shouldn't have told him what you did, but that is neither here nor there now. Dretta, it sounds like he is trying to steal the group."

"You know, Kenny, I was thinking that and didn't want to say it. You know he got the girls thinking that he is the manager now and I'm just working with him. I'm trying to make some headway and this fool is acting like he's making stuff happen and he is large and in charge. I don't need this stuff Kenny. What does Kenny-Mo have to say about that?"

Ann was upset and then we both had to laugh when she started talking about me in third person. "You know I'm sounding like your behind now when Ashley pissed you off in San Francisco."

"You know you're wrong for that!"

"I know. I couldn't help it. Heck, I'm just about as pissed right now as you were then in that hotel room."

"Seriously though Dretta, just be smart, keep an eye on him, and keep on pushing. He seems to have a good business sense, but I'm not sure what his aim is."

"He's gotten wind of them wanting Bey, and since he's the daddy, you just don't know what to expect from him."

"Well, let's just keep our pulse on the matter. Keep setting up the gigs and the opportunities and keep it moving."

"I hear you Kenny. You are always the voice of reason. Well, most of the time, anyway. I don't know about Kenny-Mo though."

We both laughed at a serious situation to stay sane with everything going on at one time.

Right before Girls Tyme headed to California to perform at the BMI showcase, Ann had a major Lupus crisis which caused her to be hospitalized. So, as the girls and their parents were heading to San Francisco to perform at the BMI Showcase on August 26, 1992, Ann was heading to the hospital. I had started a new job and was unable to travel to the showcase so it was up to Mathew and Lonnie to go.

"Kenny, did the girls get off to California?"

"Yes Dretta. I made sure everything was set. Mathew was there and everyone got off okay."

"Okay, good."

"Dretta, what are you doing? You better get your tail on up and out of here. Now you know we ain't got time for this mess. You setting up all this stuff, and your butt wanna sit back and relax."

"Kenny look..."

Ann showed me where they had to amputate her finger. She tried her best to laugh but she was not as playful as she had been before. You could tell that she was not well. "Kenny don't make me laugh... I, I can't."

"What the hell you mean I can't. Girl you better get your tail up!"

Ann was laughing as the nurse came in and I was trying to make her laugh even harder.

"Sir, you are going to have to leave. We cannot have her blood pressure going up. She needs to stay calm."

"Okay sorry."

I whispered to Ann, "You know you fakin'. Ain't nothing wrong with you."

Ann was trying to keep from laughing and getting herself worked up.

"Kenny stop it now, shoot."

"Sir, you are going to have to leave."

The nurse kicked me out of the room. I called Ann later, but I could tell that she was not her energetic and bubbly self. To start losing fingers was not a good sign of her condition as far as I was concerned. I really started looking at her health as a serious matter at that point.

Ann was recovering, as reports came back from California. The BMI Showcase was a success. Not too long after everyone returned to Houston from the showcase, Ann received a call from Daryl Simmons who contacted her about his interest in the girls. His wife had seen them perform a month earlier at the Black Expo. She told her husband about Girls Tyme and I guess word got around pretty fast because he reached out to Ann. Daryl who was the founder of Silent Partner Productions was also associated with Kenny "Babyface" Edmonds and Antonio "L.A." Reid of LaFace Records. So right after the BMI Showcase is when the first talks with Silent Partner Productions began.

Who would have thought that losing a finger could change Ann's routine around the house as much as it did. However, the fact that one of her fingers was gone created challenges for her. Different friends went over to her house to help out. Charlotte often took Nicki and Nina to go help. Daily rehearsals, conditioning and vocal training had recently been turned over to Mathew and David. Ann and I would go over to the Knowles' house once or twice a week to see the progress. They also started rehearsing at Tina's hair salon and practicing on the customers that came into the salon.

Ann was recuperating pretty well, and Nina was a big help for Ann, spending a lot of time over to her house and then heading to rehearsals. Ann observed Armon and Kelly a little closer since the conversation she had with Mathew. One day Ann walked into the living room and caught Armon and Nina kissing. Ann had thought that he liked Kelly. She did not confront Armon or Nina at the time, but the next morning when Armon was in the bathroom mirror brushing his hair, she raised the issue.

"Armon, I saw you and Nina kissing. What's up with that? I thought you liked Kelly. Which one of the girls do you actually like?"

"I like both of them."

"Well, whichever one you like the most, I will tell you this right now, Kelly is gonna be the rich one."

Armon looked at his mother with embarrassment. Ann just said what she had to say and walked away. Being that Ann saw Armon and Nina kissing, she got to thinking about the conversation with Mathew and reluctantly allowed Kelly to go stay with him and Tina. By this time, conversations between Ann and Silent Partner Productions had progressed to the point where Daryl Simmons was talking about setting up a showcase for the girls to perform for him in Atlanta.

Ann had Silent Partners on the hook. As she was pulling on that line, she received a letter from Arne asking her to call him and that the girls needed her. Inside the envelope was also a check for five hundred dollars reimbursing her for the loan she gave to Lonnie and a copy of the video tape from the BMI Showcase performance. When Ann called Arne back per his letter, she received some great news along with an ear full.

"When you were not able to make the BMI Showcase, I heard you were not feeling well. I asked Mathew to send me the pages and covers for the package. Like I said in the letter to you, I can put together about twenty-five to thirty packages to take along to meetings. Can you follow up with Mathew and make sure that I get them?"

"Yes."

"Also, I need Carolyn Davis' number. Alonzo gave her an airline ticket to use in August. I bought the ticket for him to use, and it was worth a hundred and ten dollars. It may seem like a small thing to the two of them, but it's my money and he had no business giving it to her without consulting me about it first."

"Uhm. I see."

"I want Carolyn or Alonzo to reimburse me."

"I understand Arne. What's the good news you had?"

"Oh, the good news. The girls got accepted to perform on Star Search! I hope you're going to Florida wth them, because, Ann, they need you."

"I know they do Arne. I'm here and haven't gone anywhere."

"Well the great news is…Girls Tyme has a spot on Star Search. It's next month and will be aired sometime in February."

"That is great news. Arne, why didn't you say that first, instead of giving me all that other crap?"

Things were popping and Girls Tyme had very little time to prepare for the Star Search taping which was scheduled for November 4, 1992. In one of the conversations over song choices, Ann, Lonnie, Arne and I ended up in a heated debate on what song the girls should sing for the Star Search appearance.

"I want the girls to sing a song that will display all of their talent. I'm thinking they should do something like "Sunshine" where you can hear their vocal ability."

"Ann look, Arne and I think we need to feature Beyonce and LaTavia. That's who they want. Everybody else is along for the ride."

"Lonnie, that's bull and you know it. All of these girls are working hard, and I'm in agreement with Ann, we should feature the girls collectively and build on their harmony."

"Kenny, you always agreeing with Ann."

"Screw you Lonnie, that's because Ann is the only got-darn one who is making any sense right now. The girls have great harmony and we should highlight that harmony and feature the girls collectively. Ann's right."

Arne and Ann had strong words over the telephone because Arne was coming from the same perspective as Lonnie, "Bey and LaTavia are the real stars here."

Because Arne said it, Mathew rolled with whatever anyone in the industry said. The song that was ultimately selected to perform at Star Search was selected by Lonnie, Arne, and Mathew. Ann and I were in disagreement with the song choice.

Around the time to appear on Star Search, I had to work so I could not go. Ann had another Lupus crisis and ended up back in the hospital. During the last hospital visit when she had the first finger amputated, she was made aware that she would need to have another one removed but they told her they would only take the one at that time. However, as she went into another crisis, it became necessary for a finger and a toe to be removed. It seemed the more Ann became stressed the more she had Lupus bouts. When I went up to the hospital to visit her, she asked me to work more closely with Mathew.

"Kenny, I need you to start working a little closer with Mathew. I told him what to do and he says he feels pretty good about what he's doing, but I want you to work with him. He has a corporate background and I trust he can work well with things.

"I don't know Ann..."

"I trust that Mathew can do that. He says he's okay with things, plus there's this group I want you to take a look at. They are playing at the Sky Bar and they're supposed to be this girls group that is a lot like EnVogue. Heck I'm laid up in this darn hospital and won't be out for about a week, so I need you to do this for me Kenny. We need to continue to look for new talent."

I agreed. This was the first time that Mathew and I went to take a look at groups together. Usually it's just Ann and me. So, I picked Mathew up from his house and I drove to the club.

"You know Kenny, everyone is talking about Beyonce being a future star…"

"Yeah."

"But the truth is…Solange is way more talented than Bey. She will be the real big star."

When Mathew said that to me I was like, "You crazy as heck."

However, instead I responded, "Mathew man that would be great."

Mathew and I clicked well that night. Things were cool. The group we went to go scout out was pretty good, but we didn't approach them that night. Instead, we took note of them with plans to speak with them at a later time. We reported back to Ann. When Ann got out of the hospital, I went over to her house.

"Dretta, the act that we went to go see…"

"Yeah, what about them? What did you think?"

"There's some promise there. I think they have something."

"Well let's deal with them after the Star Search piece, because things are pretty hectic right now."

"Yeah, I know, and this job doesn't allow me the time off to travel as much as I was able to before."

"Heck, this Lupus is kicking my behind. But we're gonna keep pushing. I go into the hospital with my darn fingers and toes, and it seems like every time I leave something else is cut off and left on the table."

"I know one darn thing, you better keep yourself out of that hospital. We ain't got time for that. Do that mess when we close this deal."

"I won't be able to make it to the Star Search appearance. I am still in a lot of pain though and I guess they say I'm still in a crisis. But this stuff is not going to get the best of me. I might not have any fingers and toes when all is said and done, but I sure in the heck will have my mind and my mouth."

"I don't think anything can stop that darn mouth of yours."

"You know what...you see this tape here where my middle finger used to be...I can still say screw you nigga."

"I'm glad to see you getting back to yourself."

"When you see this tape go up, just know I'm sayin' screw you...better yet, when we in our darn meetings and you see this tape go up right here..."

Ann took the part where her middle finger was replaced with surgical tape and stuck it in her nose. "...I'm sayin' screw you. And when Mathew or Lonnie get to talking they stuff...and you see this go up here like this...I'm saying screw you. That way, you know I ain't agreeing to their bull."

We laughed and continued discussing everything that was on our plates, the girls' schedules, as well as how we would work everything out. Girls Tyme had been working hard getting ready for Star Search. Ann and I went to see the rehearsals. Lonnie grew more impatient and Ann and I witnessed more yelling of the girls to get it right. Things were amping up to the next level and the pressure was on to win Star Search. Because Ann was not one hundred percent and I had this new work schedule, Sheryl stepped up to the plate and offered her assistance to help Ann coordinate the girls' schedules, especially since her daughter LaTavia was quickly becoming one of the group's stars.

After pushing to get things perfect, everyone who was scheduled to fly out headed to the Star Search appearance. The girls went up against the champions which were an all white male group by the name of Skeleton Crew. The champions remained the champions with a score of four stars while Girls Tyme, the challengers, received a score of three stars. After the performance, some of the feedback was that it was not a good song choice and three stars were far too generous. Everyone was upset that the girls did not win. They called back to Houston to share the somber news.

"Ann, this is Mathew. These are some racist folks out here. The girls didn't win."

"Okay, what happened? How did they do?"

"They did great, they nailed the song. What happened? I will tell you what happened. These are some racist cats that's what happened."

"Okay, I will let Kenny know. Let's talk when you all get back."

"Alright, see you soon."

Ann called me right after she hung up from Mathew.

"Kenny?"

"Yes."

"This is Ann."

"I know who this is nigga. I talk to you every darn day. Don't you think I know your darn voice by now?"

"Shut up Kenny. Look…the girls didn't win."

"What?"

"The girls didn't win. They lost against some man band called Skeleton something. At least that's what Mathew was saying. He's pissed."

"Well, how did he say they did?"

"He said they did great but honestly, that song was screwed up, but you couldn't tell them nothing. So I'm not surprised at the outcome."

"That's something."

"The way he was sounding and the way he said the girls were taking it, we are gonna have to do some damage control. I'm not sure if the girls would've chosen that song for themselves if they were given the chance. See what I'm saying?"

"Valid point Ann. When does this stuff air?"

"Arne told me it will air in February. We are gonna have to make some headway before it airs. I'm not sure of the impact of this loss."

When the crew arrived back into Houston, everyone was very disappointed at the fact that they lost. This also took a toll on Ann's health and the stress of this played a role in her suffering another minor bout with Lupus. This time Ann managed to stay out of the hospital. It only knocked her down a few days with a lot of pain. When the Lupus became an issue, it was just too hard to tell how long she would be down for. The only thing we could do was not to cause her unnecessary stress and to handle our business so that she would not have to keep cleaning up everyone else's stuff. Being that Ann was having more frequent setbacks with Lupus and was in need of a little more support at home, a woman by the name of Ms. Penny came over to Ann's house to help her until she felt much better. In addition, to take some of the burden off of Ann, the team met at her house for meetings.

Ann did not let the fact that she was not feeling well get her down. Although she was not feeling her best, business kept moving and so did she. Ann continued to make things happen. She received a call from a man named Dick Griffy who was the owner of Solar Records. He wanted Tillman Management/Girls Tyme Entertainment to come out and meet with him. Because Ann was not able to go to the meeting as a result of her more recent health crisis and I could not go because of my job, the two of us discussed the situation at great length and with great hesitation, decided to let Mathew go and attend the meeting on his own and talk the deal.

Ann paid for Mathew to fly out to Los Angeles to speak with Griffy. Our thinking was, "If he screws it up, at least we are still in talks with Silent Partners. It's worth going to see what can come of it."

When Mathew returned from the meeting he and Ann met to discuss what happened. She was not able to really get much out of him other than the meeting went well. After the two of them got together, Ann and I met so that Ann could provide me with the feedback that Mathew had shared.

"Kenny, Mathew said the meeting went well. He did not provide a lot of details. He just said it was a good meeting. Not really sure about where things are with this one."

"What did Mathew say Griffy said?"

"Well, he said that Solar was interested in the girls, but he really didn't give any concrete information. I'm gonna have to follow up to see what is what."

"Huhm...okay."

The interesting thing about the Solar situation was that Mathew went to speak with Griffy, but as things played out, I got the distinct feeling that something wasn't right. Whatever Griffy said or whatever those conversations were, we knew that it changed Mathew. He wasn't the same after that meeting. I started to do some digging and learned that Griffy had a reputation of manipulating and stealing from his artists. Some of his acts included Yarbrough and Peoples, the Gap Band, and Rolls Royce.

When I found out that Griffy worked with Yarbrough and Peoples and the Gap Band, I made a call to Troy to find out as much as I could in order to satisfy my own scepticisms.

"Hey man, we had a meeting with Solar Records. What's up with Dick Griffy? I'm not sure how comfortable you are talking about it but we really need to know what's up with him. How is he…I mean what type of person is he?"

"Kenny man, the guy's a crook. He robbed from us and black-balled Yarbrough and Peoples. He ain't right, man."

Troy and I spoke for some time, he was a reliable source and I was appreciative of how direct and straight-to-the-point he was about his experience with the man. Once Troy shared with me what type of character Griffy was I, called Ann.

"Ann, I just got off the phone with one of my contacts. You remember I was telling you about Troy People's right?"

"Yes. What about him?"

"He told me that this Griffy guy is a character and not someone you can really trust."

"What specifically did he say?"

"Well Dretta, the long and short of it was that he is a crook and he steals from his acts. In other words, if you really want to get ahead, Griffy is not the one to get you to where you are trying to go."

"Well, we need to just move on past that one then. What do you think?"

"I think you might be right."

After a long discussion about it, Ann and I was prepared for nothing to come of the meeting that Mathew had with Griffy. Therefore, we moved forward as if the meeting didn't even happen. As we continued to have our management meetings, I began to notice how Mathew was speaking. Prior to the meeting with Griffy, he was being a parent, a daddy, and a team player. However, what Ann and I started seeing was something very different.

"Shoot Ann. You listening to Mathew? What the heck he mean he is in the business of exploiting people? He wasn't talkin' that stuff before LA, what's up with that?"

"I heard that too, Kenny…Huhm."

"I don't know who this nigga is right here, but he on some stuff."

"I wonder what really transpired with the talks with Griffy."

"Takes a lookin' into you figure?"

In one of the meetings involving Ann, Mathew, and me, I confronted Mathew when he got to talking crazy again.

"Look ya'll, I'm in the business of exploiting people. That's what I do now."

"Mathew man, you can't be going around talking about you going to exploit people, man. That's not cool."

"That's all the industry is; it's about exploiting people. And that's what I'm gonna do. I'm gonna exploit people, and do what we gotta do."

Mathew mentioned to Ann and I that Griffy said in order to control the acts, you have to own the name. So we immediately went to file a trademark on the name Girls Tyme. The trademark went under Ann Tillman and Mathew Knowles as the owners of the name Girls Tyme. What that did was give management the power if any of the girls got out of line, they could be kicked out of the group because we owned the entity of Girls Tyme. We went on with business and did not think any more about this. We figured, we owned the name and that gave us more control over the girls as well.

After all of this took place, the conversation with Daryl Simmons and Silent Partner Production began to catch fire. Talks were progressing with them even more. At this time, we started to go out and look for more acts. Once again Mathew and I went back to the Sky Bar to follow up with the group we saw before Star Search. Ann and I discussed it and we definitely wanted to sign them as an artist. So that night we went to another one of their performances and approached them afterwards to express interest.

"Hi, my name is Kenny and this is Mathew. We are with Girls Tyme Entertainment and we are interested in signing you and having you to join our stable of artists. Right now we have Girls Tyme, which is an up and coming act. We have Tayste, which is an all-boys group similar to a Boyz II Men, and a few other acts. We are interested in bringing you into the fold."

"We're interested."

"Good, so what we would like to do is talk to each of you to find out a little more about you."

"Cool."

So, we talked to the girls one-by-one. By the time we got to the fourth girl, we learned that she was a model. She was very beautiful. She had a light skinned complexion and beautiful hair. She was gorgeous. Mathew and I sat at the table and spoke with all the previous girls very professionally. We had a couple of drinks. This girl came to sit down and speak with us, and this was the first sign where I saw that Mathew had some issues.

When she sat down, Mathew leaned back in his chair and reached down in his pants.

"I'm just horny as a mug. I just wanna screw right now. I'm horny as heck."

I looked at the girl and she looked at me. I was still in professional mode. Mathew was sitting there holding his crotch.

"…huh, I am so sorry ma'am. I am so sorry. He's a little drunk…"

"I'm not drunk. I told you! We're in the business of exploiting people, and I'mma exploit you and if you wanna be a star, you gonna have to come on and do something for me. Heck, I know what I can do for you' but what can you do for me?"

The girl looked straight passed me and right into Mathew's eyes.

"Look, I don't know who you think you are! But, I don't need this mess! I'm a professional model. I do this stuff because I sing with my sister, who's one of the singers. This is just a past time for me. I don't need to be no singer. I have a kid at home to take care of and this stuff here I don't need!"

She got up and stormed off and went straight to the other girls. They all started talking, and looked over at us.

"Mat, what did…what wrong with you?"

"Oh man, they gotta understand…my job….everybody gonna be exploited that's what it's about. Heck you wanna get on, you wanna get with what we are about, then you gotta put out."

"Mathew, you can't do this type of stuff! This is not the kind of business I agreed to do. I don't get down like that dude! I'm not with this stuff! I'm not rollin' this way!"

"Oh, man, this is just the way it is. If we gonna get some where this is…"

"No Mat…I'm not with that!"

We sat and talked for a while. "Man you could've at least leaned over and whispered that stuff to her. Heck, don't put me in the middle of your foolishness! I don't roll like that man."

I was outdone when we finally left the Sky Bar. I drove Mathew back home and being pissed was an understatement. When I pulled up in front of his house to let him out of the car, he tried to talk to me about the situation again.

"What? You think I did something wrong?"

"Heck yeah nigga. You screwed up! That was real screwed up."

"Man that's just the way the business is, you know. Ya'll back-wooded country asses, you and Ann, ya'll gotta understand this business is about exploiting people. That's the way the business is and that's what we're gonna have to do to make this a success. That's what we're gonna do!"

"Man, get out of my car!"

I let him out of my car and he walked in his house. I wanted to drive over to Ann's house that night, but it was way too late. So when I got home, I called her and told her that we needed to talk. When I hung up from Ann, I shared the situation with Cassey. She was like, "What?!"

The next day, I went over to Ann's house so we could talk.

"Dretta, we gotta problem on our hands! This sucker is out of control!"

"Darn, Kenny…what happened?"

"That Mathew! This fool is a major problem."

I explained to Ann what happened. She was like, "What…what…you kidding me…what?"

She couldn't believe what she was hearing. "Come on Kenny now, Mathew didn't do that."

"Yeah the heck he did, and I don't know what happened with him and Dick Griffy, but something happened because he's not the same guy he was two weeks ago!"

"Kenny look…I need you and we gotta balance this fool. So please…hang in there with him so he don't screw us up. I'll keep him working with the girls. We'll handle dealing with the labels."

"Okay."

"If he has to go out again with you, just keep him on a chain."

"Dretta, how can I stop a grown man from doing what he wants to do?"

"Tell him you gonna tell Tina or she's gonna find out. I don't know."

When Mathew and I went out, that is exactly what I would say and he would calm himself down at least in my presence. Mathew had issues, and they were not the kind I was really interested in trying to manage in order to get business done. However, for Ann's sake, I tolerated him, but I did not like it. I love my wife, and I just didn't deal like that. I preferred not to associate with someone who did. So it was hard for me every time we had to go out together to see acts.

With the conversations Ann and I had regarding Dick Griffy and what he did with Yarbrough and Peoples, he was out the picture. That thing there was a wrap. We kept communications open with Daryl Simmons. We laid the ground work and discussed how we would handle Simmons. We let Mathew work with the girls and agreed to just carbon copy him on the contracts and things of that nature.

New Years nineteen ninety-three had long passed and the new contracts were signed where Mathew was actually listed for the first time as co-manager on the contracts that Girls Tyme signed. Every year Ann had the team resign contracts to make sure everyone was on lock-down.

With all the mess going on with Mathew, the conversations with Daryl Simmons and getting past the Star Search loss, Ann was hit again with another fire to put out. Carolyn met with her about Ashley.

"Ann, I no longer feel that Girls Tyme is in Ashley's best interest. You are featuring other artists. Ashley needs to be either a solo artist or the lead artist."

"Alright Carolyn, Nolan…Give me a day to talk it over with management."

Ann called me in on what else had taken place.

"Kenny, Carolyn's getting ready to take Ashley out the group."

"Ann, the group is now like Michael Jackson and the Jackson Five. Beyonce is who everybody is talking about…and LaTavia. They're not talking about Ashley. So if Carolyn wants to make that mistake, let her."

"Huhm…"

"…But, I feel you owe Ashley because of the way everything went down. At least still try to get her a solo deal."

So Ann and I agreed that Ann would talk with Carolyn and even if she took Ashley out of the group, Ann was willing to make every effort to sign Ashley to an independent artist deal and continue working with her, because we already had all the contacts. Carolyn agreed. Ashley Davis left Girls Tyme officially and signed a solo artist management deal with Girls Tyme Entertainment. Everyone was shocked that Ashley left the group. So with only five girls left, we started to observe at the rehearsals that Beyonce had taken on the persona of, "This is my group now."

Beyonce started driving the rehearsals and the girls to work harder. In truth, it had become her group. She and LaTavia had begun to choreograph the moves. Surprisingly, Beyonce's personality did not change in how she would communicate with Ann and me, but her attitude in rehearsals changed and the manner in which she related to the group. David, Lonnie, and Mathew reinforced this new attitude as well. If she had any issues with anyone, LaTavia was her hedge man. In other words, she would pull everyone in line.

When Daryl Simmons' wife saw Girls Tyme perform at the expo she saw six girls. Also, Daryl was aware of a six-girl group. At that point, Mathew and Ann auditioned other girls while I was working in order to replace Ashley and deliver six girls. One primary contender was a young girl by the name of Letoya Luckett.

"Alright Kenny, we got a new member, lets go to rehearsal."

"What?"

"Yeah! We gotta new member, Letoya."

"Darn Ann that was quick."

"Heck we ain't got time to waste. You gonna like her though, Kenny."

At the rehearsal, I met Letoya and her mother Pam. They were very nice people. Letoya was bubbly and a "jokey-jokey" type. However, Ann was right, she fit like a glove. The strength Letoya brought to the group was her ability to move and work the stage. Yet her voice was not as powerful as Ashley's. Therefore we ended up having to put more pressure on David to make Kelly a stronger vocalist. Letoya was a great harmonizer but was not a lead singer.

The way the talks were going with Silent Partners, we knew that an Atlanta showcase was coming up very soon, so the girls had to ramp up things and work even harder than what they had been working before. Plus, Kelly had to bring in more vocals to fill the void of Ashley. On top of that Mathew was really starting to spin even more out of control. He started going over to Ann's house almost everyday attempting to interfere with the meetings Ann and I were having. There started to be a lot of uncalled meetings, where Ann would often have to call me and tell me that Mathew was there at her house and she needed me to drive over immediately.

Mathew was starting to drink a lot more and he would come to Ann's house high as a kite. He threatened Ann yet again to take Beyonce out of the group if she didn't let him co-manage Ashley's solo management deal. All of this was going on when Pam, Letoya's mom, started raising questions about why Letoya couldn't be involved in other things besides Girls Tyme. Ann and I were strategically working to juggle a lot of irons that were on the fire.

While there was no respect for Mathew's crap, Ann and I both respected the fact that Pam was willing to challenge the contract in order to get the best deal for her daughter. Her approach was very different from Mathew's and with much more class, professionalism, and fairness. So we wheeled and dealed and handled things the best we could.

NO TIME TO CRY

Although the group dynamics and Ann's health were ongoing issues, we continued to move forward and work hard to bring about tangible results. It was a rollercoaster ride to say the least; but we kept the faith. Girls Tyme, their parents, and the entire management team were doing their best to cope with the disappointment surrounding Star Search. Regardless, there were still labels expressing interest in signing the girls and we did not waste time in exploring those options.

Rap-a-Lot, a record label owned by James Prince aka Little James that focused on "gangsta" and southern rap, was very interested in signing the girls to his label. One of the most notorious groups signed to that particular label at the time was Geto Boys led by rapper and performing artist, Willie D. He helped both the group and the label reach national acclaim with songs such as "Mind Playing Tricks on Me" and "Scarface."

After brief discussions with Little James, Ann and I decided that Rap-a-Lot Records was not the best fit for Girls Tyme. Although the label was known in the rap game, Ann was not interested in positioning Girls Tyme as a rap group. She wanted to secure a much bigger deal for the girls as well as sign with a more established label.

Although Ann did not "get into bed" with Rap-a-Lot, she became good friends with Willie D, who was interested in getting into the management side of things. It was not unusual for me to go by Ann's house and see Willie D. Regardless of the many people doing a whole lot of talking, there was no record deal yet, and mine and Ann's concern was to get a deal – the best deal for the girls.

"Kenny, this is bull. We need to get these girls signed."

"I'm with you on that, Dretta. When you think about who we have on the hook, something should close, whatcha think?"

"Heck, I would think so. Who else can you talk to that could maybe walk us through?"

"Let me put in some calls, Dretta."

"Let me know. This stuff is getting old, something's gotta give!"

I reached out to a friend of mine named Robert, who was a travel agent for So So Def Records in Atlanta as well as co-manager of the group Whodini along with a guy named Frank. At the time I reached out to Rob, Whodini was on the downslide but they were still a popular group, so it didn't hurt to give him a call.

"Hey Rob, can you guys help us out?"

"Whatcha need B.K.?"

"We are trying to keep this ball rolling and I was wondering if there were some record label execs you all could possibly walk us through?"

"Uhm."

"What about Jermaine Dupri. Can you speak with him?"

Rob went and spoke with Jermaine Dupri's father who was over So So Def at the time and then came back to tell me what he said.

"Okay Kenny man. He thought your girls were interesting, so he said he will talk to a couple of people and see what's up."

"I appreciate that man. It means a lot."

I followed up with Ann regarding my conversations with Rob. There was some talk out there about the group and we didn't want the devastation of the Star Search loss to leave a bad taste in the mouths of some of the people who might otherwise be interested in Girls Tyme or for them to be associated with losing. Consequently, we changed the name of the group from Girls Tyme to Something Fresh. Ann ultimately made the call to change the image and name. At that time, you had groups out there such as Kriss Kross, Da' Brat, and The Boys, who were really jumping.

Ann put out a lot of money to get the name changed and create a new image. She spent a lot of money making sure the girls were on point for the showcases and so forth that she placed her house in jeopardy of foreclosing. Ann was spending money on the girls as opposed to paying some of the bigger bills. Although she had money set aside for her sons, she refused to dip into that. So it was as if she did not have it. After being confronted with the necessity to make some really tough decisions, Ann decided to let her house go and downsize in order to cut her overhead.

"Darn Kenny, this is our dream house. I feel like I've let them down."

"Dretta, you didn't let them down. You did the best you could."

"No I didn't. I know darn well I should have been paying the mortgage. How could I have been so stupid?"

"Dretta, you are not stupid, so stop all that beating yourself up."

"I messed up stuff!"

"Ann, you've been running on ten. You have kept a lot of stuff together for some time. So stop knocking yourself. Look at what you have put together to make Dwight's dream and your dream and the dreams of others come alive. If Dwight was alive, he would be proud of you."

This was the first time I saw water well up in Ann's eyes. She was really going through it during that time. I spent a lot of energy trying to lift her spirits and assure her that things would be okay.

"You know, Kenny, it just makes me do a lot of soul searching. All these people sending me in all these circles. I just wanna make this stuff work. You know what I'm saying...I just want it to work!"

"I know Dretta. We're gonna do this. It's okay...we're gonna do this."

Ann almost whispered, clearing her throat as she attempted to get the words out of her mouth. "Oh, Kenny..."

"What are you going to do?"

"I bought another house."

"What the hell...!"

"No! Wait. I bought a house down the way that is smaller than this one. It has pretty much the same floor plan. The boys can still have their own room... It's just not this house. This was our house Kenny. This was the house me and Dwight picked out!"

"I understand, but you are gonna be fine, Ann."

"I know Kenny, it's just bull! I ran through a lot of money. Sometimes I wonder if it's all worth it. Do they even understand or appreciate the work that we do?"

It took some talking to Ann to help her get through this period of being confronted with leaving her home. As Ann packed her things to move out of the house, a flood of emotions overwhelmed her. It appeared that all the old feelings of losing her husband and daughter resurfaced. While she had to leave her dream home, Ann stayed in the general vicinity of the same neighborhood so that her boys could continue with the same school and before long got moved into her new dwelling place. She could not yet call it home.

With all of the stress of what was going on in the organization, the foreclosure, and the move, Ann landed back in the hospital from another Lupus crisis. This was the first time that she had to bring home an oxygen machine. However, she would only use it when she was in dire straights. After Ann got out of the hospital, I made my way over to her new residence.

"Hey Blackie! Is your mama as Black as you?...Dretta? Where your Black tail at woman?"

Ann came out from the kitchen. "Hey girl...with your Black tail. Is your mama as Black as you? Is ya Mama Black as the ace of spade like you? You know your butt is faking and stuff! Ain't nothin' wrong with your lying tail!"

Ann just continued walking back into the kitchen with this smirk on her face and chuckling under her breath. I followed right behind her playing the dozens and dancing. I even started singing the dozens and stepping side-to-side. I was loud with it too.

"Hey...I'm a roll tonight girl! Whoop...ten for Kenny Mo!"

I continued playing the dozens and laughing. Ann just kept walking to the kitchen, and I was right behind her clowning.

"Hey Blacky...with your Black tail..." When I got into the kitchen, I stopped dead in my tracks because I had not realized that someone else was at her house. Then Ann turned to me. "Kenny this my mama."

Ann started laughing almost hysterically. My mouth dropped wide open. I was completely stunned. "Uh…how you doing…uh…I'm uh… Kenny."

I reached out my hand to shake her hand. She looked me up and down with a disgusting look on her face, and then said, "Uhm huhm," then she rolled her eyes at me, turned her back and went and sat down with her cup of coffee.

"Now…uh…uh Ms. Brown…uh…you know I was just joking when I said what I said when I came in now…"

Ms. Brown just looked straight through me and had this look on her face as if to say, "You jackass!" However, she just kept looking at me with her nose turned up then said, "Uhm huhm."

Ann just laughed. I was trying to figure out a way to get out of the fools place I put myself, when Ann finally helped me to somewhat get out of the situation by pulling me aside to talk. We walked into the other room where the piano was.

"I got your butt this time nigga!" Ann said laughing.

"Ann, you know you wrong for that, you didn't even tell me your mama was here."

"That's what your Black butt gets nigga! I fixed your butt this time…Talking all that stuff!"

"Seriously though, how you feelin' baby girl?"

"I'm okay. Just a little down. I didn't really want to have to make this change. And getting out of the hospital and coming here…it's just not the same. It feels a little weird for me."

"It's a nice house Ann. It ain't too much different from the one you were in. It's suitable for you and the boys. You can still keep things rolling."

"Yeah, I guess you're right…it's not home yet though, you know what I mean?"

"You gonna be alright girl. You know I'm here for you...me and Cassey, we're here for you."

"I know Kenny."

"Shoot don't let them niggas get to you. Heck if I need to kick some butt you know I'll do it!"

Ann's mother heard a lot of what Ann and I were talking about. She walked passed us and the look she gave me let me know very clearly that she was watching me. Her look also communicated to me that she was appreciative of the support that I was offering her daughter, and glad to know that someone else is actually looking out for her.

Although Ann was still recuperating from her most recent Lupus crisis, she was more concerned with Tayste rehearsals and the girls' new image. I explained to her that it would be fine and although she had a detached garage now, Tayste could still rehearse in the garage. I told her the fact that she moved wasn't going to stop things from moving forward.

Ann continued to work on getting the girls a fresh image, which meant a whole new wardrobe as well. As she was paying closer attention to her finances under the circumstances, Ann noticed that things in her bank account were not balancing out. So she went back to the bank. Ann found out there were a number of checks that had been written on her account made out to Lynn with her name being forged.

"Kenny, this fool been stealing my money!"

"Whatcha talkin' about Ann?"

"Lynn! He has been writing checks on my bank account, forgin' my name...Shoot!"

"What?"

"Really Kenny?! What part of what I 'm saying to you don't your butt understand?"

"Wait a minute Dretta, cool down."

"Cool down? I left the bank today. I found out this idiot...it ain't enough that this mofo done bought cars, drugs, and stuff on money for the group, but he done gone and started screwing with MY money!"

"Are you saying that Lynn wrote hot checks on your account?"

"That is exactly what I'm saying."

"Darn!"

"That fool gots to go! Ain't no ifs, ands, and buts about it. His tailis history!...Darn drug addict!...What the hell?!"

"So he'd done burned through the other money and now he done wrote checks on your account?"

"Darn skippy."

"Okay Ann, the first thing we need to do is limit Lynn's access to anything."

"Limit him my behind, cut his behind the heck off!"

The next meeting that was at Ann's house, she informed Lynn and everyone else of what Lynn had done. They had discussions about it in the meeting. While she was cordial to Lynn, she really had nothing to do with him. He continued to come by the house for a few more meetings after that, but finally Ann just told him he was completely out and no longer a part of the team. The challenge for the team was that Lynn established a friendship with Tayste.

Harlan and Mitch were wooed by Lynn's fancy cars and women. They always invited him to their rehearsals, which was in Ann's garage. They also asked him to find producers for their music. This made for an uncomfortable situation as Ann was managing Tayste. Mitch and Harlan's attitude was that management's focus moved from all of the groups to just the girls.

Lynn became Tayste's sounding board for their complaints against the management team. To To and A.J. were in Ann's corner all the way. This created a rift within the group and thus the ultimate demise of Tayste.

Things were happening in every camp of Girls Tyme Entertainment group. Ann loaned Lonnie money and flew him back and forth from California. She gave T-Mo money. She gave me money to compensate me for my time and efforts since I was spending all that time at her home and really was just getting started on my job. That assisted with me going to buy groceries and take care of other household expenses. She paid the Girls Tyme (Something Fresh) members' parent's bills. Tina and Mathew started having more issues in their household and marital problems. She was being as supportive as she could on that front as well.

In essence, Ann was taking care of all of us. In truth, in terms of intimate comforts and satisfactions, there was no one really looking after her. One guy who came by frequently, attempted to pass himself off as a manager of one of the Clark sisters.

The problem with Tina and Mathew began to manifest itself when Mathew became a part of the management team. It gave him the needed excuse and the opportunity to be gone away from home. Often, Mathew was either not at the meetings or he would show up for a minute, then disappear to go be with other women. Whenever Tina called, people answering the phone would tell her that Mathew just left or whatever Mathew told them to tell her. I never lied for Mathew and neither did Ann. To avoid being placed in an uncompromising situation, whenever there was shadiness going on with him and his habits, Ann nor I would even answer the telephone phone. Mathew's shenanigans didn't sit well with us.

"Ann, that nigga is dirty, and I ain't lying for his funky butt!"

"Shoot, Kenny, I ain't lying for him either. Let Lonnie's get the phone. If Lynn was here he could get it too. All of them are some shady mofos as far as I'm concerned. So let Lonnie get it. That's two got-darned peas-in-a-pod."

"I don't understand what he is doing. He has a beautiful wife at home, I mean gorgeous, and he screwin' around with some darn, whateva the heck he's doing. I don't want nothing to do with it."

"He gonna keep on and I'mma tell Tina on him. I am not down with that Kenny."

"I'm with you on that Ann."

Although all of this mess was going on with Mathew, we still had to focus on business and not let any of that cause us to lose sight of what we were supposed to be doing at the time. There was this hot singing group called, The Boys, that came to town. They were four brothers out of California. Their names were Khiry, Hakim, Tajh and Bilal Abdulsamad.

So Mathew, Lonnie, T-Mo, and I went to go see them perform to compare them to what we had in our stable, specifically with respect to the girls. Their father was their manager. At that time they were on the MCA and Motown label.

They were hot! We were thinking strategically that perhaps we could connect them with the girls to get the girls to open up and perform better and maybe one of the girls would like one of the boys. We were thinking marketing and publicity. Their hit song at that time was, "Dial My Heart."

After the show, we met the father.

"Hey how ya doing? I'm Mathew Knowles, and this is our team. We're part of Girls Tyme Entertainment."

"Hi, how are you? My name is Jabari, I am the Boys manager and father."

"Well, we are just interested in talking to you about The Boys and your group and any advice that you can give us."

"Well Mathew, I really don't have any advice to give you, I really don't think... you really got nothing. My boys sell millions of records, and little girls buy their songs! Now...who gonna buy your girls' songs?"

"What!"

"Little boys don't buy music."

After Jabari said that to Mathew, he walked away from us like we were nothing. Mathew got mad as heck after that.
"Who he think he is? He's an arrogant son-of-a-gun! How in the heck he gonna say my daughter ain't nothin'?!

Mathew called that man every name but the child of God. He was so mad. He went off so bad that we all just had to laugh. He invented curse words I had never heard and the combination of words had all of us on the floor rollin'.

Mathew flipped the guy the bird while his back was turned, still cursing him out under his breath. Mathew flipped the bird again. The guy was long gone. We laughed so hard, but Mathew took it personally. I guess because his daughter was the one in the group. The rest of us didn't have children in the group, so we were able to let it roll off like "water off a duck's back."

"Mathew, man-to-man, he had a good point. It's something we have to think about."

"Kenny, screw him, and screw you too...and screw you Lonnie, and screw you T-Mo...!"

We kept laughing while Mathew was going on. "Kenny, your country-ass don't know stuff!"

"Fool you from Alabama how are you gonna call me country?"

Mathew and I went back and forth until it got so bad that we both just burst out laughing.

"Kenny, I'mma show that fool!"

The good thing about that whole situation was that for the first time I saw in Mathew a strong sense of, "My daughter's gonna be something" attitude. He let it be known that night that Beyonce was going to be a star. He took on the attitude that, "This is gonna happen!" Mathew wore his passion on his sleeve that night. He demonstrated straight fatherly love that none of us could deny.

That night was the first time I started to respect Mathew. At that moment, I felt that he was in this with us. He was serious about making it happen. I became more open to accepting him as a teammate. Prior to that night, I felt that he just forced himself on the management team because his daughter was a main staple of the group. However, he demonstrated real passion that evening and I felt that he shared our passion for the group at that point. That was a good time for our relationship.

I shared with Ann what had happened that night, which made for good light-hearted conversation in the midst of her stress. Ann told me that the money was starting to get low. The only thing left was for her to start tapping into Armon and Christopher's inheritance. The deals were taking longer to close than anticipated. Everyone started working extra hard. Tina was pulling more hours at Headliners, which was her salon, to help support her family. Mathew was not working so he was able to support the day-to-day operations more.

I worked more hours on my job. Ann worked overtime on her job. We all did what we could do to take some of the weigh off of Ann. Everybody was pretty much busting their butts while Mathew had free time because he quit his job. He sat all day masterminding stuff and then would bum rush us when we got off work. Mathew showed up everyday at Ann's house asking her questions and complaining about who didn't call him back. This presented an extremely stressful situation for Ann on top of the fact that her resources were getting low. Mathew was overbearing to say the least.

He started calling all of Ann's contacts and telling them that he was now in charge and the primary manager and if they needed to talk to anyone, they needed to speak with him. If they spoke with Andretta, he requested them to carbon copy him on any correspondence. We also found out that he was at the rehearsals telling the girls the same thing.

Ann did not want to dip into her sons' inheritance, so before she had to turn to that she decided to seek assistance from her cousin, Belfry, believed to be a drug dealer. I personally didn't know he was a drug dealer and neither did Ann. Although, she suspected it, she couldn't prove it at the time because it was not unusual for Blacks from East Texas to come into money from time to time, because of farm and cattle sales. Regardless of how Belfry made his money, he was very supportive of Ann. He and his girlfriend Sha Sha started coming to Houston frequently and visiting her. Belfry probably had an idea that something was about to break and I am sure in the back of his mind, he was trying to find a way of getting in on the action.

"Ann, instead of you stressin' out and everything, why don't I just loan you a couple of dollars."

"I don't know Bel...I gotta think about that one."

"Whatcha mean you gotta think about it? Let me help out."

"I'll let you know."

After hesitating and much thought, Ann decided to go ahead and borrow $25,000 from Belfry to tide us over and keep her from going into the boys' money that was set aside for them. He agreed to give the money to Ann in three installments. She agreed that once we got a deal, she would give him the money back. Belfry was making so much money at the time that he really didn't care about loaning the money. He was more concerned about helping his cousin out, but Ann had a lot of pride, and didn't want anybody giving her anything in that sense.

After Ann accepted the money from her cousin, Silent Partner also stepped up their game. Finally after all of the discussions and time passed, we finally were at the point of signing the agreement with them.

As we were working on finalizing the terms for the deal, squabbles crept up prior to signing because Silent Partners were not interested in signing dancers to a label. Their attitude was that they can get dancers anywhere.

Simmons attitude was, "Here today, gone tomorrow, I'm not signing!" Simmons and his partner, Sylvia Rhone, were both of the belief that there was no need to sign dancers. They also felt that some of the background vocals could be stronger. Their goal was to get more control of the girls because at that point, Tillman Management and Girls Tyme Entertainment had complete control. His move was to kick the dancers out and replace one of the singers with a better singer.

The first target was LaTavia. They then reconsidered her because they felt that if the group went down, then LaTavia could be their, "Left Eye." Instead they wanted to groom her to learn to sing. At that point, LaTavia went from being a rapper to a singer. After they decided to keep LaTavia, the target then became Kelly. Ann shot that idea down immediately. Silent Partner Management started to complain that Kelly was a little stiff; she had not blossomed, and had an attitude of "we can accept one dark girl, but not two." Ann challenged that mindset.

"Regardless of what you wanna do, there will be dark-skinned girls in this darn group!"

They felt that they could get a lighter-skinned singer who was a stronger vocalist to come in and be part of the group. So there were consistent talks of getting rid of Kelly.

There were rumors that Silent Partners were pursuing Ke Ke Wyatt to be one of the replacements. The deal hit a snag because Andretta had an ecliptic fit when they tried to kick Kelly out of the group. I had never seen Ann so irate in my time of working with her. The way Ann fought for Kelly was as if she was fighting for her daughter, Shawna.

"They are not kicking my baby out of the group! Hell to the naw! They can screw all this stuff. Kelly stays and I can't believe that Mathew agrees with this foolishness!"

"What?"

"Look Kenny, he just wants to get a deal. If Kelly goes, ain't no deal. I'll call the whole thing off! And... if his behind screw with me on this one, I'll sue him and screw up all his stuff...and he knows what I mean!"

"So what are you gonna do, Ann?"

"Ain't no deal unless Kelly is a part of it, that's what I'mma do. They can take it or leave it. I will fire Mathew's behind and make his life a living hell! He can take that stuff to the bank and he best not screw with me on this. He best not attempt to write checks his behind can't cash!"

"Okay, Dretta, I support you on this!"

"Darn skippy! Aint no other way around this one. Now as much as I want them in the group, they can dismiss Nikki and Nina, but they ain't getting rid Kelly. Aint no price right for that stuff!"

There was nothing that Lonnie or Mathew could say. They insisted that Ann was messing up the deal. Ann's position "was screw the deal, you ain't taking my girl out the group! I promised her mother, and ya'll ain't taking my baby out the group! That's all to it!"

After Ann took such a strong opposition about letting go of Kelly, Silent Partners, whose arguments fell on deaf ears, conceded on getting rid of Kelly. The battle lasted all but a week. Kelly stayed, but Nikki and Nina were let go. At that point Something Fresh formerly Girls Tyme consisted of four girls: Letoya, Beyonce, LaTavia, and Kelly. Looking back at how passionately Ann fought to keep the girls in the group, I know inside she was fighting for them as if she was fighting for her daughter Shawna.

Silent Partners, Inc. at One Capital City Plaza, 3350 Peach Tree Road - Suite 1500, Atlanta, Georgia finalized the deal including Kelly Rowland and they signed the agreement on June 11, 1993. To that point, as far as Ann was concerned with girls being replaced, Silent Partner could "Shut up!"

Although Nikki and Nina went to Atlanta along with the others to do the showcase for Simmons under the auspices of Something Fresh, with the hopes and dreams of being part of a record label deal, they returned only to learn later that those particular dreams at that time were shattered. Ann continued to allow them to come to rehearsals for awhile and she pampered them as long as she could. Ultimately things got more hectic and she did not see them as often as she would have hope to.

After the fire was put out, Silent Partner Productions took over the production of the girls. That meant that Lonnie was pushed to the side and Arne was completely out of the picture. Lonnie was not happy, but Ann kept Lonnie around in case anything fell through. Her thoughts were if something happened, at least she would still have her producer. After all the delegating and acting as drill sergeant in preparing the girls, he was relegated to only being able to submit material to the girls through Ann. Ultimately that satisfied Lonnie as he was still able to have some involvement, no matter how minimal. However, overall A & A Productions was not too happy with the situation.

Silent Partner Productions handled their business and had an established track record. Lonnie was not a part of that. They didn't need a Lonnie because they had Baby Face and L.A. Reid. Consequently, T-Mo lost his voice as well. He fell with Lonnie. So things moved along with some adjustments. Ann noticed that things were lagging. Although they signed with Silent Partner Productions and were working on some things, almost four months had passed and nothing was really happening. Ann wanted to keep things moving.

"Okay Kenny, I need you. I need you to help me balance Lonnie, and keep an eye on Mathew."

"Ann you know I gotcha."

"Heck, I need you to help pacify Lonnie. There's no need for him to fly back and forth from California. Also, we need to keep Mathew's tail at bay, before he screw some stuff up!"

"Okay so what is Lonnie gonna do?"

"Well he is staying with me right now. Instead of flying back and forth, he will just be here for now. I need you to help with that."

"Oh okay."

"Also, Silent Partner is dragging their feet. I don't want to take a chance on them not being able to get everything done in a timely manner."

"Okay, so whatcha ya thinking?"

"Kenny, this is taking too long. They seem like they are dragging their feet. Every time we take one step ahead, they seem to be coming back wanting to change something else or saying some stuff like 'there's a snag'. I don't know what the heck to think!"

"Uhm…what are they saying?"

"The question is not what are they saying, it's what isMathew up to? He is steady kissin' Daryl Simmons'. That's why I need to watch him and keep him on tight reigns."

"Shoot, that fool just can't be trusted. He blows like the wind!"

"And…Kenny…get this…Letoya's darn mama is playin' up telling me some stuff like we still haven't given them a clear answer as to why Letoya cannot do other things other than singing."

"She is still on that stuff, Dretta?"

"Heck yeah!"

"These are some ungrateful folks. I don't get it!"

"It'd be different if someone was putting up some darn money."

Pamela Luckett, Letoya's mother, and Mathew started going back and forth. She ended up hiring the law firm of Warren M. Fitzgerald, Jr. to represent her and do her talking for her.

Mathew took an aggressive position with her and sent a letter on Ann's letterhead without Ann's knowledge stating "...if you cannot abide by what management has said and the agreement in place, while it has been a pleasure working with you, I will inform Mr. Simmons that we are having issues with you, and that Letoya is no longer a part of Something Fresh. He sent this letter to both Letoya's mother and her attorney.

The Luckett's attorney fired back stating that they did not agree with the contract and felt that the requests were unreasonable. Mathew responded and said they would find a new singer. At the same time all of this was going on, Simmons was trying to get another singer in the group anyway, so for him this was not a problem. After Mathew was willing to eliminate Letoya out of the group and there was no resistance from Simmons, the Lucketts pulled back and decided to drop the issue for the moment.

What Pam didn't understand at the time was that when she made the move she did on challenging the contract, it gave Mathew the opportunity to give Simmons what he wanted and that was for one girl to leave the group so he could put his girl in. What I do not think she anticipated was them threatening and willing to follow through with kicking Letoya out of the group with no regrets. So when she realized that it was not going to go the way she thought, she settled down. Mathew was quick to send the letter because he knew that Simmons had someone (that someone being Ke Ke Wyatt) in the wings to step in, but Pam had no idea of the politics going on behind the management scenes.

Andretta was dealing with all this madness while working her tail off to get a real deal for the girls. She was complaining that things were not happening fast enough and that is when we decided to go get the money.

"Alright Kenny, it's time for us to make a move. This stuff ain't rolling like it's supposed to be."

"Okay, Ann so whatcha you want me to do?"

"I want you to go get the money. We're burning through capital too fast and nigga's aint bringin' in stuff!"

"Let's do it then, I can go back to my boy William. The truth is Ann, we are producing hits, and we just need to be able to get them pressed."

"So see what he says."

"Alright."

I reached out to William again. I spoke with him to see if there was any interest. William pretty much just shot me down. He wasn't willing to invest in a studio, but then Lynn resurfaced. When he did, he came back in a new Porsche.

"Hey, I got the money for a studio and ever' thang, you know... I can help ya'll out, you know."

Lynn was tried to get back into saving grace. Ann and I were not interested in dealing with Lynn. With Lynn came too much other baggage that was not worth carrying.

"Man, it sounds all good, but we ain't interested..."

"Come on Kenny man, let me help ya'll out. We got something here."

"Lynn, you ain't right and Ann is not interested in dealing with you. She doesn't trust you and you got too much goin' on that ain't good for these girls."

Once we turned Lynn down, he blew the money and went right back to doing what he had been doing before. He was messing around with drugs, women, and planting seeds in Tayste until they had disdain for the management team. He divided Tayste. Ann and I got together and said we could not deal with

Lynn at all and didn't want him coming around under no circumstances, Tayste or otherwise.

While this is happening, Mathew got wind that Lynn had gotten some money and blew it on cars, drugs, and women. He was livid! Mathew started hounding Ann after that.

"Andretta, you let this dude blow all this money! He had the money that we needed and you let him blow it on bull!"

"Mathew, get back, I ain't let nobody blow nothin'. Lynn is his own man and we pushed him back some time ago, so how you gonna put that stuff on me?"

"You didn't get the money. You let him take it and blow it!"

"I didn't let Lynn take crap. Hell your butt know he stole money from my account, so whatever he went out their and got in my darn name is his crooked stuff...so don't be sweatin' me with that mess, Mathew!"

"Well it's like this...this record deal is getting' ready to come, and when we get this advance, I'm handling the stuff. This ain't gonna be happening on my watch! I'mma be in charge of the money from the record deal. I'm gonna pay out who needs to get paid, and if you don't like it, then I'll take Beyonce... go somewhere else!"

"Mathew, get out of my house. I just got home from work. I don't need your crap. Go get a job and stop makin' it your job to screw with me...please."

"I ain't playing, Andretta...I'mma be in charge of the money..."

After Mathew left, Ann called me. I went over to her house to help lift her spirits. We sat at her baby grand piano like we always do when she was feeling low.

"Look Dretta, don't let Mathew's behind get you down. I know it's a tough situation, but it's gonna be alright. No matter what you do, hold on to Beyonce, because she is gonna be a big star."

"Shoot Kenny, Mathew is just simple! I can't stand him. He get on my last darn nerve...and he always threatening with takin' Beyonce if I don't do what he says."

"We all know he's a dirty mofo...that's a given, but we will get through this."

Ann was stressed. Lynn blew money that should have been used for the girls and to pay her cousin back. Feeling that her back was against the wall, she agreed to let Mathew control the funds from the advance whenever the record deal came through without my knowledge. I found out after the deal was done.

"Look Dretta, I know you are stressed, but maybe this will help. I got this friend in Atlanta. I will contact him and see what he can do."

"Who is he?"

"My friend? His name is Al. He comes into town frequently because he is working on opening a Sally's hair supply place here in Houston...I can get with him and see what we can make happen."

"Okay. Will he do it?"

"Well, every time he comes, Cassey and I work with him helping him to find good locations. I can see what his thoughts are. We're good friends though, so..."

"Well call him then."

I called Al. He already knew that we were dealing with the girls group, and that they were a pretty hot group. When I asked him about investing, he didn't hesitate.

"How much money ya'll need, man?"

"Al man, we need about a hundred and fifty thousand dollars."

"Okay, okay…let me know…did you wanna come and get it? You know…meet with my attorney…we can talk about it."

I flew out to Atlanta to meet with Al Clark. I stayed at his big ole house up in Stone Mountain, Georgia. We did it up and had a great time. When I got there, Al scheduled the meeting for the next day with his attorney. We were getting ready for bed that night when Al called me.

"Hey Kenny, come here man. Do you know what I do?"

"Al man, I figured out what you do man. Don't forget man, I've run around with you."

Al was a number's runner. Right before the Georgia lottery came in, he was running all the numbers.

"Yeah, yeah…okay," he chuckled.

"Okay so lookie here Kenny. Got something to show you in my bedroom."

"Nigga, I ain't on no funny stuff now."

"Man shut your tail up. Come here."

Al pointed at this bag. So when I saw it I said, "What? It's just a bag."

Al just laughed, then dumped the paper bag out on the bed. It was nothing but money.

"There's your money right there. How much do you think that is?"

"A hundred and fifty thousand I guess. Shoot I don't know."

"That's a million dollars boy! Obviously you ain't seen a million dollars before."

"Obviously not, because I wouldn't swear that was a million dollars."

Al broke it down and counted it. We counted stack after stack. Then tallied them up, and it was a million dollars indeed. He put the money back in the bag.

"Come on, let's go down here."

I followed Al outside. There was this switch by these big Rottweilers in a big pen. Al hit the switch and the dog house lifted up hydraulically. Under the dog house was a cement bin. He went over to the bin where there was a safe and he put the bag of money in the safe, locked it, and then came back out of the gate. We went back into the house, wound down for the night and went to bed.

Al woke up the next morning mad as heck. He was slamming cabinets and things downstairs. When I heard the commotion, I went downstairs where he was.

"Al, what's wrong with you man?"

"Come on Kenny man, let's go walking."

As we were walking, he was huffing and puffing. He was mad.

"Kenny, what kinda man are you?"

"What man?"

"I ain't never met no nigga like you!"

"What do you mean, Al?"

"Nigga, I showed you a million dollars, and you didn't get your butt up nil one time last night…"

"Al, man I came here to get a loan from you, not rob you man. What the heck wrong with you?"

"I ain't never met no nigga like you. The average nigga would've got up…walk past my door or something." Then he started laughing.

"Nigga, what are you laughin' at?"

"Shoot, Kenny. I'm glad you didn't because I had my gun and every thang...Shoot I was sayin' this big mofo here, I'mma have some problems with him if he decided to try and take my money."

Al had three of his guys stay outside of the gate by the dog pin all night.

"Shoot Kenny man, my whole thing was, if you get me in bed, these niggas be out here, and if you got past the Rottweilers, I told them no matter what happened, don't let that fool get my money!"

Al was laughing his butt off. I was in disbelief this nigga went through all that stuff just in case I tried to steal his money.

"Man, Al, you crazy as heck! You went through all that stuff? Just for me?"

"Kenny, you's a big one shoot, I didn't know! I didn't know."

"Man, you touched in got-darned head, that's what you are."

Al and I just laughed. By then we were back at the house from the walk. Al then turned to me and said, "Come on, let's go see the attorney."

We went to the attorney's office. I thought we were going to a regular criminal attorney's office. I thought he would be a typical guy in Atlanta. Since Al ran numbers, it had to be someone who could get him out of trouble. When we walked into the attorney's office, I noticed all of these pictures of records on the wall of TLC, La Face Records artists, and others. There was more of TLC than anyone else. TLC was like "The Group" to the girls. As I witnessed this I was like, "Oh my God, this guy must be in the music industry too."

As Al and I were talking to Darryl, I realized that this dude really did know what he was doing. So I gave him my whole pitch. Attorney Darryl said, "I like you and I like your girls." He turned to Al and said, "Al, I assume you are going to give them the money, right?"

"Yeah."

"Okay then, well, if we are gonna do it, we gotta do it right."

"Okay."

"Now, Kenny, you are one of the managers, right?"

"Yes I am."

"Well, I tell you what...you go back and you bring them here and we'll get it done, we'll get it done right."

When Al and I got back into his car, I called Ann from his brick phone.

"Hey Dretta, Dretta..."

"What!"

"Baby girl...shoot! I got something to tell you."

"Kenny, I got something to tell you too."

"What...what?"

"Naw, naw you go first."

"Got-dammit, I done got here, I done got the money baby for the studio."

"What?"

"Yeah, and you know this attorney, his name is Darryl...he got TLC and all their pictures on the wall..."

"That's great."

The next day, Ann called me back.

"Kenny...let's keep them in our pocket...but...you might as well come on home, we just got a deal."

"Got a deal with who?"

"We just got a deal with Elektra! Now Kenny, who did you say that attorney was?

"Attorney Darryl...why?"

"That's interesting because we just got a deal from Elektra and either he knew someone or someone knew you got to him... That's odd because as soon as I spoke with you, then the next day, we get the news that Elektra wants to sign the girls."

"Somebody in the Simmons camp must have gotten wind that I got to Attorney Darryl. Since they were dragging their feet..."

Ann and I was always under the impression that perhaps Attorney Darryl might have called and said hey, "he was sittin' in my office and he got someone who is willing to put up the money and he is one of my clients..." Consequently perhaps that made Silent Partners speed up the process and secure a deal. Now if we had signed with Attorney Darryl, we most likely would have signed directly with La Face Records and side stepped Silent Partner Productions all together. However, we went ahead and agreed to sign with Elektra.

LET'S MAKE IT HAPPEN

I packed it up and returned to Houston. Everyone kicked into high gear knowing that the talks were much more serious regarding a record deal with Elektra. It was unfortunate because a lot of disrespect was starting to happen. With Nikki and Nina being gone, Charlotte was out of the loop in terms of rehearsals and details with respect to the group, but she still maintained a good friendship with Ann. Her presence was more to check on Ann to see how she was doing.

Since there was a growing focus on Latavia as the "second star" of the group, a kinship began to evolve between Cheryl and Mathew. As a result, there was also a growing trend where Cheryl started assisting Mathew instead of going through Ann which would have been the appropriate thing to do. The talks about Mathew taking the lead in terms of managing the group could have been some of the motivation behind her disrespect.

The girls traveled back to Atlanta to start recording with Silent Partners. Many things were happening at one time. Ann was having daily bouts with Lupus. She was more jittery and not quite as strong as she had been in the past. Belfry and his girlfriend Sha Sha came down and started hanging around a lot more. Whenever Belfry had to leave and go to work, Sha Sha stayed with Ann to help out around the house and provided support to Ann wherever she needed it. Mathew started coming around more causing unrest. He started to change drastically and became more aggressive in his demeanor. Mathew often went in Ann's garage to do cocaine or other drugs, then would come back in ranting and raving. He often called Darryl Simmons, then afterwards would come back to Ann yelling and carrying on.

"We gotta get this stuff going! Shoot Ann you ain't makin' it happen fast enough!"

"Look Mathew, we are doing what we can. There are a lot of people involved and you just have to be patient. Things are moving."

"They ain't moving fast enough! Make some stuff happen, Andretta!"

Mathew consistently harassed Ann, telling her she needed to get a deal done, while telling others and giving them the impression that he was in charge. Mathew was becoming even more aggressive. He was also hard to get in contact with so the record executives felt more comfortable contacting Ann and talking with her when it came to handling the business. These antics caused unnecessary stress and pressure on Ann. The way Mathew had started overtly behaving and telling the girls that he was their primary manager and leading others to believe the same, it gave rise to additional disrespect toward Ann. All the while, he had to "kowtow" to Ann to get things moving. However instead of talking with her and asking her questions, he had tirades, shouted, and threatened her to get answers or his way.

Mathew's drug use was becoming a major problem. In addition to his constant criticisms of Ann and accusations, he also kept demanding money for various things. He started to identify a host of bills or other items that needed to be paid and insisted that Ann write checks so he could take care of the things he outlined. The excuses Mathew presented to get money from Ann ranged from mailings to photos to producing new tracks with no name producers. Mathew saw how Lynn stole checks and manipulated money, and he too began to take on an air that he would get money from Ann and do whatever the he wanted to do. Although Ann knew that some of the reasons Mathew gave for needing money were not legitimate reasons, he pressured her to no end to give him money and if she didn't, he threatened to take Beyonce out of the group.

During that time, Ann became fearful that Mathew would take Beyonce, because word had gotten back to her that Beyonce was the key. I had heard that Beyonce was the key to the success of the group as well, so I kept reiterating to Ann that whatever we did, we could not lose Beyonce. I encouraged Ann to stick it out. So many times Ann often gave into Mathew's ridiculous requests just to keep from losing Beyonce.

Sha Sha witnessed a lot of Mathew's behavior and became very upset with how he kept showing up every day at Ann's house causing her even more stress than what she was already dealing with. Sha Sha was a light-skinned, very attractive young girl around nineteen. She was accustomed to being at the house and Mathew showing up unannounced, often in a tirade. There were times that Sha Sha would be on the couch sleep with short pants on, and would feel Mathew staring over her. For awhile she would get spooked.

"Look Ann, I don't know what's wrong with him, but somethin' wrong with that fool, and I don't trust him."

"What he do?"

"He keeps standing over me, staring at me like he is undressing me with his eyes. He's weird."

"Huhm."

"Ann, he got some problems, and the way he be acting trying to look under my clothes and stuff...heck I'm afraid that he's gonna try something with me."

"I'll keep an eye on that Sha Sha and I will also talk to Kenny about it as well."

"I'm tired of that fool looking at me like that!"

It became almost a routine that when Mathew came over, he would stare her down. She got to the point where she would ask him, "May I help you?"

Instead of responding, Mathew, who was almost always high on something, would just walk off. It became so excessive that Sha Sha started speaking up more assertively to try and encourage a behavior change on his part.

"What's wrong with you? Stop staring at me all the got-darned time! Ann, this fool is perverted! He got some got-darned issues! Get the heck out of my face you pervert...before I get someone to whoop your butt!"

Ann had to take Sha Sha aside and talk to her.

"Sha, I know something is wrong with him, but we gotta get it done."

Once Ann talked to Sha Sha to give her a better understanding of what was going on, she tolerated Mathew's behavior.

While Mathew's erratic behavior was going on and he was adding additional pressure on Ann, another Atlanta showcase came up for the girls to perform as Something Fresh. At this point it was officially – Beyonce, Latavia, Letoya, and Kelly. All four girls had been recording in Atlanta with Darryl Simmons already. Right before the Atlanta showcase, Ann had a Lupus episode where she needed to be hospitalized again and another finger removed. She ended up going into surgery two days before the Atlanta show.

Ann insisted on going to the showcase. She wanted to demonstrate that she was okay and still in charge. Ann had the itinerary for the show and as far as she was concerned everything was set and ready to go. As I was unable to go to Atlanta this time, I asked Sha Sha to escort Andretta due to her recent operation. Once Ann and Sha Sha arrived in Atlanta and checked into the hotel, Simmons had a meeting with everyone. When Ann was at the meeting, she felt that Darryl and Mathew made some type of pack because of the way that the two of them were talking to her. It was as if she did not have control when in fact she did because the contract was between her and Silent Partners as the lead manager.

"Well Ann, we made a few changes and we want you to take a look at them."

"Okay, Darryl, that's cool!"

Ann didn't think too much about it, nor was she alarmed. Ann had confidence in Darryl's ability being that he had been in the industry for awhile, and figured he just wanted to do something just a little differently. She never suspected that anything was wrong.

Before the showcase they all went over to Darryl Simmons' house to hang out before the showcase. When they arrived, Sha Sha felt that the girls were acting funny, and she was not really digging how things were going on.

"Ann, what the heck is wrong with these girls? I mean these little brats got some darn nerve acting simple and stuff! What's up with that?"

"Sha, it's alright."

"Naw the hell it ain't alright! How you gonna let them disrespect you and stuff! What? Did they forgot who you are or something?"

"Be cool Sha, it's alright."

"Uhm...what...! Can't they even come and show you some love or something? Heck, at least say hello. They act like they got sticks up their butts! You ask me, Ann, something is very wrong here, and I ain't diggin' this stuff at all!"

"Sha, I see what's going on. Someone has been saying something."

"Darn straight! I bet anything that coke head is behind this stuff!"

"Who, Mathew?"

"Ann...who do you think I mean? You know he's a weird ass and anytime there's some stuff, I bet you it has his name written all over it! Perverted behind! And his tail is tryin to pimp his daughter...jerk!"

"Sha!"

"Screw all that nice stuff Ann! He's a got-darned trick!"

"Apparently this stuff is true, Sha. I had been hearing that he was saying he was in charge and stuff. The girls are acting really strange...and that Kelly...heck, if anyone should be showing some love over here it would be her."

"Black heifer! All of them can kiss my tail Ann. You aretoo nice to them ungrateful wenches! You're better than me. Heck, I go get me another group of girls and they all could kiss my high yellow tail!"

"We can't do that Sha. We've come too far. I've invested too much in these girls to throw my hands up and walk away or be moved to one side."

"I guess you're right, but something's gonna have to give, 'cause this stuff ain't right Ann, and you know it!"

Ann got up and walked out and called me to talk on the telephone.

"Hey Kenny, this is Ann...are you busy?"

"What's up?"

"You know, we had been hearing about this jerk saying all kind of stuff."

"Yeah…what about it?"

"Everybody's acting a little strange."

"Whatcha mean, Dretta?"

"The girls are walking around here, half speaking and stuff. Others looking at me like what the heck am I doing here and stuff…"

"What?"

"Yeah Kenny, I'mma ask what's up because even the girls are acting all funny. If I hear that this jerk has said some stuff, I'm jumping all in his butt."

While Ann was on the phone talking to me, Sha Sha went around the house talking to the girl's one on one. Latavia was the one who actually spoke up and told Sha Sha that Mathew said he was taking control of managing the girls and that Ann was going to work with him. Once Ann got off the telephone with me, Sha Sha told her what Latavia had said. Ann was livid!

"Ann, this fool is crazy! That girl…Tavi, Latavia… whatever the heck her name is said that that fool done said some stuff!"

"What she say?"

"She said that Mathew told them that he was in charge and you were now pretty much answering to him."

"What! I had been hearing a bunch of stuff, but this takes the cake!"

"No wonder they ignoring you…he's ignorant if you ask me!"

"Let me handle this stuff, Sha!"

Ann went up to Mathew while he was standing talking to Darryl Simmons.

"Mathew, why the heck you runnin' around telling the girls and everybody you are in charge when you know I'm the darn manager and your tail is working with me?"

Darryl was taken aback at the abruptness and straight forwardness of Ann in her confrontation of Mathew. He seemed surprised at the whole situation.

"Hey…whoa…whoa…whoa…What ya'll gonna do?"

"Darryl, what do you mean what we gonna do? Mathew knows darn well what the deal is."

"Andretta, I ain't got time for this stuff right now, we here at the man's house chillin out and this ain't the time for this bull!"

"It's just the time for this stuff Mathew!"

"Look we can talk about this stuff later, we got a darn showcase!"

"Fine, but we gonna talk about it!"

After that, Ann and Sha Sha headed back to the hotel, as did Mathew and the girls to get ready for the showcase. Somewhere between Darryl's house and the showcase, something was said to the girls. As Ann and Sha Sha walked into the venue for the showcase, she heard the new music. However, the ultimate disrespect followed.

When Ann walked into the room, there was no acknowledgement of her presence.

The girls were all sitting with their parents, and there was a separate table for Ann. The centerpiece on all the tables had "Baby Dolls" on it. Ann soon found out that Darryl Simmons and Mathew had gotten together without consulting her and changed the name of the group from "Something Fresh" to "The Dolls."

She was mad as heck, but kept her cool because there was a room full of executives and more arriving as the night went on. All she could really do without causing a scene was whisper to Sha Sha to observe.

"Sha, look at this bull. They have changed the girls' names. Haven't consulted me or said anything to me about it."

"That's bull Ann."

"You just wait, I'mma get in Mathew's butt."

When it came time for the girls to perform, they were introduced as "The Dolls." As the night moved on, Ann became so upset that her fingers started to bleed through the bandage and for the first time she was about to cry.

"Andretta...don't you cry. Don't you dare cry!"

Ann was tearing up, but fighting the tears back.

"Don't you let these heifers see you cry!"

Ann was working on getting her composure, while Sha Sha continued to offer support.

"Don't you let them see you cry. You can cry all you want back at the hotel, but don't let these fools see you cry! They ain't worth it!"

Ann was able to get herself together and keep it together. However, what was extremely hurtful that hit to the core of her soul was seeing Beyonce, Latavia, Letoya, and Kelly over in the corner pointing looking at her hand and laughing. She heard them say, "Look she got her fingers cut off..."

Words could not express the profound pain that Ann felt at that moment seeing young girls, especially three of them that she had mentored and cared for, for years behave in such a manner. The very deal which made it possible for them to even be at this night was because of her hard work. Being young and lacking understanding in some areas is natural. Yet, the ignorance and level of insensitivity these girls showed at that moment was beyond comprehension. Ann was devastated, but her love still allowed her to look beyond their cruelness to believe that behind it all was the manipulations from adults. Yet, that belief still did not change the fact that Ann was extremely hurt and almost broken from the girls making fun of her.

Ann made it through the show. Afterwards the girls came over to her asking if she was okay. It was more two-faced than anything. Ann showed very little emotion toward them to protect her heart. Sha Sha looked at them as if to say, "Get your, black and high yella behinds out of my darned cousin's face! Heck naw she ain't okay…! Go back to that darned pimp daddy coke head and…bounce, before I put my foot up where the sun don' shine!"

However, Sha Sha only rolled her eyes while the words stayed in her mind and on the tip of her tongue. By the girls' actions, they had been prepped on what to say and do. Ann had no idea that their names had been changed to "The Dolls" and in her observation, they knew that she didn't know, but pretended otherwise.

"You know Sha, Darryl Simmons knows what the he's doing. I believe he is guiding Mathew and he's souping Mathew's head up talking about how Beyonce's the star and stuff!"

"Mathew is a perverted jerk Ann, and Simmons…well, this is some crap!"

"They think they got the group, but it's not that easy, Sha!"

Ann ultimately made it through that trip to Atlanta, however, the disrespect continued because Mathew increased his trips to Ann's house and well as his drug use. It was getting out of control. He started lying even more to Tina and giving her the impression that there were meetings going on at Ann's house when, there was not. When there really were meetings going on, they usually lasted between three to four hours. Mathew used them as a cover for extramarital affairs with different women. Mathew might show up at the start of a meeting and then leave or he would come at the end of one after screwing around and getting high. There were many times that he would be so high that he ended up sleeping on Ann's floor or couch because he couldn't drive home for being so high.

Ann knew one of the girls that Mathew was having an affair with, and when she first found out about it, she was very angry at both the girl and Mathew because she knowingly was messing around with a married man. Even worse, the girl knew Tina. While she knew Mathew better, she knew darn well that Mathew was married to Tina. They spent so much time together she was darn near living with the man. Ann would often say, "That's a dirty son-of-a-gun, and mark my word...his stuff gonna come back on him!"

Ann felt so bad for Tina, who started calling excessively looking for Mathew. Ann got to the point she would not even answer her own phone because she was not going to lie to Tina. Lonnie was still living with Ann. T-Mo came around because of Lonnie and some of the others who were coming in and out, really didn't know what was going on. When any of them would grab the phone, they would say whatever Lonnie or T-Mo yelled in the background.

"He ran to the store...he's out back in the garage...we had a meeting and he fell asleep on Ann's couch and is too tired to drive home..."

The excuses were numerous. After a while when even the clueless became clued in on Mathews behavior, he convinced them to stick with him because he would take them places. They believed him because Beyonce was the key focus of the group. Mathew played that trump card as far as he could take it. Beyonce, being a young girl, was almost completely oblivious to all this background mess going on around her.

When Mathew did stay the night at Ann's, he would be walking around when everyone else was sleeping. Sha Sha was very uncomfortable, so she started sleeping in Ann's room. What made her most uncomfortable was that Mathew was always looking at her and undressing her with his eyes. She was afraid that he might try to do something.

Mathew was completely out of control as if someone had given him some gas and he was pushing the "metal-to-the-peddle." Mathew was not stable and Ann was not feeling the best about how things were going. I was still communicating back and forth with my friend Al. So knowing this, Ann wanted to make a shift.

"Kenny, let's go back and talk to Al, and back door this stuff."

"I'm with you on that Ann."

When I called Al back, he agreed to put up the funds. Attorney Darryl was waiting on us to come back with the girls to sign the agreement. It was a catch twenty-two because we needed the girls, and we could not figure out how to get the girls to go back to Atlanta to sign a new contract without Simmons and Mathew knowing. While Ann and I could sign as the managers, Attorney Darryl's position was that he could not go to one of the major labels and by-pass this deal that we were in with Silent Partner if he could not be sure we had the girls.

Ann and I did not want to "stir the pot" to alert them that we were after a side deal. Although were in the deal with Silent

Partner, we could have gotten the money from Al for the studio and kept working. With the dynamics of the deal and the sensitivity around the matter, that put a hold on Al giving the funds. However, he continued to come over to see how things were progressing. His position was that the girls were hot and he was ready to go, but we just couldn't pull the strings without Mathew and Simmons knowing. Around the same time, the girls were also performing another showcase in New York for Elektra.

Even though the behind the scenes conversations were taking place, apparently the meetings with the attorney Darryl helped the Elektra deal get expedited. While we had agreed to sign with Elektra a while back, Elektra still had not come forward with the paperwork to sign. The reality was there was an agreement for a deal, but the deal had not closed. The conversations we were having on the side with Al and Attorney Darryl changed that reality because Elektra finally came to the table to sign us.

Once we finally signed with Elektra, we had a signing party and it was a much lighter time because finally we had a record deal and Ann felt that some of the stress had come off. She had accomplished what she was after. She got the deal and now she could really get the girls out there in a much bigger way. Getting this deal was a big accomplishment because we had a stable of artists and it was not just "The Dolls." Our position was all we needed was one deal and then we could get the other artists in the stable going.

The advance from Elektra came through, and as Ann had agreed, the advance went to Mathew to manage the distribution of funds. This advance was to cover the budget for the recording of the album. The girls moved to Atlanta to record. The advance that Elektra gave was to cover all production costs with mainstream producers to end up with a high-quality product.

"Look, I ain't gonna pay all these fools that kind of money."

"Mathew, naturally the main stream producers are gonna cost more, but they are the best and you have name recognition which is going to make our stuff better."

"Nigga, why in the heck should I pay these producers to do the same stuff we can go get a no name who's just as good? Why should I when I can get people like Lonnie and all these other cats who can do it? I can pay them five thousand dollars and get the stuff done and keep all this other advance money!"

"Mathew, you can't do this. You have to use the money what it is for."

"Look Ann, I ain't paying all this money to produce these songs. We got people who can do this!"

"We have to get the people they said to get. We have to show the label that we used their money properly, Mathew."

"Shoot, I got the advance, I'mma say how the stuff gonna get spent, and I told you, Ann got-darn it, I ain't payin' them all that got darn money to do what Lonnie and 'em can do!"

Mathew would not listen to reason, he ranted and raved and insisted on doing it his way. There was nothing that I or Ann could say to get him to cooperate. Lonnie was like a hungry gremlin so there was no way he would turn it down and even if he did, Mathew was still gonna find a way to short cut and short change the process.

Mathew went and got some local producers and some people around Lonnie that had songs that the girls recorded. While "The Dolls" were in Atlanta recording the album, Mathew spent a lot of time traveling back and forth. His marriage started to suffer drastically from the travel, the drug use and the rumors that Mathew was having affairs with a couple of women in Atlanta. While we were trying to manage all that was going on as best we could, things on Mathew's home front started to get completely out of hand. Although the girls were making progress on the album, the songs they were recording were "so-so." Ann knew that it was going to fail.

"Mathew, we must use this money to record using these other mainstream producers, so that they will help to push the album and their names would be on the album."

"Got-darn it Ann what's your problem? I got this!"

"Mathew, you cannot mess over Elektra's money, you got to do it their way."

"Look, I got this stuff! I'm controlling the money, and this is how we gonna do this!"

That fight with Ann and Mathew went on and on. Ann kept insisting that Mathew use the money for what it was intended, and Mathew kept threatening Ann and insisting on doing it his way. It was not too hard to see from where I was standing that Mathew was doing exactly what Lynn was doing whenever he got money.

While the songs were being produced, after about a year and a half of working on the recording of the album and getting polished as young artists with a major record label, the product was completed and finally turned over to Elektra. We listened to it, and Ann and I felt that it was no where near what a major label would expect. However, it was turned over to the label as requested. They reviewed it and after doing so decided that they could not push the album and consequently, dropped the girls. That album was completed but never released.

Ann had known that it would be a failure. Yet Mathew's habitual drug use, extramarital affairs, and ego hindered him from listening to reason. He and Ann stayed in constant conflict that entire time. While she knew that the record would need to be tightened up, she had no idea that the label would drop the girls. Everyone was devastated and extremely disappointed.

When Elektra dropped the group, Mathew had no other avenues and thus crawled back to Ann with his tail between his legs. So on top of messing up his marriage and his relationship with Ann and the management team, he also messed up with Silent Partners.

"Darn Ann, we are back to square one!"

"That fool is a screw up! Now let me see his tail try to threaten me over Beyonce's now. At this point, we be lucky if anyone in the industry even gives us a second look."

"Man! That jerk!"

"Kenny, what we gonna do?"

So Ann, Mathew, and I had to have a pow-wow.

"Ann we need to get another deal…we have to…"

"Look you messed up the last got-darned deal!"

"Screw you Kenny."

"Screw you! You low down dirty stank behind!"

I was so pissed off watching Mathew back begging her to go make something happen, when he was the reason why everything was in the state it was in. I mumbled under my breath, "Punk behind…"

I needed a breather because I was very angry at the situation. Here we worked our butts off to make something happen, and had to tolerate his mess to make it happen, then he went and screwed the whole think up with his mess! I walked in the kitchen to take a pause from the meeting. Sha Sha was standing in the kitchen.

"What's up Kenny?"

"That punk…"

"You ain't gotta tell me…If you only knew how I felt about his stank tail."

"Baby girl you ain't never lied."

"I feel sorry for Tina. He is special. I can't stand that nigga. If you only knew how many times I wished someone would take his behind in alley somewhere and beat the crap out of him."

"Heck, I came real close to it…"

"I wanted to screw him up myself. I was thinking about all sorts of diabolic stuff. Why don't he just go away! Darn, do ya'll need Beyonce that bad that ya'll have to deal with his bull? Heck it don't seem worth it Kenny."

"Sometimes I wonder Sha Sha."

I finally walked back in the room where Mathew and Ann were still talking. Ann was explaining that some major changes had to take place for us to continue.

"Tillman Management and Girls Tyme Entertainment cannot go any further, because people are already associating us with messing up the advance from Elektra."

"That's true Ann. It's like the Star Search piece."

I looked at Mathew, rolled my eyes, and then said, "Association is a mutha!"

"That's right Kenny," Ann said shaking her head.

"Heck, no major label is gonna give us any money, and regardless as to who screwed up, we are the management team and no major label is gonna give us the money."

Mathew sat there looking pitiful. I was completely pissed off I mumbled under my breath, "This fool come with a bogus album…"

Although Mathew completely messed up, we all re-grouped and formed a three-way partnership between Ann, Mathew and me. Mathew took fifty percent, while Ann and I each took twenty-five percent. Mathew's argument was that I was Ann's boy so it would give him a level playing field. Hence, this was the birth of Music World Entertainment. Ann kept Tillman Management for all the other acts. The girls however transferred to Music World.

Belfry stepped in again and provided more funding for Ann to keep things moving and to keep her from tapping into the boy's trust fund. We got back on the horse to make things happen again. Ann got back on the telephone with some of the former players, and Teresa resurfaced giving advice again. Things started to pop! The girls started coming around again and spending more time at Ann's house, but Sha Sha was not thrilled.

"Kenny, what the heck…they trifling tails want to start coming back around talking about hey Aunt Sha. Screw them!"

"Girl you know you crazy."

"I can't stand no fake folks Kenny. You know I am as real as they come …"

"Girl, be cool. We tryin' to handle some business."

"Yeah, Kenny…I'mma handle some' business alright. They plastic! And that Mathew…after all that bull, I hope Ann set that dude straight!"

"Things are gonna roll alright Sha Sha."

"Alright Kenny, I've been here for Ann and my sentiments is that now that all they stuff done fell through, now they need her again and they wanna be all fake and stuff. They are a bunch of users!"

"You right."

"You darn right I'm right. That's right…kiss her butt. Lick all up in her Black butt…I can't stand them Kenny."

"I know Sha Sha, but it's all good, girl."

Although things were starting to look up with the girls and it looked like things were moving forward again, along with that also came more stress. Ann ended up back at the hospital with another Lupus crisis. Sha Sha called me to let me know that Ann had been taken to the hospital. I rushed up to the hospital. We could see Ann's health deteriorating so it wasn't a total surprise that she had another crisis. Me being the cheerful support that I was, walked into her hospital room with the normal banter.

"Hey Blackie! Where is yo Black behind at? Your mama so Black, I bet when she get out the car, the oil light come on…"

I was loud in the hospital cracking all kind of Black jokes. This was the first time that I came to see her up at the hospital and she wasn't really laughing. She gave some half shallow laugh, but not the from the gut laughter that she usually gave. "Kenny don't make me laugh. Please don't."

When I looked at her this time, it really hit me that this was very serious. I was taken aback and a little afraid.

"Kenny, I really wanna talk to you about something."

"What Dretta? What?"

"If something was to happen to me…"

"Ann, I don't wanna hear this stuff! I'm not finna listen to this…Ain't a got-darned thing gonna happen to you so I don't wanna hear that stuff! We gonna get this stuff done and we finna roll!"

"Kenny…"

"No Ann, you can't start thinkin' negative because we hit a bump in the road…and that's all it is…a bump in the road. We are where we need to be. We got it back in hand. We back in charge, they learned their lesson and ain't none of them runnin' stuff and it all gotta come through you if they want this stuff to happen. Let's just make sure we emphasize that a little more and I'll step up and handle the meetings and dealings with Mathew and kind of keep the pressure off."

"I know…I know…but if something was to happen to me…"

"Dretta, I really don't wanna hear this but…what?"

"Kenny, if something was to happen to me, I want you to raise my boys."

"Huh?"

"Yes, I want you to raise my boys. I want them to have a stable environment…and uh…I just want you to raise my boys. They love you. You like a dad to them anyway. I want you to rais ethe boys and then that way…You'll already know what percentages and my contract…so if something happens to me…you would run the estate and…you'll already know my percentage of…uh…with the new management company."

I sighed and said, "Yeah Ann."

"I know you will take care of my boys and you'll give them their inheritance and all of that."

"Ann, why would you want me to do that? Why would you want me to raise your boys? You know…it would seem to me that your sisters and brothers…you know would be better."

"They would be but…a lot of times people be all about money, and…it don't necessarily be out of love…you know when something happens. I'm just sayin'…I'm not saying somebody's bad and wouldn't give my kids their money and all of that but…I do know folks act funny, especially your family. They will feed your children and everything else. When they turn eighteen they put them out and keep the inheritance and the kids ain't got nothin'."

"Well Ann, put it in a trust and..."

"I already have."

"Okay, I am not going to keep this conversation going. Quit talking like this and get your Black butt up and out of here, and cut all this other stuff out."

This was a very touchy time and while I was attempting to make it a laughter situation, Ann was very serious.

"You finna have this conversation Kenny..."

"Alright Ann, we'll have it another time.

Ann spent a couple of days in the hospital. When she finally got home she rebounded a little faster this time. I was at her house when we went to the piano to talk.

"Dretta, you remember all that stuff you were telling me when you had all those drugs in your system at the hospital?"

"I meant what I said. As a matter of fact, I'll tell you exactly what I said."

"Dretta, you are not gonna have to do this. I'm telling you with my gut, Bey, is gonna be on that some Michael Jackson stuff! I'm telling you. When the Commodores sang Machine Gun, I say Lionel Ritchie was a star, so your tail ain't going no darn where. This is finna happen! It's gonna happen, we just gotta ride it out Dretta."

"Yeah."

"It's always darkest right before the sun comes out. I'm telling you. We are going to ride this thing out. Something good is gonna happen. Trust me on that. So let's just hang on in here...and keep rollin'."

"I'm tired of carrying all these folks. Mathew and Tina done broke up. They don't live together anymore. Now I'm having to send money and stuff over to Tina to kind of help her out so she can buy food to feed Beyonce and Solange."

"Huhm."

"Shoot Kenny, Tina footin' everything and having to work all these hours while his lazy and trifling ass done went and started living with this other darn woman."

"That's some crap."

"Yeah Kenny, and my behind is caught in the middle because I know who it is, I know where his Black butt is, and he still running here trying to have management meetings and stuff. He needs to handle his business. Now his family is in an apartment some darn where."

"Ann you kiddin' me."

"No, and it pisses me off because while he is laying up with some woman, I'm sending money over so Tina can feed the girls."

Ann recuperated and was getting her strength back. The girls were still coming around and appeared to be getting back to themselves. Ann felt like things were getting back to normal. Beyonce and Kelly were getting back to being Bey and Kelly. Just as Ann was feeling like things were getting back to a reasonable environment, all of a sudden a shocker hits the whole camp.

Not only were Mathew and Tina having problems, Cheryl and her husband were also breaking up. During this time every thing was extremely tense.

I called Dretta because it was so bad but nobody was saying anything.

"Dretta, what the heck is going on?"

"Kenny, come by the house tonight."

"What's goin' on?"

"Just bring your tail by the house. I'll talk to you when you get here."

"Alright, I'll be by in a few."

"Talk to you then."

When I arrived at Ann's everybody was just quiet, too quiet.

"Dretta, why you so quiet? Why you and Sha Sha all tight-lipped and stuff? What goin' on?"

"Kenny, you know that jerk has been molesting LaTavia…"

"What! The police dude?"

"Yeah."

"You're lying, Ann."

"No, he's been molesting her for years."

"What in the heck…"

All of this was just coming out. We just sat there.

"How in the heck could Cheryl not seen that this man be messing with my baby?"

"Wow."

"I don't understand these hoes for mothers and…"

Ann went off. She was beyond upset.

"How can you be so in love with a man that you can't see he's screwin' you and you can't see he's screwin' with your baby?"

"Shoot."

"How can you be that darn blind to this?"

Ann was so mad that she started planning things for LaTavia and then called Charlotte.

"Charlotte tell Cheryl to just go ahead and let LaTavia come and stay with me."

Charlotte replied.

"No Ann, she can come and stay with us."

Ann's goal was to make sure she got out the house and everything. While Cheryl and Charlotte was dealing with the family issue, Ann and I was like, "What the heck"

Then while me and Ann was sitting there, she had an "ah-ha" moment.

"Kenny, darn...I should have seen it. I should have seen it."

"What?"

"I should have seen it."

"What, Dretta?"

"Out of all the time we've been rehearsing, or they've been performing, LaTavia has always appeared to be more sensual than the other girls. Bey butt be buck wild. Kelly was stiff, Letoya had her funny way on stage, but LaTavia was always sensual with hers. I should have seen it. I should have seen something."

"Ann you can't see stuff like that. You wouldn't expect a darn Houston police officer to go and be molesting his step-daughter, especially as public a persona as she's had. Heck she's been a model for a national product line and she's been in Girls Tyme and now The Dolls. She's been in Something Fresh. Heck Ann, she's been in all these groups for all this time. You can't expect no stuff like that."

Cheryl kicked him out and the family worked to get LaTavia some counseling. The whole situation sent shockwaves through the entire camp. We asked all the questions. How do we deal with this? How do the girls deal with her? Will they treat her differently? These were the questions and concerns from all the parents and adults. The blessing was though that Beyonce had a way about her that when she really realized that LaTavia had been damaged, she was very compassionate.

Beyonce seemed as if she felt LaTavia's hurt. One of the reasons why I even love her today is because of this special way about her. She and LaTavia were already close, but Beyonce drew closer and more protective of her after learning about what had happened to her. I believe it was this situation that caused Beyonce to become like the mother hen of the group. It was like Beyonce said, "How dare them. How dare they hurt one of us?

After this, Beyonce started to develop thick skin. She was still sweet but she was more edgy and protective.

You could see Beyonce sort of grow up with LaTavia and the realization that this has happened. That buck wild personality that LaTavia had was still there, but you could see that the innocence had been stolen. She was no longer like a young girl with her innocence. People had come to know what had happened. So she was somewhat forced to be a young lady instead of a little girl. She was robbed of her virtue. She was forced to be a little more mature.

After it had come to light what had been happening to LaTavia, I really did not hear too much else about the case of LaTavia's step-father or what happened to him. The group didn't talk about it because we did not want LaTavia to be treated differently or for her to feel like something was wrong with her. We actively worked to overcome this major issue and did our best to help LaTavia and the girls to overcome it as well.

HARD TO GET, EASY TO GO

The bad news about LaTavia left things somewhat gloomy and added to the extreme disappointment of being dropped by Elektra. Mathew was driven by his greed and worldly vices, mishandling money and spending it for frivolous pursuits of women, and drugs, and as a result costed us what we had worked so hard to achieve. He lost favor with Elektra executives. They were embarrassed by the whole situation and made sure everyone knew about the bogus album production. As a result, word ran through the industry like a brush fire and no one wanted anything to do with Girl's Tyme Entertainment because of Mathew's actions.

We were in a tough situation. Mathew had worked tirelessly to usurp Ann's position as lead manager and when she gave him a little leeway, he screwed things up for everyone.

He forced his way into every conversation or negotiation that he could and used Beyonce as a pawn and bargaining tool. He was messy and this was one of the biggest messes so far. If there was one bright spot during that time, it was that this one messup he was unable to clean up, so it forced everyone to run back to Ann for guidance.

At the end of the day, Ann was the one making it happen and if the crew would have just followed her guidance without trying to compete to be the HNIC, then we would have undoubtedly been a lot further and would not have lost the first major deal we signed. Some people had their own agendas and were dead set on getting their agenda across regardless as to what the cost and believe me, it cost us big. It was apparent by the attitudes that they were not prepared to face the consequences, but as the saying goes – "It costs to be the boss!" Unfortunately, no one at the table was prepared to put out. So once again they expected Ann to come to the rescue. They wanted to know what she was going to do.

As Sha Sha said, "Now their Black behinds wanna come and lick all up Ann's tail, sticking to Ann like flies to crap and begging like dogs for a bone. They act like some got-darned crying punk babies. What we gonna do Ann...How can we make it right Ann...Screw You! Do it your darn self!"

Sha Sha was upset because she saw first hand what was going on and how they handled Ann nearly bringing her to tears in Atlanta. That was enough for Sha Sha to tell them all where to go.

"See Kenny, those fools can eat crap and die treating her like that. They get what they get. Mathew is out for what Mathew can get and he don't give a darn about nobody but his self or who get hurts in the process!"

"I want to make sure that Ann's stress level stays down because whenever this bull with Mathew is going on it stresses her out more."

"I know. And the thing is Kenny, since the Elektra thing went down; he has started lurking around even more. Somebody need to pull his crooked tail in an alley and whoop his butt!...Coke-head bastard!"

"Sha Sha, just keep helping Ann and doing what you can to minimize some of the stress off of her."

"Oh you don't have to worry about that. I'm just not sure how much longer I can stay, but I'll be here as long as I can! Bank on that!"

"Well I hope you have some time."

"Kenny to be honest, my major concern is Ann. Belfry left me here to help with his cousin and I don't give a crap about the group if it means Ann's health. And I sure in the heck don't give a flyin' flip about Mathew and his bull."

"You don't like Mathew very much I can see."

"What the heck?...Boy...I will throw this got-darned pan of hot water on you."

I laughed at Sha Sha's response to that statement. I knew that would work her up more than she already was. I allowed her the room to vent. I realized that Sha Sha was young and although she was strong, what was going on got to her too. So I offered as much support as I could.

"And your ass don't like him either, Kenny, and you know it!"

"Shoot...He's dirty, I give you that."

Sha Sha and I continued talking in Ann's kitchen while she was cooking. Ann was in her bedroom resting.

"You know he's on some bull and I ain't as forgiving as Ann's. Personally I think he's a user, and those girls are ungrateful as heck. I believe that coke-head bastard would sell Beyonce's little yellow tail on the got-darned street corner if he thought he could get away with it. And Kelly got some darned nerve being all simple and stuff for everything I hear Ann did for her nappy-headed butt."

"Oh yeah! Mathew didn't hesitate to get rid of her when Darryl Simmons and 'em was closing the deal."

"All he is interested in is making a dollar, and he don't give a darn about how he does it either. Kenny, you should see how he be pushing up on Ann and pressuring her."

"Darn, Sha. I see him in the meetings and how he is when I'm here, but you mean to tell me that fool comes around on other times with that bull?!"

"I ain't lying, you should see him. He's creepy and the way he be looking at her sometimes...ugh...It's creepy man."

"What?"

"Ann is too darn trusting and forgiving. She should have cut him off a long ago. She loves those girls though Kenny and I don't get it."

"Yeah Sha Sha, there's something to that though. She know they are gonna be stars and they keep saying to her that Beyonce is key. So she works hard to not let that slip through her fingers so she has to put up with his sorry behind."

"Mathew is getting over on some trick stuff Kenny, dangling Beyonce like a piece of meat, and he's willing to sell everyone else down the river if it means more money for his dope-head behind! I tell you...I don't get it."

I sat there for a moment, thinking back on the intimate details Ann shared with me about her husband Dwight's death. I sighed and realized that Sha Sha had no clue about much of what was driving Ann.

"Yeah, you're right, Sha Sha."

"Heck Kenny, I might only be nineteen, but it doesn't take a rocket scientist to figure this crap is bull no matter how you sling it! This house is a revolving door. Do you know how many darn people come in and out of here? She's too nice to people and they don't deserve it. They screw up her stuff, then they go screw up theirs, and then like some bad kids who got their butt kicked out on the street they wanna come running back to Ann to make it all better."

"Uhm."

"She buy them clothes, she pay their bills, she pay their got-darned mama and daddies' bills, she pay for their crap while they flying all over the darn country like they got something...and for what? So those little heifas can stand over in a corner in Atlanta and laugh at her hand bleeding and stuff! So those punks can go behind her got-darn back and try to cut her every chance they get and take her stuff like she owe it to them?"

I just shook my head while Sha Sha was going off.

"Like I said, now that the Electra deal unraveled Mathew's been kissing all up in Ann's tail."

That day, Sha Sha and I ended up talking a while. It just goes to show that one person on a team can impact the entire team. When Mathew thought things were on the up with Elektra and was dealing with the no name producers, he had gone out and got a couple of acts that he intended to manage on his own and put them out there. However, when the situation crumbled, he was forced to look to Ann again for help.

Things were tighter in Ann's house. She started getting calls from Tina telling her the electricity was off at the apartment or she didn't have food for Beyonce and Solange. Ann was in a catch twenty-two because Mathew was at her house excessively, while Tina was busting her butt to make ends meet. So Ann shelled out money to help Mathew's family. Tina didn't get any money from him for support and whatever he got from Ann or stole; he spent it on women and drugs.

Given LaTavia's situation, Charlotte started coming around the house more to help Ann more. It was just in time because Sha Sha ended up having to move back to Tyler. Since Ann was by herself more again, Charlotte and her girls ended up spending more time at Ann's. Ann was working on regrouping with everything that went down. She reached out to me and Lonnie to see what the next move was. She asked me if I thought we should go back to Al in Atlanta to try to get the money for the studio.

When I reached out to Al, his attorney advised him against it and had turned a cold ear to the idea of giving us the money because of what happened with the Elektra advance. Al's attorney's position was that we did not know how to manage money. Mathew's dumb move, although we insisted against it, had killed the Elektra contract and shot down any funding through Al. Now with all these doors closing, creating Music World really became a smart move given what we were facing. With these conditions, no one was going to talk with us. We had to present a new brand and image as we did when the girls lost on Star Search.

As we were working to reorganize and pick up the pieces of what was left, Mathew started talking about taking Beyonce solo.

"You're gonna screw the girl's life up Mathew. Leave her alone. She has the talent, we all know she has the talent. Leave well enough alone. You done already screwed up her first major deal. Leave her alone!"

"I know she got the talent, Ann, that's why she should go solo."

"You already screwed stuff up, you done screwed up the money, don't screw up her life too. Let me fix it. Let me think about it and I'll get back with you on how we need to move forward."

"Well, yo' butt need to hurry up and fix it."

"You broke it. Like I said, give me a got- darn minute and let me see how to clean up your stuff! Let me do what I need to do!"

"We need to make it happen now. People are talking bad about us and everything."

"Fool, they are talking bad about you."

Ann still had a lot of support in the industry. Teresa began advising Ann again as she was loyal when everyone else had shied away. Willie D started coming by again helping Ann to chop it up. Ann had quite a few people at her beckon call that she could call to use as sounding boards in terms of how to regroup and how to go about rebuilding.

Willie D, Rob, and Dwayne Wiggins all pretty much said the same thing. "Nobody is gonna give you money anymore!" They said we would have to get a surrogate to basically take us back in. This gave us some leverage because no one wanted to put their name out there in terms of dealing with Mathew when they knew that he was the one who blew the last deal. Unfortunately we were branded too, but everyone knew we were under the situation of a parent with a star child.

"Okay Kenny, this is the word. We have a lot of people still on our side. They know Mathew's dumb behind don't know what the heck he is doing. They are still willing to work with us, but they don't want to touch Mathew."

"So what are we gonna do Ann?"

"Well the good thing is although we are in a partnership with this fool, in the contract I am the manager, so I still have control and the industry is back in my corner. They will not deal with him at all."

"Okay so what you saying?"

"Well, what I am saying, Kenny is that it is our game again now."

"Ann, what we waitin' on?"

"Lonnie mentioned to me that Dwayne is still interested in the girls and thought that we should go through his company."

I started laughing at how things were playing out, and then said to Ann, "Lonnie's slick tail is something. Mathew threw him under the bus so this is his way of getting back in charge I guess."

"Lonnie is gonna be who he gonna be, Kenny, but, if this is the way we need to get back into the game, so be it!"

"Shoot, Ann, I'm with you on that. Lonnie ain't been no issue with me. I know how to handle that. He ain't a problem. It's Mathew who is the real dirty punk we gotta worry about and watch."

"Lonnie ain't messin' with Mathew. I think with the A & A stuff and now this Elektra thing…Heck I wouldn't be surprised at what Lonnie would do. He might be wishy-washy, but he ain't fooolin' with Mathew, mark my word. Heck he know Mathew would sell him to a pack of wolves if it meant getting what he wanted."

"Girl, you ain't never lied. He ain't got a darn loyal bone in his body."

"I know we need to keep him at bay so he can't mess up another got-darned thing. I mean that stuff!"

The group's name was changed again and they signed a contract individually as LaTavia, Beyonce, Kelly, and Letoya and collectively as Destiny under our newly-formed entity – Music World Management. We started meeting with Dwayne Wiggins of Tony, Toni, Tone. After hashing things out with Dwayne and his company, Grassroots Entertainment, Inc., located in Beverly Hills, California, Music World Management entered into an agreement in the spring of nineteen ninety-four for them to be a surrogate and work with the girls. Grassroots Entertainment, Inc. were represented by the law firm of Bloom, Deckham, Hergog, and Cook. This was about six months after we were dropped by Elektra. LaTavia, Beyonce, Kelly, and Letoya were all around thirteen at the time.

Lonnie and Ann met with Dwayne to iron out the production details and start production. They discussed who they would pitch to once the recording was done. The girls started flying back and forth to and from Oakland, California to work with Dwayne and Lonnie.

"Kenny we got things moving again. Teresa is on board and said that she would be willing to follow the deal."

"That's great Ann, but do you trust her? I mean, how are you feeling about that?"

"Kenny, Teresa is cool. It's Mathew, Darryl Simmons and Sylvia Rhone that I don't trust. All three of them stabbed me in my got-darned back! Heck Mathew wants to take over and since Beyonce is his daughter and Darryl and Sylvia feels she is the key, Heck..."

"Alright, as long as you know."

"It's fine Kenny. As a matter of fact, Teresa advised me to take the deal to Tommy Mottola."

"He's the one at Columbia or rather Sony right?"

"Yeah. They are one and the same."

"Oh I remember that."

"Teresa has been helpful through all of this stuff. She knew how I was embarrassed at the showcase."

"Wow, I didn't know that."

"Heck yeah, Kenny. She's been there."

"Okay."

Although Teresa was not tied into the Elektra deal, she was consulting with Ann and remained loyal to her even when others bailed on her.

"I really believe that Simmons was coaxing Mathew along. Heck TLC was crying about their stuff as well."

"You know something was going on Ann, because Attorney Darryl was ready to do the deal from under them. He must know how they operate."

"All of them were probably some crooks anyway. That's probably why they were so darn comfortable with Mathew."

"I hear you."

"Heck Kenny, all Mathew's butt-kissing and sweet talking ain't doing a got-darned thing! Do you know that fool still have the nerve to threaten about taking Beyonce out the group talking about going solo and stuff!"

"What?"

"I told that no good dirty punk he don't scare me with that stuff because ain't nobody foolin' with his greedy behind…bastard! Just pisses me off to even think about this stuff. He don't listen to no got darned body. He wanna be the big man…ain't got a got-darned thing."

"He's still clowing Ann?"

"Heck yeah"

"Sha Sha mentioned he was coming by a whole lot more."

"He is here so got-darned much that you would think he lived here. Tina has called him numerous of times. He out screwin' around and snorting stuff that he can't even help his got-darned wife and kids keep the darn lights on or food on the darn table. And he has the nerve to threaten me…trifling butt."

"What…he tryin' to screw up Beyonce's chances?"

"I told him to leave her alone; he is going to screw up her stuff to. That threatening stuff ain't working with me no got-darned more. Everybody knows what he's about, and they don't want nothin' to do with him. He knows it too."

"That's why he's harassing you with his bull. You need to stop him from coming over so much Ann."

"If I knew how to move him back, I would do it in a heartbeat, Kenny."

Ann was on a lot more medication around this time than before. While Charlotte and the girls came by more frequently, Cassey and I would stop through often. If Cassey couldn't make it, I would still pop over to her house. However, Ann was still alone quite a bit. So there were many times that Mathew was there and no one else was there with her.

I started to notice Ann acting a little funny and out of character.

"What the heck is wrong with you girl?"

"Oh no Kenny, I'm fine. I'm just handling a few things that's all."

"What the heck is going on? You haven't called me in a couple of days?"

"Kenny, I just really need to talk to you."

"Okay, you gonna have to do something because this stuff ain't cool now."

Ann came over to the house. She kept trying to talk to me.

"Kenny, I need to talk to you about something."

"I figured that's why your Black behind was here girl."

"No seriously Kenny, we need to talk. We need to revisit that conversation from the hospital."

"Now Dretta, you're doing fine. We don't need to revisit this."

"Shut the heck up Kenny, I really do have something I need to tell you. I just really need somebody to talk to."

"Dretta, I really don't wanna have the conversation with you..."

"Ann, you know Kenny don't wanna talk about if something happened to you," Cassey said who was sitting there listening. "He can't handle it, that's just him."

Cassey motioned Ann into the kitchen. As they started to talk I was listening through a little opening to the kitchen.

"Cassey, if something was to happen to me...uh...I want you and Kenny to raise the boys."

"Ann, we're praying ain't nothing gonna happen to you. Honey things are gonna be fine. You're looking stronger, things are going better."

"I know Cass but I need to know that if something did happen that you and Kenny would do that for me. Every now and then I get sick. Nobody's there at the house with me and if something happened to me who gonna know. Heck if I wake up dead...I'm just saying if something happen."

Cassey was very comforting to Ann rubbin her back and stroking her lovingly. For the first time I listened intently, but neither Cassey nor Ann knew it. It was a tough situation because Ann was almost pleading Cassey to promise her that we would take care of the boys. As I continued to listen, they talked about the boys, the insurance.

"Cassey, the boys would financially be fine. I have their money in a trust for them. If something were to happen, Armon and Christopher will not be a financial burden on you and Kenny. I know you have Brian and they can be like big brothers to Brian."

"What about your family, Ann?...One of your sisters?"

"I know how families can be, Cassey. They'll get the boys and get the insurance and when they turn eighteen throw them out on the streets. I'm not saying that's what my family would do, but I know how people get to arguing and fighting and I just don't want that for my boys."

"Okay."

"I know you and Kenny will provide a stable environment for them. I know ya'll love the boys and the boys' love ya'll. I know you won't throw them out on the streets or misuse their trust fund. Plus they will be in the general area where they can stay in the same school."

Cassey just continued to listen to Ann talk.

"That's all you would have to do is use some of the insurance money and buy a car for Armon and he can drive them back and forth to school from here."

"Ann, we don't need to talk about this, but whatever you need us to do you know we will do it."

"Thank you Cassey."

"Ann...why is this such an issue all of sudden...I mean, what is going on?"

Cassey started to seriously probe Ann's mind because she was sensing something else.

"Do you need me to start coming and staying at the house with you or Kenny to come over? What is it?"

"Well I need somebody."

"Why..."

"Cassey I've been having the weirdest dreams."

"What?"

"Well I would take my medicine and I would wake up as if I had been having sex."

Cassey started laughing. Then they both started laughing.

"Got-darn it Ann, shoot can't you tell if you been having sex?"

"Well heck Cassey, its been so darn long, shoot I don't remember. I don't know if I'm having flashbacks and dreaming about Dwight or what's going on."

"Ann you know you crazy as heck, don't you?"

"No for real the other night…I realized someone was in the bed with me."

"What? Who?"

"I don't know…but…when I took my medicine, Mathew had came over and I told him that I was sleepy and too tired to even talk about business and that I had just taken my medicine."

"So what happened then?"

"Well he said he was just gonna lay on the couch. And I went back to my bedroom to lie down. As I was drifting, I saw a silhouette of someone walking toward me as I was nodding off."

"So…what happened, Ann?"

"Well this time I realized that I had had sex…"

"Ann, are you telling me you were taken advantage of?…Cause you know if you are sedated because of your medicine and someone had sex with you without your consent, you know what that is don't you?"

"What I'm saying is that…when I woke up, I realized I had sex, and I did not consent to having sex with anyone…but because I had my medicine I don't remember…and that the only person who was at my house at that time was Mathew, and I sure in the heck did not give him my darn permission."

"Ann why didn't you say something before?"

"Cassey, my medication puts me completely out of it when I take it. That is the only way that I can get some sleep. I really thought I had been dreaming those other times, until the other night. When I woke up I knew without a doubt that I had sexual intercourse because of what was going on down there."

I came into the kitchen after hearing that.

"What the heck! Ann are you saying that Mathew took advantage of you?"

"I don't know Kenny because I don't remember. But I know my body and I do know that I had sex that night the way my body felt and the way my private parts felt."

"Shoot!"

"Kenny, heck…when I take my medicine, I can't do anything. I can't move my muscles, I can't fight back. I can't do anything. I just don't know."

Ann was very upset.

"Well Dretta,that explains why the last couple of times when I have been over to the house, this jerk was walking through the house like he owns the place…going into the refrigerator and all kinds of stuff like that. Heck, nobody ever did that before."

Cassey nodded her head in agreement.

"Heck, he's comfortable and probably thinking, 'I'm sleeping with her or I did this for her, I can have my way.'"

"You don't think…"

I didn't even let Ann get her comment out before I started back up.

"That's what he act like! He act like he got a run over the house and stuff."

I was livid. At that point, all bets were off for me. Here my friend is on about thirty pills a day and busting her butt to make everybody successful and I hear this? All bets were off. I started pacing and drinking, walking back and forth into the kitchen where Ann and Cassey continued to talking. I said to myself, "I gotta do something. I gotta figure out a way to protect my friend. Okay this stuff is happening…she can't control herself. I gotta put something in place."

At that time Cassey's younger brother Chauncey and his partner were staying with us. They were up and coming producers. Whoosy was also a choreographer. They were working with some local acts down in Acres Homes. When they came home that night, I had a conversation with them.

"Hey Chauncey man…Whoosy…I know ya'll lookin' for a place to stay. I need ya'll to get ya'll stuff and I'mma take ya'll to a place where ya'll gonna stay."

Chauncey had already met Ann. He said, "What?"

"Get ya'll stuff. Ya'll finna go over and stay with Ann, and I'll fill ya'll in on the ride over."

On the ride over, I explained to them that I had good reason to believe that Mathew was taking advantage of Ann when she was sedated from her medicine and to help run her day-to-day operations. I told them I needed them to spend the night there; make sure ain't no stuff happening.

"I'll make sure Ann give you one of her cars to get around in. But if anyone of you has to be in the studio, at least one of you have to be here to help take care of the boys."

"No problem, ma'am. We got it."

"Thanks Chauncey."

"You cool with that Whoosy."

"You know me man."

Whoosy was from Mississipi and was country as heck, but good people.

"You gotta make sure Armon and Chris gets to school and all that."

"Alright."

We finally made it over to Ann's house and busted up in there like the police.

"Kenny, what the heck ya'll doing here?"

"Ann, you remember Chauncey, you remember Whoosy?"

"Yeah."

"Well, they need a place to stay and since you got an extra bedroom upstairs, I think that would be the perfect place for them to stay."

"Huh?"

"I think this will be the perfect darn place for them to stay!"

"Well Kenny you know…"

"Ann, I said they are gonna be staying here!"

"Uh…okay."

Ann just looked at me.

"Chauncey and Whoosy your bedroom is up there on the left. That's where ya'll be staying. Go put your stuff down and then come on back down here so I can show you through here."

When they came back down, I walked them through the house and pointed out everything they needed to know.

"This is the refrigerator. This is the stove. This is Ann's bedroom. Nobody but Armon and Chris goes in Ann's bedroom. Are we clear?"

They nodded.

"If there is anything ya'll need to say to Ann or if Ann needs your help, stand at the door and she'll invite you in. Are we clear?"

I went through the whole routine with them and basically took over the house.

"Here are the car keys. One of you is to be here at all times. Are we good?"

Chauncey was cool with it.

"Oh yeah Mo…yeah, yeah…"

Whoosy was fine as well. So Ann and I went to the piano. She was sitting and playing with the two fingers she had.

"What are you doing Kenny?"

"Dretta, I heard what you told Cat. Now...I'm been telling you all these screwin' years just stick it out, just stick it out. But the stuff done got out of hand. So...I'm just gonna put some things in place to make sure that you are okay."

"Okay."

"You already said that you can't take care of yourself when you're on the medicine. Sha Sha's gone and I don't wanna call her back up here. Heck, Chauncey and Whoosy ain't doin' snothing. We can talk to Sha Sha about comin' back up at a later date. They gonna be here for six months or just until you get to feeling better."

Ann looked at me.

"Ann, are you sure?"

"Yeah."

"What I'm asking is are you sure he did this to you?"

She said, "Yeah."

I looked at her as if to motion the question again.

She said, "Yeah, I'm sure."

"Okay."

Belfry came back into town. I had heard from reliable sources that he was in fact a reputable drug dealer. He was driving through with some friends.

"Hey Belfry, let me talk to you."

"Yeah man, what's up."

"You ever give Mathew some cocaine or something?"

"No man, I ain't give that nigga nothin'! He ask me all the time but I never gave him none."

"I ain't gonna tell you what to do, but I'mma tell you this. If that fool ain't off balance, he gonna kill your cousin. I'm tellin' you point blank. I ain't telling you to give him drugs or what to do. If you ever around him and he acting funny, do what you gotta do. But keep him off balanced."

Belfry listened.

"I see his game now. It's at any cost now; he's out to get her. He's a crook. He wanna be close to her and have access to her to see what's going on. This jerk on some different stuff."

"You really think so man?"

"That's what I think."

I didn't tell Belfry that Ann said that Mathew raped her. I just told him to keep him off balance if he is ever around.

Chauncey and Whoosy were set up at the house. They were cooking and taking the boys to school. Any studio time that needed to be coordinated, Chauncey would do it. He also handled the books and anything that dealt with Lonnie and Dwayne Wiggins. He became like Ann's secretary. Pretty much anything that needed to be done was handled by the two of them. They were right there and they were good at it. Ann was so appreciative she gave them a shot on one of the girl's songs.

The first night that Chauncey and Whoosy were at the house after I went home, Mathew showed up. He bammed on the door and busted all in and saw Chauncey and Whoosy in there.

"Hey, who the heck are ya'll?"

"I'm Chauncey."

"I'm Whoosy."

"I'm Kenny's brother. We just moved in with Ann."

"What the heck ya'll just move in?"

"We helping Ann. Kenny asked us to come over and help out."

"What? Kenny!"

"Uh...uh...How he gonna tell ya'll you can come and stay over here?

"He told us we can come and stay and Andretta agreed so we are staying here."

"Oh...oh...so, what do ya'll do."

"Chauncey said, "I'mma producer."

Whoosy followed with, "I'm a choreographer and I write."

"That's good stuff, let me hear something...you know maybe I can do some good things for you."

Mathew got ready to try to walk into Ann's bedroom.

"Hey, Kenny said can't nobody go in the bedroom. Ann's sleep."

"I gotta talk to her."

Whoosy said, "No man, naw man. Mo said naw!"

"What?"

"Mo said heck naw man! Can't nobody go in the darn room, so can't nobody go in the darn room man."

"You a country backwoods mutha ain't you?"

"It's just like that. I gave Mo my word! And I don't need Mo and the boys comin' down on me. So you can't go in the room man. You gonna have to talk to her when she wake up."

"Yeah, yeah...whatever. Tell her I'll be back to talk to her in the morning."

Everytime Mathew came over, they called me. I told them not to let him near her. It got to the point that I would pop up just as much as Mathew did. He would come by and see me or he would be there and I show up.

"What's up Mat, whats going on?"

"Nothing. What the heck you doing here man, ain't no meeting."

"What the heck you doing here, since we ain't got no meeting?"

"I...I...just came here to talk to Andretta!"

"I was too. That's funny ain't it?"

He wasn't feeling me and I wasn't feeling him, but we got him under control. It got so funny over time that Ann started laughing at the situation. Her health started to come back and she was regaining her strength. She wasn't trying to cook or anything, she mainly rested and kept the stress level low, while Chauncey and Whoosy blocked Mathew's access to her. She recuperated tremendously to the point of going back to work. Although, I was acting out of anger, the way we were handling the situation, helped to bring my friend back to a healthier state of being.

We kept working with Grassroots Entertainment. Soon, we started to hear from Sony. The girls had basically moved out to Oakland with Dwayne for a brief while to keep things moving forward in the most cost-effective way. Teresa was helping Ann to get things set up to keep them moving on. Finally a couple of nice tracks came about including "No, No, No" and "Killing Time." When Ann called me to come over to listen to the tracks, I thought they were on point.

Dwayne along with Taura Stinson wrote the song "Killing Time" and Dwayne ended up negotiating to get it placed on the soundtrack for Men in Black. Everyone was getting excited. For a moment Ann had begun to lose faith, but once her health returned, she too was back to herself. We started to get a lot of calls to get the girls to be in their videos and sing hooks on their projects. Things finally started to happen again but in a much bigger way. We were gaining momentum and Ann regained her health.

"Come on Kenny, let's go get this big record deal. I have a master. Now it's time to go get a deal."

"Well come on then, shoot!"

"I've been talking with Teresa and I started talking with an executive at Columbia/Sony Records."

Ann was excited that the executive loved what he heard. He liked the girls, and he thought that we had something. He said to Ann, "I am not about to give you all a four hundred thousand dollar advance for nothing when one of the girl's daddy already blew the money from the Elektra deal. I'm not going to do it!"

Ann asked the executive, "What do I need to do?"

"I don't know Ann, you have to go figure that one out."

After the call with the executive, Ann then called me.

"Kenny, what we gonna do? I got four hundred thousand dollars, a major record deal, he loves everything, but I can't get the darn deal signed."

"What?"

"Teresa banging her head up against a wall trying to figure out what we gonna do."

"Dretta, uh…well…they ain't gonna give us the money. Mathew screwed that money up! We know that for a fact."

"Yeah."

"Now, what would we do if we were going to buy a car, and they told us that we didn't have the credit to get the car, Dretta? What do we do? Come on Dretta…we Black folks, what do we do?…What we do Dretta?"

"We go get a co-signer."

"There's your answer."

"Huh?"

I looked at her until she got it. Then it hit her.

"You're right!"

Ann called Teresa and she thought it sounded like a great idea. Teresa said, "But Ann, it gotta be somebody we trust because it's going to be advanced to that particular person that we get to co-sign with us."

Her thing was she could go get some artist like R. Kelly to sign and he could come give us some crap music and we're right back where we were like with the other deal. The conversation went all the way round. Ann pitched the idea to Lonnie then to Dwayne. There was already a partnership agreement in place, so who better to do it than Dwayne Wiggins. So we took the deal under the Grassroots banner and said, "Okay ladies and gentleman, here's Destiny."

Ann went and got the deal, and because we got with Dwayne Wiggins, Columbia/Sony awarded us the contract for Destiny as well as the advance of four hundred thousand dollars.

She told Dwayne, "Okay, Dwayne, you have the advance. Now you know we have to get the album recorded with reputable people, and give some of the advance to the girls."

Ann continued on with the ground rules for the agreement.

"I want the master for every recording to make sure things go the way they are supposed to go and you do what needs to be done. This way, I can make sure you don't give me no crap!"

Dwayne agreed.

"I'll have the master recordings to show Columbia/Sony executives that I either approved or disapproved of the recordings, and I can go sound the alarm if you start messin' up."

Ann was not tripping about the money. She wanted to make sure that everything went the way it was supposed to go. Immediately after this happened, Mathew stepped back into the picture.

"I need the advance for the girls. I need to make sure they are okay and that they are compensated."

Ann and Mathew fought over how the advance should go. Mathew continued pressuring, Ann until she agreed to give him the fifty thousand dollars to distribute equally among the girls. She was not concerned because she knew that Dwayne understood that she was due her portion from the deal as well as future royalties from Destiny and the album sales. Mathew was steady trying to get his hands on the advance.

"I need that darn money."

"No you're not getting it. We're going through the proper channels."

It was a constant battle with Mathew once money was seen. Ann was more focused on getting the other acts now built up. Her whole thing was to solidify everything and get the girls out there. Her conversations with me were about the business and making it stick now that we had signed with Columbia/Sony.

"Kenny, let's get the videos done, and everything else done that need to get done."

"Okay."

"We can take the money from that and I need you to be my road manager and be my eyes while the girls are on tour."

"Alright. Shoot I'm feeling you. Heck we rollin'."

We started to build and map out the plans. We were still waiting on the money. Then Dwayne was said, "Well Ann, I got to send fifty thousand dollars your way, what do you want me to do with it? Do you want me to send it to you?"

"No, the girls have waited, let's get it to them. Give it to Mathew to let them split it."

"I will send the other part after this second wave when I send the next recordings."

"Dwayne, I'm okay for now, I'll get my money then. I can wait. You know. Everbody still a little hungry."

Ann was still financially okay. Her position was to take the first advance and give it to the girls; they earned it. She wanted to put a couple of dollars in their pocket. Mathew wanted to be all big and everything so she handed the money over to him and instructed him on how to distribute it. He didn't like that too well. He wanted complete control. Although Chauncey and Whoosy were still at the house, there were times where neither of them could be there. Since Ann had her strength back, it wasn't too much of a concern.

Mathew would be hiding behind trees and things to try to catch her by herself. He started fighting and pressuring Ann again over the money now that he knew money was coming.

"Ann you got any more money from old boy?"

"Mathew, I put the deal together. You ain't did jack. You need to get on before you screw up this deal like you did the last one. Be the quiet and let me handle it."

"I got a deal and I've been talking to people and I'mma take Beyonce out the group. In fact, I have guardianship over all the girls."

"Mathew, you know I just got out the hospital, I'm not for your stuff today!"

"I don't give a crap about you just gettin' out the hospital."

Unbeknownst to Ann, Mathew had been demanding the parents turn over guardianship. Mind you, he still had been telling them that he was in charge and he wasn't telling them what Ann had been doing to secure the deals. So, the parents were thinking everything going on was because of him. They were only going to rehearsals and hearing from Mathew and David. Mathew brought some paperwork over to show Ann. Kelly's mother had given him guardianship. Of course he already had guardianship of Beyonce, and he had two contracts pending where he was trying to get Pam and Cheryl to sign. The contracts were already documented and legally drawn up.

"This is what I have and I will have full guardianship of all the girls by the weekend. They are still minors and I'm taking the group from you right now and I'll kill this deal and go get it myself."

Mathew came with all sorts of threats. This went on for about a week. He was making demand-after-demand, particularly as it pertained to money. I am not sure what all happened with that situation, but what I do know is that Ann eventually conceded. Her health began to deteriorate again. As Chauncey and Whoosey's Production Company picked up steam, they weren't at the house as much. Consequently, Mathew's visits increased.

Because of the guardianship papers, Ann agreed to partner with him again, and give him the lead on management of the girls creating a fifteen/five split of the management partnership for the lifetime of Destiny. In other words, Ann would receive five percent of the management royalties for the lifetime of the girls, while Mathew received fifteen.

"Kenny, I'mma let this nut think he's in charge, but we get fifty percent of the management royalties for the lifetime of the group. But I'mma show him one last time. When the final album is done, then it's will be turned over to Tommy Motolla. I'mma show him who he gotta go through to get it turned over to finalize the deal."

Ann had worked the deal where she knew she was going to have to turn the masters over to the label once all the songs were complete.

"This fool is runnin' around like he's the boss. I'mma have one last laugh on his butt!"

OUR SECOND CHANCE

Over the course of two years we were working very hard on getting the ball rolling and the recordings done so that Ann could have something to turn over to Columbia/Sony after signing with Grassroots. While Mathew was still being Mathew Ann knew at the end of the day that she would get the masters for each of the songs from Grassroots because that was the arrangement. During that two-year period, things were stagnant off and on and it wasn't as easy a sailing as one might have hoped it to be. There were many conversations with Columbia/Sony and Grassroots in putting things in order.

We had to iron out many details including the travel back and forth to Oakland, how we would structure things so that it could work for everyone involved, and take Ann's health into consideration. Things were not as peachy as it appeared to those who were not behind the scenes. It was hard work. For Ann it truly was a labor of love and things did not move nearly as fast as we wanted.

Because things moved slower with the deal, the advance took a little longer to come through. One of Ann's worst nightmares came upon her – to go into the boys' inheritance. More monies were needed to get the girls back and forth to Oakland and for other expenses. So, with the deal not coming in a timely manner forced Ann to use some of the boy's money from their trust; but things changed fast. Everyone was excited and looking forward to what was to come. Ann started talking seriously to Tommy Motolla and working the deal, hashing things out in terms of the type of deal it would be. Tommy liked what was recorded by Dwayne. Tommy and Ann worked everything out. By this time we were rolling into nineteen ninety-seven. The album Destiny was being recorded and the girls were floating on "cloud nine." Everyone was chanting "Destiny, Destiny, Destiny…"

Because there was already an R & B disco type all girls group from the seventies named Destiny, there was a discrepancy when it came time to signing the record deal with Columbia/Sony. The label felt that there could be some confusion on the name and confusion in terms of which group was which. The other group was Alton McClain and Destiny.

As we discussed the matter, we decided that we could not just use the name Destiny. As we threw it around, Tina came up with Destiny Child from the Bible. So, Ann took the name to Columbia/Sony and we ended up signing the contract with Columbia/Sony under the name of Destiny's Child.

Once the contract was signed, Mathew started back up with that same mess about being in charge. This time Ann was not as hot around the collar as before. She knew it was coming. She knew he was going to react and do the same stuff that he did with the Elektra deal. She laughed as if it were a joke to her.

"Kenny, here this fool come again. Here he comes again."

"What?"

"I done got the deal, now he wanna step back to the front like he doing all this stuff. He's a screw up but wanna act like he's Mr. Big Stuff and running things."

"Uhm."

"…But I got something for his butt this time!"

"What?"

"Well, he's talkin' all that stuff but when the time comes for the album to go back to Columbia/Sony, guess who got the master?"

"Who?"

"I do!"

"What?"

"I got the masters and when the stuff is done, we gonna have a listening party…me and you. Just me and you gonna have our own got-darn party to hear it."

"Well shoot, cool! I'll come on over to hear the tracks."

"Yeah, I have the masters."

When the payment from the first advance came, Ann wanted others to get their money first since so much time had passed. Although Ann was upon hard times herself, she was still willing to wait until another allotment came through because she knew that push come to shove she had access to resources in an emergency situation. She let the first advance money go to the girls and others to tie them over, while she used the boys' money to tie her and her family over.

Although this was going on and her health was not one hundred percent, she was still upbeat. After going into the boys' inheritance, Ann was confronted with her own bills piling up. One Saturday evening when I was cooking at home, I got a call from Ann.

"Hey Kenny, whatcha doing?"

"Dretta, you know I'm over here barbequing."

"Oh okay."

"What's up baby girl?"

"Well, I'm waiting on my money to come on Monday. You know, me and the boys over here hungry."

"Ann, how in the heck you hungry and you ain't got money and you done paid all these other fools' bills...What did you do with the advance?"

"I gave Mathew the advance and...well he was gonna divy it up and make sure everyone got something."

"You trust that son of a gun again? What the heck is wrong with you?"

"No, no Kenny listen...there was only so much... and I broke everything down exactly how it should be split and Mathew would only get part of it."

Ann gave me all the details of how it was broken down and once she explained to me it made sense.

"Kenny, I will get mine on the next wave. I am cool with that. I only took a loan out of my boys' money to tie me over until the next payout came from Dwayne, and then I was going to pay it back."

"Girl, I got so much food over here, why don't ya'll just come on over?"

"Okay, then we on our way."

At that time I was financially doing okay. Things were flowing pretty well for Cassey and me. When Ann and the boys came over, we had a good time. After that weekend of having Ann and the boys over to eat with us, it developed into a routine almost every weekend. It became like our family ritual. I would buy the food and Ann and the boys came by. This drew our families even closer together. Brian, Armon, and Christopher were like brothers. Ann and Cassey got along well. We all became a close knit family.

"Shoot, I had to go into the boys' savings to keep things moving until I get my money from the deal."

"Ann I don't see how you do it."

"I sometimes wonder myself Cass."

"Dretta you know if you need something me and Kenny got it!"

"Naw we good…but he can keep this barbeque going."

Ann and Cassey laughed. Then Cassey said, "Shoot, you ain't never lied."

They both continued to laugh as they were eating ribs. I continued over at the grill listening to them and making jokes.

Time passed and when it came time for the next payment to come from Dwayne, Ann was anticipating getting her portion from that allotment. However, for whatever reason, the monies did not come. That placed Ann in a situation again where she had to go back into the boys' inheritance a second time. Ann was postponing bills and buying time with bill collectors waiting on this payment and it didn't come. Ann was so upset and got irate. She started cursing everybody out at that point.

"Ya'll screwing around, now ya'll screwin' with my boys' money. What's the problem Dwayne? Now I gotta go back and get some money from my children to deal with this stuff, cause ya'll screwin' me around!"

Ann was getting agitated and the stress was getting to her. She came over during our weekly barbeque night and she was still livid.

"Dretta, what are you so pissed about?"

"Kenny, they messing with my got-darn money."

"Whatcha mean?"

"You know they still haven't given me the advance?"

"What?"

"They are on some bull Kenny and now I had to go right back into my boys' money."

"Dretta, you know I told you that me and Cass got you and the boys."

"No Kenny! I know you mean well. But heck, I still have money to pay you from the advance as well."

"Ann you know I ain't worried about that. When it comes, it comes. I know you will handle your business. Heck your Black butt won't take it from me, what about Belfry?"

"No he is tapped out, and ain't trying to give me no more money. I went ahead and took out another loan. So I'mma give them a chance to get this thing right."

Ann was able to keep things moving a little longer with the second loan from the boys' inheritance. She calmed herself down and kept moving forward. Then one day she got a call from one of the team members who happened to stop by Mathew's house. Ann called me extremely upset.

"Kenny, get your tail over here right now!"

"What's wrong?"

"Just come over."

"Alright, alright, I'm on my way. Heck give me about fifteen minutes."

When I arrived at Ann's she was pacing the floor and very upset.

"Kenny, one the team members just called me about thirty minutes ago with some bull!"

"What Dretta? Calm down so I can hear your Black behind."

"Kenny this ain't no got-darn play time."

"What's his name called me and said he happened to stop by Mathew's house and when he walked in he saw Mathew in his underwear and Kelly was in the bathroom. It looked inappropriate."

Ann was talking so fast in giving the details of what was said to her that I had to tell her to slow down.

"Dretta, slow your ass down...now what you say about something inappropriate going on?

"I don't know what the heck is going on over at the Knowles' house. One minute Tina is kicking Mathew's trifling behind out, the next minute she is taking him back."

"Dretta, calm your ass down so I can get what you are saying."

"Kenny, the word from one of the team members is that there's some inappropriate stuff going on between Mathew and Kelly and we need to watch him with these darn girls. He said he popped up and walked into something going on that didn't look right."

"Where was Tina and the other two girls?"

"Heck I don't know! He just called and told me what he saw and said it didn't look right to him. I now that son of a gun is crazy, but I know he better not be messing with that little girl!"

"I know that fool has done some lowdown stuff, and even given your situation on what may have happened to you, Ann, but he ain't is not that darn crazy!...I know he ain't that crazy!"

"Kelly is really timid, man, and she..."

"...yeah but, Dretta, no...if you look back...Tavia had some tell-tale signs that you could kind have looked for. She was a little more seductive and everything. You don't get that from Kelly."

"Kenny, I sure hope not."

Ann and I held that information close to the chest. Ann spoke discretely with the other adult members outside of Mathew and asked them to be very observant and watchful to see if there was any sign of inappropriate behavior going.

Ann said, "Look, the last thing we want to get out is that we have some internal bull like this going on here in our camp from someone on the management team."

None of us were sure as to what really happened, but we were going to make sure as far as within our scope of control and power of what wasn't going to happen if we could help it. However, we could not control what happened behind close doors at the Knowles' house.

As Ann and I examined what may have been going on, we saw a disparity in the treatment of Kelly compared to the other girls. Mathew appeared to be extremely hard on Kelly. He was verbally and emotionally abusive to her. It seemed that he was always mad at her, telling her things like, "You can never do nothing right!"

I felt that if he was messing with her, it would seem like he would let her "have her way," but he was very hard on her. I personally felt he was aggressive with Kelly and treated her differently in that he was dominant toward her especially. It could have been because her mother was not present. Who knows, but we were keeping a look out and it was a hard signal to see. What many of us saw and discussed was that he was extra mean to Kelly. We talked amongst ourselves in private meetings to see who saw what.

"That son of a gun is overly mean to her for whatever reason. But heck, I don't see no touchy-feely."

"Well, I think there's an anger there that can be taken either way if you ask me."

"Well shoot, if he's screwin' with her, this is his dominance over her."

"What do you think Kenny?"

"Ann, to me, a lot of times that Mathew's screaming at Kelly, she's not even messing up, so I don't know. His ass is mean as heck to her in my opinion."

As we listened to everyone's take on the situation, Ann and I always had our one-to-one conversations about it. We thought that if something inappropriate was going on when no one was looking, that maybe this was his way of humiliating in the public and showing her that he was in charge, with the thoughts of something like, "no one's gonna listen to you anyway."

It was really hard to discern the truth in that particular situation. Andretta was going to confront Mathew, but my concern was not knowing what sort of sparks might fly as a result of the confrontation.

"Ann, we are in the thick of the music deal and we don't need no extra stuff with Mathew's name associated with it!"

"Why you say that?"

"If word gets out that something like this is going on and Mathew is tied to it, there's no way they're gonna keep us."

"Well after the Elektra screw up, you might be right!"

Ann was not willing to rock that boat, knowing Mathew's temperament and instability.

With all the madness going on within our camp, I decided to call my family and see how they were. My older sister Louise and I were very close and she was always encouraging so I wanted to hear her voice and get a little boost from dealing with all this stuff. It was on a Tuesday, and I hadn't spoken with my mom and sisters for some time. When I called Indianapolis, my sister Armelda answered the telephone and said that Louise and my mother all went to the church. So I called up to the Greater Shepherd Missionary Baptist Church where my uncle Shep Banks was the pastor. My cousin Jeanette answered the telephone.

"Hey, this is Kenny, is my mom or any of my family there?"

"Uh, hey Kenny, yes Aunt Liz is here and Louise is here."

"Well, let me speak to Louise."

Louise came to the telephone and we talked for a good minute.

"Girl, I'm so proud of you."

"Man, I'm proud of you. I love you man. It's been too long, but I know you are doing some great things so I will let you off the hook."

"Oh."

"No Bae, I wanna tell you something. You have been the best brother I could've had. I love you, I love you, I love you."

"I love you too girl!"

"No matter what happens, you gonna be somebody famous, and I know it and I know you know you gonna do great things."

"I love you too. You gonna do good too."

My sister Louise and I left things just like that. It made me feel good and took my mind off of some of the mess that was going on in Houston. It was good to hear her voice and as always she knew the right things to say and when to say them. I hung up the telephone feeling better about things.

That Thursday night, I got a call from my niece telling me that my sister Louise died in a car wreck. I was devastated and in disbelief. I had just spoken with her two days prior. After that news, I flew out to Indianapolis for her funeral. On the flight I was fine, but when the plane went into the descent, that is when it actually hit me, that I was going to bury my sister. I completely lost it on the plane. People were asking, "Is he gonna be okay? Can we do anything for him?"

After the funeral, I went into a state of depression and walked through life during that time in a daze. I withdrew from everyone and everything.

Upon my return, Ann kept calling and checking to see how I was doing. I wouldn't talk to her nor see her. She kept asking Cassey how I was doing and if I needed anything. Cassey would talk to Ann, but I remained withdrawn. Everyone else pretty much left me alone and gave me the space to grieve in my own way. One day, Ann came by while I was moping around the house and the garage. I was pitiful and feeling down dealing with the pain of losing my big sister. I had painted a mural on the entire wall of the garage of what heaven looked like and where I thought she was. It was my way of grieving with the loss of Louise. Ann looked at me and looked at that big picture on the wall and had a look on her face like, "How in the heck am I gonna reach this nigga."

I was scruffy and looked like I had not seen the light of day in forever. I had been in a state of depression after my sister's death.

"Kenny, there's some exciting stuff going on. Things are coming around. I need to talk to you. How are you doing?"

"Well Dretta, I'm okay."

"Kenny, you got to come out of this. You just got to. We gotta keep going."

"Dretta, I know, I know."

"Well..."

"But...Louise was always that sister who told me I could do it."

"I understand Kenny. I really do, but you have to keep going."

"Louise was the type that she just wanted me to get on a bus and go to California because she knew I could make it."

I took a deep breath and Ann just listened as I talked about Louise. As I told her how Louise's accident happened, Ann saw the irony of how our lives were truly crossed. My sister was leaving my sister Amelda's house on her way to church when the accident occurred. Ann recalled how she and Dwight were leaving her sister's house after leaving church when their accident occurred. My sister was forty-two when she died along with the driver's seven-year-old daughter. Ann then compared this to Dwight and Shawna dying in her tragic accident. The final irony was as my sister died at the corner near my sister Amelda's house as my sister and brother ran to see Louise take her last breath. This reminded Ann of stories of her sister telling her of Shawna and Dwight taking their last breath. As I often reflected back on the last time I spoke with Louise, I could not help but to think that possibly she knew somewhere deep down that she was not going to be around.

"Kenny, I know it's hard, but I need you. You gotta come on out of this."

"Dretta, you don't understand. Do you know how my sister died?"

"Kenny, I understand exactly what you're feeling."

"Dretta, how do you understand what I'm feeling?"

Ann gave me a looked of disbelief, then said, "Really? Really?!"

"Oh, yeah...I forgot."

"Look, its' gonna take a minute, but you can't quit. You can't give up."

I just listened to Ann for a moment.

"Kenny, I know exactly where you are."

"I ain't giving up, Ann, it's just..."

"...Well then get your butt on up. You know she wanted you to do something famous and big. So let's get on up and do something famous and big."

"Okay, Ann...you think you bad ...you ain't the boss of me."

After we laughed, Ann said, "Look, I tell you what...can you barbeque for me next weekend?"

"Yeah, let's do that."

"Come by the house this week and I got something to share with you."

After that conversation with Ann, I started to come out of my depression. I got back to the point of functioning and back into the swing of things. Ann was nudging me telling me what was going on with Dwayne Wiggins and the new music.

"We have been working. Things are going good Kenny. We got some nice songs coming out."

"That's good, Dretta."

"Just come over later, I got something to show you."

"What now Ann?"

"You know the song "Killing Time", which the girls recoreded?"

"Yeah?"

"Well, that's the one Dwayne Wiggins did. It's gonna be on the Men in Black movie soundtrack."

"What! Okay! That's great!"

I was happy, but I was not as happy as Ann wanted me to be. I was still coping, and finding it difficult to jump for joy. Ann could see right through me and it bothered her because I was not as jolly, and her friend and partner was not as fully present at that moment as I normally would've been under different circumstances. It wasn't "Blackie this or Blackie that." I was strictly professional with her and giving short unemotional answers and comments.

"That's great. Okay, good…"

Because of the promise of having one of our songs on the soundtrack for a major motion picture, things were looking very favorable and everything was in place to make this major deal a success. Teresa was still talking with Columbia/Sony for us, ensuring them we were on point, and still advising Ann on our next moves. She was even ecstatic about it. The girls were happy and hanging out with Dwayne Wiggins and other celebrities from Tony, Tone, Toni. They were also starting to get calls to do cameos in hooks for a lot of the local Houston and New Orleans rappers. The excitement for the album was building. Everything was just starting to fall in place.

During this time, Mathew was trying to wedge his way in between Ann and Dwayne Wiggins. However, Lonnie was in California with Dwayne and was telling Mathew, "No you taking your butt through Ann."

Mathew could not really weasel all the way in because Lonnie knew he would get kicked to the curb like in the Elektra deal. To protect himself, Lonnie used his connection with Dwayne as leverage. Ann also saw to protect herself, as in the back of her mind she knew that her health was deteriorating. So, she signed a new deal with Mathew to secure her and her boy's future.

"Kenny, I signed a new deal with Mathew."

"What?"

"Well...at the end of the day he is Beyonce's father and she is the star of this group. It's just that whatever happens...with me or with this deal, for the lifetime, as far as the management is concerned, I'mma be fifty percent manager for the lifetime of the group."

"That's smart as heck, Ann."

"Then, Mathew will get his half. Of course you know...you get half of mine."

"Dretta, whatever...when some money come through, we'll deal with that then."

"No, that's the way it's set up."

"Okay, fine."

"Here, Kenny, sign this."

Ann handed me a contract for the first time to sign as all of our other agreements were contracts we reviewed but never signed. In the contract, it certified my twenty-five percent ownership Music World. I signed the contract and then told her to hold on to it.

"No, you take your copy."

"Andretta, we don't have to go through this."

A couple of days went by and Ann gave me my copy of the contract. It was in an envelope and until this day I haven't even opened it to look at it again since signing it. I went home and put it in my box. I said to myself, "Man, this is really finna happen."

Ann and I had gone through everything and we did everything. Our word was good enough for each other. For the first time, Ann was adamant that we sign something. The excitement in me started to build by this time and I started drawing logos for Music World. I would take the drawings to the meetings and show the team our logos. I used to draw a globe or the world spinning on a needle on top of a record and the record was on fire. Our slogan was "Music World is taking over the world."

We had it all mapped out. Everyone was starting to get their place now. We knew that Mathew wasn't going away and we had to pacify him. We knew that he was working with the girls, so Ann and I made sure the rest of the team was strong to compensate for anything he might do to the detriment of the deal and camp. Ann started to tighten things up. She used Lonnie for some of the production so he would be credited on the album as a reward for riding with the team the whole way. David was there as the vocal coach. I was going to be the road manager for the girls and to be her eyes on the road. I really didn't want to do it, but I agreed.

PLAY IT AGAIN

The team was in place and the excitement was building. The girls were back and forth to Oakland recording the album. The results of some of the production were coming forth. Ann received the masters for about half of the album from Dwayne. In her excitement, she called me one day just as tickled, laughing.

"Kenny, Kenny!"

"What girl?"

"I got some of the music!"

"What!"

"Yes, I got some of the masters. I got some of the musics for the recording already! Oh my God, we got some hits, we got some hits!"

"Alright Ann, whatever whatever."

"Get your tail over here!"

"Stuff girl, I ain't got time for that right now. I got stuff to do. I gotta cook and stuff..."

"Just get your tail on over here!"

"Heck, I gotta stop and get me some beer or something if I gotta come and sit with your Black behind."

"I already got it, come on."

"Oh heck alright... You know you get on my darn nerves don't you."

"Screw you nigga, just get your Black butt on over here."

"I'm on my way."

When I made it to Ann's house, she was just giggling like a little girl.

"Ann, what the heck..."

"Ok, here, get you some beer first…come on."

She led me into the kitchen. I looked around shocked. Ann had cooked a spread. It was the first time that she had cooked in forever so I was like. "What in the heck is going on up in here?"

Ann had cooked a spread for a stadium which included her famous smothered rice and pork chops.

"Nigga, you done lost your ever-lovin' mind."

"Just get your beer, get your food and sit your butt down."

So I fixed my plate, got the beer and went and sat down.

"Now you ready?"

"Yeah girl, now what."

"Listen."

Ann played the song that went, *You'll be sayin no, no, no, no, no…When it's really yeah, yeah, yeah, yeah, yeah, yeah…*

It was a very slow version of the song from what you hear today instead of the fast rap. When I heard the song, I was shocked. It was on another level from the Elektra tracks.

"That is nice!"

"I know Kenny."

"You can hear the maturity of the girls. You can hear the changes in them."

"There is a big difference between these and all the other recordings. We got something here."

"I have to say we do. Man, Bey's voice is a lot stronger. The harmonies are much tighter than before."

"Let's listen to some more."

"Shoot then girl, bring 'em on! I didn't know you were doing it like that."

Ann laughed and then we listened to several other songs on the album. When we got to the last one of tracks, we then listened to a song entitled, "My Time Has Come."

"I just love this song, Kenny. Oh I just love this one."

After she played that song, she went back to "No No No" then back to "My Time Has Come." Ann kept playing those two songs over and over again.

"Dretta...Why you keep playing the same two darn songs? You got seven songs let's listen to all of them."

"No! I just love these..."

We kept listening to those same two songs, laughing and talking. She got so excited as we went back and forth between those two songs.

"Ann, I ain't finna listen to these two songs no got-darned more now."

She played it again like she didn't hear a word I said. Then she said, "Give me one of them darn beers!"

"Dretta, now you know your Black behind ain't supposed to be dranking with all them got-darn pills you takin'."

"Well, I'm dranking one of them tonight..."

She was drinking a beer, I was drinking and we were just a laughing. We really were laughing because Ann didn't drink and hadn't drank as long as I knew her. It didn't take much for her.

"You drank one darn sip, Dretta and you drunk as heck."

"What you talking about I ain't drunk."

"Look at you sluring your words, laughing at everything and stuff. I told you not to be drinking when you taking all those got-darn pills and stuff!"

We just laughed. That night everything was funny, and in the background was playing those same two darn songs.

"I know, Kenny, I know…but I'm celebrating. We did it didn't we? We did it! After all this darn time, after all them little heifas spending my money…we did it…we did it!"

"Yeah Dretta, we did it! We did…"

"I told you we were gonna do it!"

"Yeah you did."

"Remember we were in California, I had to get your butt on the balcony talking all that stuff! Had to calm you down about Ashley…You wanted to quit then."

"Yeah…if I knew I had to go through all this stuff, I wudda quit."

"Your big head talking…I'm Kenny Mo, got darn it…Who these little heffas think they are…I'm Kenny Mo…got dammit! Yeah"

"Yeah I remember."

Ann and I laughed so hard reminiscing over all the little incidents and things we had gone through to get to that moment.

"Do you remember when Mathew screwed up the Elektra deal? But we stayed the course didn't we…didn't we?"

Ann was drunk as heck, but we continued to laugh and talk about old times.

"Shoot Dretta, he screwed that one up real good, no good son of a gun! I was ashamed to even come around that fool! Shoot, all my boys in California and thangs and the ones I was in the music industry with was doggin' me out…saying 'Man what the kind of camp ya'll running down there and stuff?'"

"That jerk was trying to come gansta and stuff because of Beyonce being his daughter. You should've seen him almost on his knees when we lost the Elektra deal."

"Naw I tell you who thought he was gangster…that darn Lynn…"

"Ah stuff Kenny, don't get me started on his dumb butt!"

"Now that's one crooked punk…"

"His dumb tail gonna write some got-darned hot checks on my account to himsulf…You would think if he was gonna steal he would have at least had sense enough to have some of them other crooks or hoes he' screwin' to have the darn check written out to them where it couldn't be traced back to his dumb self as quickly."

"That's because he's is greedy…he ain't got no darn sense."

"Shoot T-Mo is the dumb one… done sold his darn songs for a dollar or penny or some stuff like that, then they kicked him to the curb…"

I fell out rolling on the floor, as Ann was talking about T-Mo.

"Lonnie and Arne wrote him out the picture with one stroke. He's got to be the dumbest one of em all. Knowingly signed away all of his darn rights trusting Arne and Lonnie's crooked tails."

"Oh, Dretta, I almost forgot about that.. I bet you he ain't gonna do that stuff no more."

"Heck naw! He probably knows he can't trust Lonnie's selfish self. And don't get me started on David, trying to be some darn opera singer and vocal coach…with his big head!"

"You know you wrong for that Dretta!"

Dretta started mimicking the opera sound. "Ahhhh, Figaro Figaro…what the stuff is that!"

"You are crazy as heck, girl!"

"He wanna be an opera singer but teaching R & B vocal…what kinda stuff is that, Kenny!"

"Oooh weee!" I just laughed. Ann was on a roll.

"Shoot though, ain't no darn body as stupid as or as big of a screw up as Mathew's retarded behind! He even screws up screwing up! Ain't that some stuff!"

"You know your Black butt is crazy Ann."

"He's a got-darned ho! I can't wait 'til Tina find out, cause she gonna kill him."

"He's a dirty one for sure!"

"You know though Kenny, it's sad that Nikki and Nina didn't make it this far...now that hurt. I know it was probably the best decision, but it would have been good if they could have continued on the journey with the girls."

"Yeah...but..."

"Those are my girls though. I still wanna find a place for them...but...oh well."

"Same about Ashley. What's going on with her?"

"Yeah...huhm..."

Ann took a deep breath at that moment and appeared to allow her mind to wander somewhere else. Ann and I talked about getting past Carolyn to help Ashley. We talked about Tayste and all the mess surrounding them and how Lynn contributed to the confusion within their group whereas Harlon and Mitch was on one page and A.J. and To To on another. We talked about several up and coming groups such as Shay Atkins and Flag. We talked about still going after Kathy Taylor who had maintained a good local following. As Ann let her mind continue to wander, for a moment I could tell that she was thinking of Dwight and Shawna. She briefly looked to the sky and smiled and at that moment when she was saying, "We did it," she was not only talking to me she was also talking to Dwight.

We laughed and talked for hours. It became so redundant that each time the song switched tracks and went back to the other one we laughed.

"You wearing them got-darned songs out girl!"

Ann and I have always been professional, but this was one of the few times where we actually embraced in appreciation for one another.

"I love you Kenny."

"I love you too Dretta. You're like my sister baby girl."

"I know what you mean. It's hard for me to say that, but I really do love you man."

"I really love you too Dretta."

After we unlocked from the embrace, Ann hit me on my shoulder, and said, "We did it man. We did it."

I nodded. "Yeah, we did, didn't we?"

"What you gonna do out there on the road Kenny Mo, whatcha gonna do out there?"

"Ann if these heifas be acting like they had been acting all this time…shoot…I'mma catch it. You tryin' to kill me. I'mma have to keep these niggas off these girls. Heck, four girls, man you gonna have to give me a posse and niggas with guns and stuff."

"Yeah…I didn't think about that." Ann said laughing.

"Heck yeah! You gonna have to get chaperones and everything!

We had a really great time laughing and talking that night. We talked about everybody. We talked about the good things and all the bull. We had a barrage, discussing everything we had went through and experienced. We talked about friends and so called friends.

When I left Ann's house that night, she was bubbly and happy. Over the next couple of days we spoke and continued laughing about that night. She was still very upbeat. The next thing I knew, she ended up back at the hospital. This time I noticed that her breathing had become very heavy and she was hooked up to a breathing machine.

"Ann, not this again. What are you doing? We done got the contract and stuff. Get your ass up."

"Kenny, I want you to raise my boys if something happen to me."

"Ann, I already told you I would do it, but ain't nothing finna happen to you okay? Just get up! Come on now I ain't playin' witcha."

"Kenny, I want you to promise me."

"I promise…I promise."

"I got some stuff I need to tell you."

"Great Ann, just tell me when we get you back home."

Ann began to tell me about the arrangement with Mathew. She shared with me that she had fifty percent of the girls' management for the lifetime of the group. It wasn't a contract that was going to end and that her estate would get that fifty percent if something happened to her.

"Okay Ann."

"When my boys get up…whatever money that comes in, my boys will still get it. So you will be over that. Make sure my boys are taken care of."

"Ann I got it. What else?"

"The masters…you know where my safe deposit box is up there at the Krogers…it's at the corner…"

"Yeah…"

The Making of a Child of Destiny

"I got the safe deposit there…all the masters are there, that's where I'm keeping them until I turn them over to Sony."

"Okay girl…fine Ann!"

I was agitated with her, but she felt that she needed to tell me so this time I reluctantly listened to her go on. "What else?"

"Well the house and everything…well…I got the insurance that's gonna pay that off. My insurance is a big policy, so the boys should be fine, Kenny."

"Okay…?"

"Yeah…it doubles if it's an accidental death, but it's less if I just passed."

"Okay…Well heck, I need to get you out of this bed and take you out and let you just run into some stuff got-dammit."

We both laughed, but then she began to voice her concerns about another matter.

"Also, Dwight's brother, Keith been coming around a lot more like he expects something to happen to me or something."

"Well that's your husband's brother."

"Naw, Kenny it ain't like that. Like I tell you, these folks think I'm finna die or something. They waiting to get my insurance and stuff like that. That's why I wanna make sure. Now I done already told my mama that if something happens that you get the boys. Make sure you and Cassey get the boys."

"Okay…"

"You played football, Brian's playing football, Chris is playing football, and Armon is playing basketball…so you know all about the sport and recruiting…NCAA stuff so you'd be perfect you know."

"Okay, Ann that's fine."

The conversation was subdued. You could tell she was sad and somewhat scared. As she lay there from time/to/time I could hear her humming the melody to "No, No, No" and another time she would hum "My Time Has Come."

"Girl, when you get your butt up out of here, I'mma throw you the biggest barbeque ever."

"Okay. You know that's the only thing that'll make me happy."

It was a short stint in the hospital. We talked on Wednesday when she was in the hospital. She got out on Thursday, and on Friday, I threw her the barbeque. That barbeque was so big; you might as well have said we killed the fatty calf basically. We had everything from potato salad, baked beans, ribs, chicken, hamburgers, hotdogs, and sausages. You name it, it was there. The one way I could show my love to Ann was to have a barbeque feast she would never forget. Ann, Armon, and Chris came over. We all sat down and said a prayer and ate. Ann ate and ate and ate.

"This some good stuff...this some good stuff, Kenny Mo."

"Girl you better quit before you trigger something and get yourself sick again, trying to digest all that darn meat."

"If I'mma die, I'mma die full and happy as a pig eating me some of Kenny Mo's good ole' barbeque."

We laughed and had a good time. The boys were playing basketball and Ann, Cassey and I sat there talking.

"Kenny, my advance from Dwayne still has not come. So, I need to file bankruptcy or take more money out of the boys' trust. I really don't know what to do."

"For what Ann? Ain't the money came in?"

"No, I'm still waiting on it from Dwayne. But I need to file bankruptcy or something to hold off everything until stuff else happens. I don't wanna go back in my boy's money."

We sat there talking about it for a moment. Then Ann said, "I've got until five o'clock to call this lady if I'm gonna file bankruptcy."

"Ann, you a mother and widow! You gotta do what's best for your kids. You have given every darn body ever darn thang. I understand where you at. But heck naw! Everbody else is sittin' there with money from the advance in their pockets, and if it wasn't for you, none of them would have stuff. And you the one that's sittin over here broke? Heck, if it was me and my kids...
I 'm the type of mother that would go and sell some tail if my kids were hungry. So I ain't sayin' what you would do or won't do!"

Ann burst out laughing and said, "Darn Cassey, I hear you...I don't think I could get as much as I need to pay them bills in my condition."

They both laughed then Cassey said, "Shoot you can stand on the corner with one leg..."

After a good laugh, Ann said, "What do you and Cat think I should do, Kenny?"

"Ann...screw that! You need to go on and file bankruptcy. Hold them folks off; keep a roof over your babies head. Now this is a darn shame. All this darn money you spending and you sitting here in this stuff because you helping these heifas! You helping these little heifas' dreams come true and you over her trying to eat and tryin' to file bankruptcy. You call that woman and tell her you wanna file bankruptcy. Then everything will work out later. Plus that will take some of the stress off you. You ain't gotta worry about folks taking the roof from over your babies' head."

So, at about four-fifty, Ann picked up the telephone to call the lady to tell her to go ahead and start the proceedings for bankruptcy to hold her debtors off. She was not willing to touch

Armon and Christopher's inheritance. After that we went on with our evening. We played a little basketball and football, and Ann and Cassey continued to talk. The evening came to a close and Ann left in a very good mood.

That following Thursday, I went by her house.

"Dretta, you still lisenting to them got darned songs."

"Man…"

"Dretta…really? I'm sure Beyonce's throat is hurtin'."

"Why?"

"Because that girl ain't stop sanging since you got that darn cd!"

"Boy…whatcha mean?"

"Heck girl, all of them heffas throats should be hurtin' like a mug. Because they ain't stop singing since you go them darn masters."

Ann laughed. Then I asked her, "What's up baby girl…you good?"

"Yeah, yeah, Kenny, I'm good.

"Okay now. You know the album's getting ready to come out. They gonna shoot the videos. Kenny Mo gonna be in the video. You gonna be in the video?"

"You gonna get in the video?"

"Heck yeah, I'mma get in the video. You let them shoot around here and there's people around here. Heck yeah, I'm getting in the video. Kenny Mo gonna be in the video Ann."

"Well shoot, I can get in the video too. I can get up there and be dancing like them girls be dancing. Shake my booty."

"Naw, now we trying to make some money, not give it back, Andretta."

We laughed and hung out for a while.

"Now, I'mma run on to the house.   I'll call you tomorrow."

So I left. The next day I called to see how she was doing.

"Hey girl, how you doing?"

"Oh, a little tired."

"You tired?"

"Yeah."

"Ann how are you tired with all this excitement going on? We're getting ready to take over the world like we planned. We need to get everything mapped out."

"Well we're dealing with the label, Dwayne and my money and Mathew's stuff.   That's enough to make anybody tired."

"Won't you just get you some rest and I will come on over tomorrow or you come over and I'll barbeque or we do it over the weekend."

"Okay. Yeah, let's do it over the weekend."

We planned the weekend and talked for a little while longer on the telephone.

"You still listening to them got-darned girls?"

"You crazy, Kenny Mo."

"I'm serious. Are they still sanging?"

"Naw I done put 'em down for a while…Kenny boy, I love you. You my friend."

"Andretta, I would say I love you but I'm afraid I might throw up."

"Ah, it's like that huh?"

"Naw, alright nigga. I…I…I…I like you a lot."

"Really, okay okay. You gonna remember that."

"Alright Ann, I love you too. Alright now, I'mma come through tomorrow. You getting' all mushy and stuff… I'll come by tomorrow and check on you. But me and Cassey gonna go out dancing tonight."

"Oh ya'll gonna go dancing?"

"Yeah I'mma take her out so she can get her dance on…"

Then Ann gets quiet for a moment, then says, "Kenny, make sure you dance with your wife tonight. You be sure to dance with her every opportunity you get, because you'll never know when you won't have that chance to dance with her."

I paused a moment, then it hit me what she was saying, as if she had the chance to dance with Dwight she would have all these years.

"Okay, Ann, I will dance my butt off with my wife. I'mma do the robot, the bump, funky chicken, the mash potatoes, and I'm slow-grind like in the basement. Now your butt happy?"

"Yeah, okay. Now remember I got all the masters…don't forget what I told you about the partnership breakdown."

"Will you shut up with that stuff? You act like you trying to go somewhere got-dammit!"

"Naw, Naw! I just wanna make sure, Kenny, you know…cause that's some serious stuff."

"Ann, I'm serious too. I'mma take care of it! I got it…we're cool?"

"You know how that Mathew is. He gonna…"

"Ann, I got everything…quit trippin woman! What's wrong with you? Cause, heaven don't want you and hell afraid you gonna take over! So you ain't going nowhere."

Ann took the telephone away from her ear for laughing so hard. When she came back to the phone, we bantered back and forth for a little while longer before we finally hung up the

The Making of a Child of Destiny

telephone. The next day I went to work and when I got off of work, I got an emergency phone call from Charlotte.

"Hey Kenny, come quickly, Ann had another attack!"

"She had another attack? What?!"

"Yeah, we had to rush her to the hospital again! Her eyes were rolling in the back of her head and she just passed out!"

"Okay, where she at?"

"She's in the emergency room."

"Alright then."

I took my time. I went and got something to eat on my way to the hospital. After eating I was like, this stuff is getting old. She is in and out of the hospital. They never keep her more than a couple of days, they ain't cuttin' on her no more. One mintue she's strong as an ox, the next she laying her in the hospital."

As I approached the hospital this time, something felt different. I said to myself, "Let me go on up here. This darned girl..." I walked through the front of the hospital. I didn't go through the emergency way, I went through the front. As I was walking in, I saw this gurney going from the the emergency room area with people rushing going to the ICU. Then I saw Charlotte run by.

I thought, "Darn that must've been Ann." So I sped up.

"Hey Charlotte...was that Ann?"

Charlotte was crying. "Yeah..."

"Charlotte, what the heck is going on?"

"Ann eyes fell in the back of her head. I kept telling her Ann stay with me, stay with me. But they kept going in the back of her head."

"Well, where they going?"

"They're taking her to ICU to try to revive her."

"What! Why didn't you call me?"

"Kenny, I did! I called you two hours ago!"

"Shoot...this stuff going on you supposed to call me back..."

Charlotte and I walked down as close as we could by the door to see what we could see. We were in the hallway waiting and waiting.

"Her eyes just kept rolling in her head, Kenny...I told her breathe, Ann breathe!"

"Shoot..."

I scratched my head. All we could do was wait. I called Cassey. Everybody started coming up to the hospital. I walked down the hall to get a soda. When I came back from getting a soda, everybody was crying. Then Charlotte said, "She's dead Kenny...she's gone."

"Girl quit it now! Quit playing."

"Kenny, she's dead!"

"Charlotte, quit it, Ann ain't dead!"

I started walking toward the rooms yelling her name. "Dretta! Dretta! I know you hear me...Dretta!"

The doctors and nurses just looked at me, but said nothing. "Ann!"

Then I looked at Charlotte. "Are you serious?"

"Yeah, Kenny, Andretta is dead."

Everyone else started coming and they just kept coming. I couldn't take it, so I just stormed out of the hospital and went home.

"Man... my friend is dead."

It was hard dealing with it. Cassey was doing her best to console me and console herself. I sat there for a couple of hours maybe longer, playing the same game the night I heard that Louise had died, as I felt myself sinking back into a similar depression. Cassey said, "Kenny, you really need to go over to the house and check on the boys. We need to check on the boys. You know that's what she asked us to do."

"You right. You right, Cat. We gotta be strong."

Cat, Brian and I went to the house. By then everyone from Tyler had made their way up. Everybody from everywhere was there. All the girls, all their parents, and everyone who knew her or liked her were there at the house. Ann's mom Buck had made it as well. There was a hug fest all the way from the front lawn and driveway to the inside of the house. People were standing around crying. I went in to check on Armon and Chris. They were dazed out. I was hugging everybody, trying not to cry. I was thinking in the back of my mind, "I can't let these niggas see no weakness."

I hugged Mathew; I hugged Tina, and some of the others. I hugged Beyonce and gave all of them a look that said, "Okay little heifas...you better do something great 'cause...she gave her life to give you this golden opportunity!"

I walked on further in the house. I looked over at a round table and saw Buck sitting there. As I was making my way, I was saying to myself, "I am not going over there. This woman is hurting and I'm not getting ready to go screw with her now."

I was kind of walking through the kitchen. As soon as I hit the doorway right by the kitchen, Buck yelled and pointed to me. "You!"

Everybody stopped because Buck was finally talking. They turned to see where she was pointing. "You!"

"Yes ma'am Miss Brown?"

"Come here."

When I walked over to her, she pat me on my chest. Then she put her finger in my face and said, "You...you were my daughter's only friend."

She then grabbed my hand and sat me down in the chair right beside her. I sat there tearing up. We just sat there and didn't say anything. She looked at me and I looked at her, and then she said, "Are you okay with the boys?"

"Yes, Ma'am."

"Okay...what we gonna do is I'mma take them back to Tyler with me for over the summer. And...uh...I'll send them back up here to you. Ann said you know where everything is...you have all her insurance information, the music contracts, and the Sony masters?"

"I know where it is...yes ma'am."

"They'll just come back up here with you. That's what she wanted."

Mrs. Brown looked me straight in the eye. "You got all her business handled?"

"Yes ma'am."

"Alright, that's what she wanted."

"Okay."

I got up from the table, needing a serious drink or somewhere to go boo-hoo. I was thinking that maybe I could go down the street, cry and then come back, but right when I was making my way back through the house without tearing up, Mathew came up to me.

"Hey Kenny, man I need to talk to you."

"Matt, not right now man...not now."

"Come on man, I need to talk."

"About Ann?"

"Naw, I need to talk to you about them Sony masters."

"Matt not right now man, please. Not right now."

"Come on Kenny man, I need to talk to you. We can't have them masters getting out to nobody man..."

"The masters are secure. Let's do this later man, not right now."

Mathew grew more persistent and impatient. "Come on man, come on!"

"Matt, Ann had everything taken care of..."

"Come on man!" Mathew said loudly.

Right in front of everyone, I said with great irritation. "Look, Ann had everything taken care of. She got the Sony contract and your contract with her locked away. She got all the information on how she put the deal together locked away. She has the darn masters locked away. She took care of all of it, it's okay, secure, and locked away! So you just chill out! She always took care of business. You know that. So it's okay. It's handled."

"But...but...what about the masters, Kenny?"

"Mathew, I've got the got-darned Sony masters. I have the masters to all the girls' songs. I got them! Ann told me where they were. I have them! I got the darn masters! And for anybody who got any questions as to if Ann was running stuff and whether or not she put the Sony deal together, I got the Sony masters now because Ann gave them to me."

I spoke to Mathew loud enough for everybody to hear me just in case there were any questions in terms of what Ann had done. Several people looked in disbelief as to how I was talking to Mathew. I was hot by then and didn't give a darn who heard me and what they thought. My friend had just died, and he was more concerned about where some darn cd's were.

"Dude, not now! Not right now bro! We'll talk about this later!" But since you want to talk you need to tell me what Tina had Ann sign today. Man a dam contract on her death bed, dude you, you, are such a (I Pause in discussed)! I then walked away from Mathew and headed out of the house. Before walking out the door I ran upon Armon and Chris. I then walked away from Mathew and headed out of the house. Before walking out the door I ran upon Armon and Chris.

"Ya'll gonna talk to your grandmother?"

"Yeah, we gonna talk to her."

"Ya'll know what you supposed to do?"

"Yeah we'll talk to her."

"Okay now. Ya'll need anything, I'm here."

Then I spoke with Ann's brother Dick.

"All her stuff is in a safe deposit box. We can get together later and go through the insurance policy and everything related to the music."

"Okay…cool."

I told Dick where the safe deposit box was. I showed him which key would open it.

"We need to talk because Mathew is…"

"Look, Dick, let's go through the process, bury Ann, then I tell you everything you need to know and what we need to do."

Dick agreed and we left it at that. I walked out of the house. I said to myself, "Can you believe these people?! The woman ain't even cold yet and they worried about some Sony masters!"

DRUMS STOP, BUT THE BEAT GOES ON

When I left the house that night and headed back home, I marinated in the fact that Andretta was gone. As I sat there in my chair thinking and replaying last moments in my mind, looking back at how she was going back and forth with "No, No, No" and "My Time Has Come," I realized that she perhaps knew that she was at a crossroads and through the songs, she was expressing her sentiments of how she was feeling and what she was struggling with internally. She may have known her time was up, but she was saying she wasn't ready. There was something about it that was very spiritual.

I missed it because I honestly thought in my mind it was business as usual and she would get back up as she always had. But this time she didn't. Sitting in my chair, the realization of me having a great task ahead was an ever present reality. As long as the boys came to me as planned, we would have control of her estate and it would be much easier for me to enforce the contract she had with Mathew and that the boys would get what they had coming to them.

The days ahead, I anticipated calls from her, and a few times even went to call her and say, "Hey Blackie, get up and out!" However, no sooner than I picked up the receiver, I realized, she was not there. She would never be there again. I would often ride by the house and see the cars there. Sometimes I just sat in front of the house, thinking, sometimes tearing up, and then pull away. I would go home, expecting a call, but it never came. I pulled out the box and went through the mounds of paperwork collected over the years and looked at all we had accomplished. It was a journey. As I was going through all the "stuff," Cassey would look over her cup of coffee and observe. It was hard to believe that seven or eight years had gone by so fast.

Those who knew that Ann and I were close friends came through to show their support. The Dunsons, my friend Vilia from the airforce, and many more of the Continental Airline flight attendants came to check on us. Mainly people who knew us and knew what we were working on stopped by. After a couple of days, the family was making funeral arrangements. I kept checking on the boys to see how they were handling things. Armon drowned his feelings in basketball and Chris pretty much stayed in a daze. Whenever I stopped by the house, I met more and more of Ann's siblings, until I was able to meet the whole Brown family.

It was an uncomfortable situation because I sensed that they were aware of Andretta's wishes for Cassey and I to raise the boys, but us not being blood relatives, you could tell that they were not totally cool with the idea of Armon and Christopher coming to live us. Many of them offered up their homes and lives for the boys, and wanted to know what my plans for them were. Some might have been genuinely concerned that it was something that I was willing and capable of doing, while others most likely wanted to make sure that I was not there to steal the estate.

Ann's estate was the furthest thing from my mind. Buck was very reassuring and made it a point to constantly tell me not to worry and that everything was all good. So, I didn't worry about it. The day before the funeral I actually finally got the chance to release what I had bottled up inside for the sake of being strong for others. This was a tough time as Cassey had a trip to go on and could not attend the funeral. Brian was there, and my friend Vilia kept coming back and forth to see about me, even my boy Rob flew in from L.A. Yet, when I had a moment alone after friends were gone and Brian was in bed, I cried. I finally cried!

It hit me. This was real. We accomplished all this. It was hard because she worked so hard and now she wouldn't even get the chance to see it.

"Man! Life is just unfair! Lord, I'm not questioning you, but why?"

All I could do was cry. The knot formed in my throat. My nose got all stuffed up. The more I cried, the more I cried.

"You lose Dwight and Shawna, then you go and do all this stuff and make all this stuff happen...you fight through all the setbacks and triumphs. We dealt with these parents, we went through all the disappointments...we make it and we're jamming...and then you go and die on me! It's just not fair!"

As I cried, I cried for Ann. I cried for the girls. I cried for the boys. I cried for Dwight and Shawna. I cried for Louise. I cried for the struggle. I cried remembering the words of Dr. Martin Luther King, "And He's allowed me to go up to the mountain. And I've looked over. And I've seen the Promised Land. I may not get there with you. But I want you to know tonight, that we, as a people, will get to the Promised Land!"

I sat there crying, shaking my head, and talking to the empty room.

"You knew that Destiny's Child would make it. You always knew and proclaimed that they were destined to be great! You knew that you would not be around to see the fullness of that greatness. You tried to tell me, prepare me, but I couldn't hear you."

I sat there on the couch crying so hard because the drum major who was leading the band was silenced.

The funeral was very difficult. Cassey and I had squared Brian away so he would not have to go endure it. I rode with friends who came along to provide support since Cassey would not able to be there. Eric and Vilia were insistent on going to the funeral with me.

"Look man, Cassey ain't here and there is no way we gonna let you go over there by yourself man."

"I agree Vilia. Look Kenny Mo, we are right there with you man!"

They drove me to the funeral. Everything was cool in the car. We talked light-heartedly as they expressed that they understood how close Ann and I were. We laughed about how they would see me and Ann playing the dozens and "Joning" on each other.

"Man, I know it's gonna be hard on you, but we're here for you."

"Thanks Vilia man I appreciate that."

"No doubt, Kenny Mo, you know we got your back!"

"Thanks Eric. I don't know what I would do without you two right about now. This is some hard stuff!"

"It's gonna be alright!

We just shot the breeze so I wouldn't cry, which would make them cry, then we all be messed up. The truth was any of us could have cried at the drop of a hat so we just tried to keep it light. Finally, we pulled up to Yale Street Baptist Church located on Yale Street right off of Cross Timber in Houston, Texas. When we pulled up, the front was filled with cars and the hearse, so we pulled around back. We got out the car and as we were going in, we saw everyone standing around. The family had just walked into the church. I told Eric and Vilia I was gonna walk on around to go inside. The last time I saw Ann she was alive. As I started to walk on around, I noticed a tall figure from a distance walking toward me. As he got closer, I realized that it was Mathew.

"Hey Kenny, let me talk to you real quick man before you go into the funeral."

"Huh?"

"Let me talk to you for a minute."

I had calmed down from the last conversation we had. So I said, "Mat, look man, everything's cool, man, everything's cool. Ann told me about the contract. I know about the arrangements. You're gonna take over management. It's your daughter. It's not gonna be a fight man, everything's cool. I'm just gonna help you wherever I fit in…and we go forward…you know…it's no big thing. We'll keep things rollin'."

"But man, I need those masters."

"Mat I got them man. I'mma give them to you tomorrow man. We'll settle that tomorrow. Let's just go in here and pay our respects."

"Kenny man, we can't have those masters…."

"Mat…the darn things are still in the safe deposit box! Ain't nobody listening to them or nothing, trust me. I don't wanna listen to them no more! I done heard them enough!"

I put my hand across his back and said, "Come on man, now let's go in here and bury our friend."

Mathew violently jerked away from me and said, "Screw that bitch! I want them masters! And I want the now!"

Mathew turned and stormed off across the street. I was standing there in shock. Eric and Vilia heard the conversation and rapidly approached me in disbelief.

"Now I just done reminisced of all the stuff that woman has sacrificed and done for his child and those girls, and he gonna go and say some bull like that!"

"Yeah man."

"She done paid his got-darned bills, covered for his dirty behind when he was lying to and cheating on his wife…and this is his gratitude? What the heck!"

"Shake it off Kenny man."

I was standing there, and I was honestly looking for the biggest brick I could find to throw and hit him in the back of his "head." Then suddenly a peace came over me as I turned to my friends and said, "Look here ya'll, after everything Andretta has done, and all we've been through, if I have to deal with a fool like that, I prefer to walk away."

So, that is what I resolved to do, that is, until I started to hear Ann's voice in my head and my darn peace was disturbed.

"Oh naw…you Kenny Mo dammit! What the heck you doing? What about my boys?"

"Ann, but I gotta deal with this nigga. If I get the boys, then I gotta deal with this fool…shoot!"

I braced myself because I was mad as heck. I looked across the street hoping he'd come back. I was thinking to myself, "Bring your butt back! I'm finna whoop your natural black butt. Bring your butt back here, I finna put a Mississippi butt whoopin on you."

Then I said outloud, "I'mma whoop his behind!"

Vilia said, "Man, just calm down, calm down."

Eric said, "Yeah Ken Moore calm down. But…if he come back, we kickin' his behind!"

"That Mathew is cold man."

"Look Vilia, that ain't the half of it."

We started to go inside. As I got up to the door, I saw family members standing around and Armon by the door next to

Beyonce, Kelly, and Nina. LaTavia, Niki, Letoya were with Chris. I walked up and leaned into Chris.

"Hey, you alright?"

"Yes sir. I'm good."

"Okay."

I then walked up to Armon and hugged him.

"Are you okay?"

"Yeah. I'm good. I'm good."

I then turned to Beyonce, and said, "Finish it!"

She nodded her head and said, "Yes sir. We don't stop."

Beyonce knew exactly what I meant and we have always been able to talk to each other and understand each other. From the studio to that day, it didn't take a lot of words to get a point across. We just understood where each other was coming from. My point was, finish it. It is not over, so make something happen from here and don't stop moving forward until we're the greatest group ever.

They all walked on into the main sanctuary of the church and I walked in behind them. When I walked into the room, everyone looked at me as if I was the preacher. All eyes in the place were on me. Even her family turned to look at me. I was thinking to myself.

"They are not gonna see me show no emotion whatsoever. I'mma going into the Kennedy's mode – like they do when one of them die."

I strutted in with pride. We had done something big and this was my girl, and my time to say goodbye. I acknowledged various family members. I didn't try to speak to them other than when I walked down to view Ann's body. She layed there, dressed in pastel pink, peach, or white. I don't really recall exactly what she was wearing. All I remember was her face because it was swollen. Whatever the trauma of what had happened to her during her final moment had inflamed her face more. When I looked at her, I noticed the hairdo she had, and thought about what she might have been saying.

"You see this stuff Kenny Mo? These mutha screwfolks didn't even comb my hair right. What kind of stuff is this?"

Ann's hair was thin from the stress and the medication. I stood there looking at her for a minute, and then turned to look at Buck. She didn't flinch. There wasn't a tear in her eye. I wasn't about to cry. I was still mad thinking about what Mathew had just said, but I was trying to smile. I finally walked on back and took a seat. There was a seat in the family section they wanted me to sit in, but I went all the way toward the back. I didn't want anybody staring at me. I wanted to observe other's reactions. All I can remember was that after this one upbeat song finished playing, I recall cursing in my mind.

"This jerk! Boy…this low-down dirty jerk!"

The preacher was up there delivering the eulogy.

"…as much as it is God's…"

But my mind was on Mathew.

"I'mma get him!"

In between the scriptures and the preacher's sermon, I was just a cursing in my mind. I said to myself, "Lord, you know I'm wrong…but this…Lord Jesus I know, I know it…but this here…"

I said, "…but this right here is some screwed up stuff!"

As I was thinking, I got madder and madder, and then the preacher said what his message was for the day.

"My message for today is, "what do you say, when you don't know what to say?"

Then he went in to talk about funerals, events like this, life…when you come across things. As he continued to talk, it brought me back to what had just happened with Mathew. It brought me back to the night Ann died.

"People…there are just times you don't know what to say." The preacher continued.

"You want to console somebody…you want to ask for something or do a business transaction in a better way but regardless as to what it is…at moments like this, you don't know what to say…"

I started to listen to the preacher and take everything in. I was angry with Mathew, but I was trying to reconcile that I've gotta take care of the boys and carry on her legacy. I finally came to the conclusion that there was no reason for me to be mad at the girls or anybody else because I had to work with them. I had to be there to watch her money and her estate.

Toward the end of the service, there was a lot of crying. The church became very loud unlike at Dwight's and Shawna's funeral. The girls cried their hearts out. There was no doubt that they loved Ann. Everything else aside, the girls were extremely crushed at Ann's passing. As I watched Beyonce, Kelly, LaTavia and the rest of the girls bawl, you could see that they truly loved Ann and the mask that they sometimes wore was because of some of the adult's mess. I had heard so much and had seen quite a bit, but I realized as I was observing them, that those girls had been manipulated because their tears expressed their pain.

They couldn't know. Yes, they knew Miss Ann was gone, but they couldn't possibly know the behind the scenes tug-of-war of the management team. Charlotte, Tina and Carolyn, I mean all of them came. They cried and appeared to be truly hurting over Ann's death. It was a sad day. The whole thing was sad because of the promise. We all took flight. There were some talented artists who got us to where we were going. They all began their journey at nine, ten, twelve-years-old. Yet here Ann was, at thirty-nine at the end of the road. We had some ways to go, but we would have to continue on without her. This was tough and everyone who was a part of the making of destiny knew, she was truly the staple of it all.

As I looked around the church drenched in flowers of every kind, and the choir began to sing the song, "Soon and Very Soon," the grieving increased as they were preparing to say goodbye forever. The preacher walked out, the casket was hoisted and carried out, and the family followed behind. I looked on and I spotted Buck. When she looked up and her eyes locked on mine and I stared her squarely in the face, I noticed that she was crying. Immediately tears began to well up in my eyes. I was holding on, fighting to try not to break down.

As each family member walked out, and each person who thought they were close to her walked by, the humor of recollecting the many conversations Ann and I had, was enough to keep me from completely breaking down. I was able to say to myself, "Boy if you only knew what Ann used to say about your behind."

Sha was bawling. The girls were bawling. It was hard watching those who you knew genuinely cared about her pass by. It was a constant battle between laughter and tears. Seeing LaTavia, Beyonce, Kelly, and Ashley crying the way they were, caused me to lose the battle, and tears won out. I didn't break down, but the tears flowed. All of the other partners who had taken the journey walked down the aisle. They were also crying. I did not see Mathew in the funeral at all. I was standing there in shock.

We all loved each other. We fought, but we loved too. When we got outside, people came up to me and asked, "Okay man, whatch you gonna do with it?"

"I got it! I'mma take care of it. I'mma take care of it."

I scratched my head and said, "What kind of people are ya'll. We just got outside from her funeral. Everyone's crying and carrying on...and now ya'll asking what we gonna do? Darn can we get through one darn night?"

It was an evening funeral, so it was dark outside. They were gonna take her body to Tyler for another service.

"Can we just get passed all this?"

Everyone was trying to talk about what's next. Her brother Dick came up to me and said, "Hey man, we need to talk about some things tomorrow. What's all this stuff Mathew keeps asking about?"

Mathew was going around asking everyone he could about what was going on with the masters and other paperwork. For years he had been telling everyone he was in charge. Now, here he is frantic because he doesn't have the masters.

I said to Eric and Vilia, "Here his no good behind, running around at this funeral asking for the masters and he had everybody thinking he was the manager and in charge and he don't have the masters...come on now...he's in charge. He is losing his darn mind over this stuff."

Eric, Vilia, and I left the church and headed over to my house. I went to Lou's place. Lou's place was in my garage with the big mural that I painted on the wall when my sister Louise died. There's a big card table, and these big high-back wicker chairs that you see in the club that guys used to sit back in during the seventies where the girlfriends used to stand up next to it. I got me some scotch and a cigar and toasted to Andretta, then turned the music on and listened to the music from the first CD we did out at The Plant in California under A & A Production.

I listened to "Teacher Fried My Brain", "Take it to Another Level", "63257 is Your Number". It was about ten songs. I just went through the whole catalogue. I cried it out to get up the strength to receive the two boys that were coming to the house. I had to prepare my family for what was to come.

"Come on, let's go handle it."

I went to talk to Dick. I handed over the masters and for him to go ahead and give them to Mathew and handle everything else how he felt it should be handled. I was not concerned about who had what, because I saw the contract. I knew what the deal was. Dick handled everything from there on out with respect to the materials. I did not interact with Mathew after that regarding Ann's estate. He communicated with Dick because I turned everything over to him.

Over the course of the summer, Cassey and I prepared for Armon and Chris. We sorted out transportation and everything else that needed to be sorted with respect to rearing them from that point on. We called to check on the boys, but didn't get an answer. We kept calling to check on them, but still no response. Shortly after that I ran into Charlotte, the two of us started talking.

"Hey, I have been calling to check on the boys and haven't been able to reach anyone. Has Nina spoken with Armon?"

"Well Kenny, you know that the boys are with Keith, Dwight's brother, don't you?"

"What?"

"Yeah. He has them and he's gonna raise them."

After speaking with Charlotte, I called Tyler, but Mrs. Brown was no where around. I ended up speaking with one of Ann's sisters.

"Where are Armon and Chris?"

"Well you know…uh…they're gone to stay with Keith."

"Oh…"

Although I was hurt, I didn't push the issue. I started to but I didn't.

"You know Ann wanted them to come with me, right?"

She got quiet, and so I backed off. At the end of the day this is their family and that is their father's brother. Yes, he might be pulling rank and while Andretta's family agreed to it, he may have stepped in and said, "Well you're not family, and regardless of what Ann thought of you, you're not family."

I took it as they were all separating me from what Ann had wanted. While Buck might have been attempting to follow her daugther's last wishes, the family could have manipulated the situation while she was in mourning and she didn't fight the issue. I thought for some time that this was what happened, but I came to find out later that it was more of a kidnapping situation. I found out that Keith came to a family outing and tricked the boys into leaving with him and traveling back to Houston to go to his house and return to their school.

Keith told the boys that he would raise them and he fought a good fight with Ann's family and they let them go, ultimately disregarding Ann's final wishes. He had the boys and claimed that they were happy and wanted to be with him in Houston. So at the end of the day, it was Keith who claimed the boys. The word was, when the family was discussing who would take care of Armon and Christopher, my name never came up.

When I received that news, I was like, "The boys are gone. They did not do what Ann wanted them to do. I do not have the boys, so there is no real need for me to be around. All the money and things going on with the girls and them blowing up didn't excite me because I still have to work with Mathew."

I resolved to get away because I was too close to everything and I didn't want to make a hasty decision. So I went back home to Greenwood, Mississippi to see my grandmother. At the time she was about a hundred and six. She lived to the age of one hundred and seventeen still in her right mind. Now, my granny was a woman of wisdom. I was emotional first of all because I had not seen my grandmother in years, and she was happy to see her Chin, which is what she called me.

"Mama, well…"

"Chin, whatcha doing out there in Texas?"

"Mama Lizzy, I got this hot little girl group, and we're coming out and taking over the world and everything…but…I don't know if I'mma stay with them."

"Chin, why wouldn't you stay with the babies?"

So I went ahead and told my grandmother the story of what I was dealing with.

"Well baby, what I always told you, 'what do it profit a man, to gain the world, and lose his soul'?"

"Yes ma'am."

"…and know this…all money, ain't good money, baby."

"So, what you tellin' me to do?"

"You know what to do…pray on it. You know what to do."

I returned back to Houston after a wonderful visit with my beloved Mama Lizzy. I came in the house and had gotten several calls from different members of our team.

"Hey Kenny, man rehearsal's going on, we're doing a couple of things…you know…won't you come through."

"Naw, I won't be comin' through."

"Huh?"

"Ya'll can have it. I'm good."

"Huh?"

Yep, ya'll can have it. I'm good."

Whoosy, Chauncey and everyone who was in the clique, was trying to suck up to Mathew. Now that he had the reigns, it was like, "I'm Mathew Knowles and this is my world."

He started to become the Mathew Knowles that the world ended up seeing.

I finally came to the conclusion that in order to wipe the slate clean, I had to move on. I didn't have the boys, everyone else was chasing Mathew or chasing the girls trying to get on. I decided, I didn't want to be a part of that. Yet, that didn't keep people from telling me what was going on with the group. I kept hearing about their successes and how they were climbing up the musical ladder. They were all over the television and in the papers. I was hearing how Mathew had taken over the reigns and how he was actually doing a great job with them. Of course in my mind I was like, "Is Mathew really doing such a great job or is he just standing in the gap and under the light from a fire that Andretta started. Is he just the one giving direction after the conductor who got the train rolling in the first place?"

I really didn't care to hear anything else about what was going on with any of them. It was hard listening to their songs. Whenever I caught an ear full of their music, I flashed back to when I was working with them. From time-to-time I would also get to thinking about Ann.

The news kept coming. Pam and Letoya must have finally gotten to LaTavia and Cheryl and pushed their point home of them needing separate management. Pam always wanted Letoya to be able to do more than just sing with the girls. Well, they must've shaken things up because they were kicked out of Destiny's Child. Both girls sued Mathew using the same lawyer that Pam and Letoya had used early on when they challenged the contract before with Andretta and Mathew, but with Andretta not being around to balance things out, there was no one to save the day.

SOMETHING KEEPS CALLING ME

Things appeared to also be going well in the girls' life. Beyonce was doing well. Kelly and Letoya had released their albums. Ashley popped back up on the scene using her middle name Tamar and was working with Prince. She was nominated for a Grammy and was with him at the awards. All of the girls seem to be doing great except for LaTavia. So as far as destiny being fulfilled, I thought things had come full circle, and I was proud of them.

I looked up and realized that everyone from the Andretta Tillman camp was having some form of success. Mathew and Lonnie must have reconciled because he was producing tracks for Kelly as well as working with Dr. Dre.

As for me through my research, I developed Dousic, a concept for getting independent artists exposure. I worked with internet radio and got on the cutting edge of the industry transition from terrestrial to the internet. I was very happy with what I was doing. After a while, life was great again.

Cassey had a group of girlfriends that would all get together when each of them had a birthday. This time it was Cassey's friend Jean's birthday and she wanted the husbands to go.

"Girl, I'm not going no darn where with ya'll. Have a good time without me."

"Come on big daddy...Let's go have some fun!"

"Jean, you lucky it's your behind...cuz I would be sitting my Black tail at home watching the game or something."

So after being convinced to go out, we all got in this long black stretch limousine. The women were about ten deep. We rode around town partying and drinking in the limo. We ended up at The Sky Bar. When we arrived, the line was extremely long. Just as they wanted to turn around and leave, I spoke up.

"No, let's stay."

I kept hearing them say Gertner. So then it clicked, one of our business partner's name was Gill Gertner. I called Michael.

"Hey Mike, this is Kenny."

"Hey partner, what's going on?"

"Is Gill related to this cat named Scott Gertner with the Sky Bar?"

"Yeah, that's his uncle."

"Hey Mike, I'm stuck outside with this darn line of about two hundred people, and I got about twenty people with me. I need to break this velvet rope."

"Hold on buddy, let me call Gill."

So Mike hung up and not even five minutes later called me back.

"Look, Kenny…go to the side by the elevator, there's a guy that's gonna come down there in a few seconds."

Everybody was waiting at the elevator because you have to go up the elevator to get to the Sky Bar. So the manager came down and yelled, "Kenny? Kenny?"

"Right here."

I motioned the rest of the crew to get out of the limo. He backed everyone up so my party could get through. We broke the line and as we were walking by we could here some of the comments.

"Who the heck are they?"

"I'm with them…"

"Can I come with you?"

We chuckled as we headed on the elevator.

When we got on the elevator, Cassey, Jean, and some of the others wanted to know what I did.

"Bae, what did you do to get us in?"

Then Jean said, "Heck, if I didn't no better, I would think you were somebody!"

Toni was like, "You know Kenny is big time around here, he just don't say nothin' to nobody."

"Jean, I'm Kenny Mo. Understand?"

We all laughed as we got off the elevator. We partied and celebrated. There were drinks everywhere. The Sky Bar has an open balcony where you can go smoke cigars. So we were out there sitting, drinking, and partying. Suddenly, Cassey got started.

"Well, I 'm going dancing since you out here with the boys smokin' cigars."

"Take your little fast tail on then, girl. We just shootin' the breeze."

Cassey went out on the dance floor. She was just a dancing. She noticed this big tall guy just staring at her. She thought he was weird, but he had a woman with him. As she was leaving the dance floor, he walked up into her space.

"Excuse me ma'am."

"Yes?"

"You gotta know me…you gotta know me."

"Baby, I'm afraid I don't know you."

"No, No, No…you know me. You gotta know me! You my mom's friend. You my mom's friend."

"Your mom? Well baby who is your mom?"

"My mom…Andretta Tillman!"

Cassey looked real close at him, the said, "Armon?"

"Yeah!" Where Pops, Where's Unc?"

"Oh baby!"

Cassey grabbed him and they hugged. Cassey started crying. He started crying. The woman with him started crying. Next thing I knew, Cassey, Jean, and the other women ran off the dance floor and headed in our direction. We saw them running toward us with this big old dude.

"What the heck!"

Me and the boys got up. "What the heck is going on?"

Cassey was yelling.

"Kenny! Kenny! Kenny! Look! Look who it is!"

I looked, and then looked again. That big 'ole dude walked up to me.

"Pop!"

"Armon?"

We both burst out in tears. Everybody started hugging.

"Man, what?"

"Ken Moore, what the heck is going on?"

All of Cassey's friends knew the story. There was not a dry eye in our party. Some of the men still hadn't figured it out.

"Who is that V?"

One of the women spoke up.

"Do you remember Andretta? Her kids were supposed to come and stay with Kenny and Cassey? Well that's one of the boys."

Everyone was talking and crying, but Armon's girlfriend was crying almost uncontrollably. Cassey looked at her and tried to comfort her.

"Baby, what's wrong?"

"Ya'll don't understand. He's been looking for ya'll forever! Ever since his mom died he been lookin' for ya'll."

"We've been looking for them too."

"Armon, what happened?"

"What?"

"Ya'll was supposed to come and stay with us…"

"Pops, somehow Uncle Keith, got us man and convinced us to go stay with him. I didn't even know we were supposed to come and stay with ya'll. Ya'll name didn't even come up from what they told me. It probably would've been better if we had come to stay with ya'll."

"What?"

Armon and I talked for hours that night.

"Man, Pops. Chris gotta see you!"

"Yeah. How is everybody? How's Buck?"

"Well she's old and not really doing too well."

By the time we finished talking, I asked about everybody from TuTu to Mop and everybody in between.

"Okay look, get Chris, round up all ya'll darn kids, my grandkids, and ya'll come on by Saturday. I'mma barbeque."

"Oh snap! Not the world famous barbeque again!"

We laughed and talked briefly about the old barbeques and how much fun they used to be. Finally Armon and I parted ways that evening, but we talked everyday the following week. I also had the chance to speak with Chris. We made arrangements for the upcoming weekend. At that moment, I was so glad I went out that night with Cassey and the girls as it was a life-changing moment. I learned that Armon had one child and Chris had five. I was a grandfather six times over or at least Andretta and Dwight were. I could not help but to think about Andretta and Dwight in their absence, Cassey and I would have to serve as grandparents.

Armon called me the Friday evening before the barbeque.

"Hey Pops, I gotta a couple of people who wanna come to the barbeque, can I bring them?"

"Yeah…no problem…cool."

So like old times, I went and killed the fatty calf and barbeque up a bunch of meat and prepared all the "fixins." We were all excited and waiting for the boys to get there. Bryanna was looking forward to meeting them because she heard us talking about them since forever. Brian was looking forward to seeing his big brothers who he hadn't seen since he was really young. All of our immediate friends came by. They wanted to be there to witness the reunion of Andretta's boys and grandkids with our family.

First Armon showed up. He had his girlfriend with him and this little girl that looked just like Andretta. She had such an uncanny resemblance to her grandmother that it was amazing that it almost brought us to tears. I looked at Cassey and she looked at me.

"Oh my Gosh! This is Ann Jr. Kenny look at this."

I bent down and said, "Hey, hey little Ann."

I went and picked her up in amazement at just how much she looked like Andretta. We all started calling her Little Ann. Shortly after, Chris arrived. He had a basketball team with him. He had four girls and one boy which included a set of fraternal twins. As I looked around and saw all of these little extensions to Ann, it was a bitter-sweet moment. All of the children had a touch of Ann in them. So, out of all these grandchildren, there was only one little boy.

"Chris, so what is the boy's name?"

"His name is Dwight."

"Oh, okay...wow."

I paused for a second before I reached down and picked him up. I said, "Well, it is finally good to meet you Dwight Tillman."

As I walked around the room holding him and talking to him, I said, "I've heard a lot about you over the years...Armon give me little Ann."

With both of them in my arms, I said, "So you got a little Andretta over here, and a little Dwight over there...Uhm. Lawd have mercy!"

I just thought for a moment to myself, "Everything has come full circle."

It was a fantastic evening. We all laughed and talked about old times. I shared stories of their mom with them and her grandchildren, maybe exaggerating a little but to the kids to make her seem even funnier. Then I got another surprise when the doorbell rung. It was Nina and Charlotte. Cassey started screaming.

"What is this? Are you kidding me?"

We hugged, laughed, ate, and talked. It was as if we had never been separated. When we finished eating, Charlotte pulled me aside and said, "Kenny, I wanna to talk to you for a minute."

"Okay, what's up Charlotte?"

"Well, what are you gonna do about Mathew and them doing all this lying? Whatcha gonna do about them trying to act like as if Ann never existed?"

"Charlotte, well…I'll handle it."

"Well, it's just not right the way they are trying to write her out of history and she did all the darn work."

"Yep, I know, Charlotte."

After this conversation, I began to wonder was there more for me to do. I had not taken the time to really listen to what they had been saying about how the group was created. That evening, as Cassey and I were talking, I wondered what was going on. First it was Tamar, then Pam, then Letoya, Armon and Chris, and now Nina and Charlotte. It was something to think about because all of them pretty much wanted to know the same thing – "What are you gonna do about Mathew trying to write Ann out of the history."

We continued to host barbeques at the house which included Armon and Chris and their families. They re-entered our lives and have once again become a part of the family. I am very grateful for that, and I know Ann is really proud of them. Armon and I got to talking about music. Then out of the blue he said, "Pops…how can we go about getting my mom's story told?"

"Huh?"

"Well, they act like she doesn't exist. They're trying to write her out of the history, like she wasn't nobody when she sacrificed a lot. Come on Pops, my family had sacrificed a lot. All I want is her story to be told."

"Well then, Armon, why don't you just tell it?"

"I can't, because when the lawsuit was settled, we had to sign a non-disclosure clause. We can't write it, and even if I could write it, I don't know everything you know. You are the only one that was there that can tell the truth about what she did. You were there."

"Okay. Armon, I'll think about it."

Armon and I continued to bond and likewise so did Chris. Armon was always pretty upbeat, but one day he heard something on the news about how Destiny's Child got started, and when he heard it, his mother's name was not even brought up. I guess it got to him.

"Man, we gotta tell my mom's story!"

Armon had this look on his face of pure disgust mixed with helplessness. If I was able to read his mind, he probably was saying, "Shoot ain't nothin' I can do to tell my mom's story!"

"Armon...you know..."

I really did not know what to say. I took a deep breath.

"Armon...I don' think I can go back down that road."

"I understand...I understand Pops."

Once again, we left it at that. Two weeks later, Armon called me and said, "Hey Pops, I got someone who wants to come and talk to you about how everything went down with my mom."

"Now Armon, you know I'm not just gonna tell anybody about this story. I mean... so who is it?"

"It's David."

"David Brewer?"

"Yeah."

"What!"

"Yeah, he flew in from Germany."

"Got-darn! What's really going on? Are they trying to draw me out? Why is everybody looking for Kenny Mo? Can you tell me that?"

"Well Pop, you the only one that know. You the only one that knows the real story and people are going to keep coming until they can get it out of you."

"Okay Armon, tell David to come on over."

David and Armon came over. We sat down in the backyard and had some scotch and cigars. My thinking was, a man not used to scotch and Cuban cigars will get drunk enough to expose his true motive.

"Well David, whatcha need? What's going on?"

"Well, they are trying to discredit me from being Beyonce and the girls' vocal coach."

"What? What's the purpose of that? You were their vocal coach."

"I don't know. They're trying to discredit me."

"Man, that's a shame."

"It's as if they're trying to write out anybody who had a part of creating the group. It's like Mathew is trying to take all the credit."

"I see."

"Well, you know I'm writing a book."

"What...you writing a book, David?"

"Yeah, and I wanna include some of the stuff about Ann being the manager. So I just wanna get some information from you because...so... I can add it in the book. No one will really only take my word for it. I need some facts, some contracts and different things like that to prove I was there."

"Well David, I haven't said anything to anybody all these years. What do you need?" Why should I start to talk now?"

"Kenny...I just wanna know why you haven't said anything all of these years?"

"To be honest David, I promised Tina when Beyonce was a little girl and we were traveling to California. Tina was crying and I asked her why. She was telling Beyonce she didn't have to do this. I told Tina not to worry, as long as I'm alive and I'm able to that I would never let anyone hurt Beyonce."

"What? For that reason, you haven't told my mom's story?"

"Yeah."

"You worried about not hurting Beyonce. What about all the hurt it's causing me?"

I thought for a few minutes, sipped on some scotch, and puffed on my Cuban cigar, and the next words that came out of my mouth was, "What do you need, David."

"Anything tangible."

"Well here are some pictures. I can email you some stuff, come contracts, some dates, and hope it helps you."

When David left, Armon and I continued to talk.

"Pops, now you know that even though he tells the story, he wasn't there behind the scenes. He was living with the Knowles' and worked with the girls, but he can't tell the story like you can."

"Yeah...yeah...you got a point."

"He can only talk about what went on at Mathew and Tina's house."

"Okay, well...Armon, I got one question."

"What?"

"Is this about your mom's story being told, or is this about making some money off of her memory?"

"Pops, it's about my mom's story being told."

The Making of a Child of Destiny

"Okay. Now if I tell the story, I'mma tell the whole story. How she came to do it, what happened. I'm not going to leave any stuff out."

"Okay."

So from there, I started to write the book that you are now reading. Often, I was asked the question, what am I gonna do about them writing Ann out of the history of Destiny's Child. I then began to ask the same question. While the first two albums were dedicated to her, gradually after that, you did not hear her name when the subject of their beginning came up. If the truth was told, there would be no need for me to write this book. Yet, I find it necessary to write so that the world can know what my friend sacrificed to get them to the greatest pinnacle of their young lives and careers.

Andretta Tillman opened the most important doors of their lives driven by the dreams of her husband and the love of her daughter. They died in pursuit of the Destiny that these girls are living. So how dare we forget where we came from? I don't know if they just don't remember, don't talk about, or just ungrateful for her as a manager and mother figure in their lives. She is the one who helped to turn on the lights so that the world could see that it was the Girls' Tyme, after all and Andretta Tillman was in fact a Child of Destiny and why Destiny's Child came to be!

For me, the original question still remains, "Do they really know what happened?"

The sacrifice of a daughter, a wife, a mother, and a friend was the greatest love she could have shown. As the Bible says, "No greater love has no one than this than to lay down one's life for a friend."

So, what's the measurement of love when three lives are laid down for a destiny? While we may not know what's ahead,

299

and none of them may ever find the courage to step forward and speak up, one thing is for sure, time will most certainly tell.

As for me, I find myself sitting in the studio again listening to hot new artists wondering,

"Can lightening strike again?"

I don't know if it will strike twice, but while sitting in the studio with my son Armon, the irony is it used to be his mom sitting in the chair. Just doing music again, the feeling, the passion and drive has returned. So, will we be able to recreate the magic that brought the world Destiny's Child? I don't know, but what I do know is, we will darn sure try. More importantly, however, is that we're back as a family; and that's what the journey was all about in the first place. So my wish for those of you who are on similar pilgrimage, is I hope that you are able to maintain your peace and integrity and in the end find your Destiny!

About the Author

Brian K. Moore the author of The Making of a child of Destiny "The Andretta Tillman Story". Sets the record straight about the making of the international phenomenon, Destiny's Child. Moore a first time author and the **President/Founder** of Dousic Entertainment, LLC. A key player in the creation of Destiny's Child, he was Co-founder of Music World Entertainment, and former Co-manager of Tillman Management. Moore key areas of expertise covered Executive Leadership, Artist Management, and Company Development. Moore also assisted in acquiring Destiny's Child contract with Sony's Records, which launched Destiny's Child to international fame. Moore later served as Vice President of the Eastlon Records. Where he was responsible for the strategic development and operations of Eastlon's records management and music portfolio. Raised in the Mississippi Delta music has always been a part of this New York born author's life. Further **his** unparalleled expertise in the development, production and marketing of digital media platforms lead him to create Dousic Entertainment LLC, which aspires to be one of the world's leading social media and entertainment content companies.

www.ingramcontent.com/pod-product-compliance
Lightning Source LLC
Chambersburg PA
CBHW020358100426
42812CB00001B/103